Family
Diversity
and
Well-Being

Volume 195 Sage Library of Social Research

RECENT VOLUMES IN . . .
SAGE LIBRARY OF SOCIAL RESEARCH

84 Gelles **Family Violence, 2nd Edition**
150 Frey **Survey Research by Telephone, 2nd Edition**
155 Russell **Sexual Exploitation**
163 Markides/Mindel **Aging and Ethnicity**
166 Steinmetz **Duty Bound**
167 Teune **Growth**
168 Blakely **Planning Local Economic Development**
169 Mathews **Strategic Intervention in Organizations**
170 Scanzoni/Polonko/Teachman/Thompson **The Sexual Bond**
171 Prus **Pursuing Customers**
172 Prus **Making Sales**
173 Mayer **Redefining Comparative Politics**
174 Vannoy-Hiller/Philliber **Equal Partners**
175 Brewer/Hunter **Multimethod Research**
176 Chafetz **Gender Equity**
177 Peterson **Political Behavior**
178 So **Social Change and Development**
179 Gomes-Schwartz/Horowitz/Cardarelli **Child Sexual Abuse**
180 Evan **Social Structure and Law**
181 Turner/Turner **The Impossible Science**
182 McCollum **The Trauma of Moving**
183 Cohen/Adoni/Bantz **Social Conflict and Television News**
184 Gruter **Law and the Mind**
185 Koss/Harvey **The Rape Victim**
186 Cicirelli **Family Caregiving**
187 Caves **Land Use Planning**
188 Blalock **Understanding Social Inequality**
189 Gubrium **Out of Control**
190 Albrecht **The Disability Business**
191 Alter/Hage **Organizations Working Together**
192 Freeman/Rickels **Early Childbearing**
193 Burr/Klein **Reexamining Family Stress**
194 McGrath/Hollingshead **Groups Interacting With Technology**
195 Acock/Demo **Family Diversity and Well-Being**
196 Midlarsky/Kahana **Altruism in Later Life**
197 Sussman/Dent/Burton/Stacy/Flay **Developing School-Based Tobacco Use Prevention and Cessation Programs**

Family
Diversity
and
Well-Being

Alan C. Acock
David H. Demo

Sage Library of Social Research 195

SAGE Publications
International Educational and Professional Publisher
Thousand Oaks   London   New Delhi

Copyright © 1994 by Sage Publications, Inc.

For information address:

SAGE Publications, Inc.
2455 Teller Road
Thousand Oaks, California 91320

SAGE Publications Ltd.
6 Bonhill Street
London EC2A 4PU
United Kingdom

SAGE Publications India Pvt. Ltd.
M-32 Market
Greater Kailash I
New Delhi 110048 India

Printed in the United States of America

Library of Congress Cataloging-in-Publication Data

Acock, Alan, C., 1944-
Family diversity and well-being / Alan C. Acock, David H. Demo.
    p. cm.—(Sage library of social research: 195)
Includes bibliographical references (pp. 275-288) and indexes.
ISBN 0-8039-4266-4 (cl).—ISBN 0-8039-4267-2 (pb)
1. Family—United States. I. Demo, David H. II. Title.
III. Series: Sage library of social research: v. 195.
HQ536.A225 1994
306.85'0973—dc20   94-11589

94 95 96 97 10 9 8 7 6 5 4 3 2

Sage Production Editor: Diane S. Foster

Contents

Acknowledgments   ix

1. **Family Structure in Context**   1
   The Traditional American Family
      and Recent Changes   9
   Major Developments in Restructuring
      Family Relations   19
   Family Structure and Family Process   23
   Prevalent Family Structures   24
   The Chapters That Follow   26

2. **Theoretical Perspectives Linking Family**
   Structure, Family Relations, and Well-Being   28
   Theories Linking Family Structure, Family Relations,
      and Adult Well-Being   28
   Theories Linking Family Structure,
      Family Relations, and Child Well-Being   42
   How Important Is Family Structure?   48

3. **Research Design and Profile of American**
   Families   50
   Identifying Types of Families   51
   Socioeconomic Characteristics
      of Family Types   56
   Weighting Versus Controlling for Relevant Variables   66

Summary   69

4. **Marital, Postmarital, and Nonmarital Relations**   **71**
   Division of Household Labor   71
   Division of Household Labor
       Across Family Types   74
   When Mothers Do Not Work for Pay   85
   Role Strain Regarding Household Labor   88
   Wife-Husband Relations:
       Interaction, Quality, and Strain   92
   Postmarital Relations With Nonresidential Parent   98
   Summary and Conclusions   102

5. **Parent-Child Relations**   **106**
   Family Values, Rules, and Expectations   108
   Parent-Child Interaction:
       Support, Control, and Conflict   118
   Summary and Conclusions   139

6. **Family Structure and Mothers' Well-Being**   **144**
   Measuring Mothers' Well-Being   146
   Mothers' Well-Being Across Family Types   147
   Factors Influencing Well-Being   151
   Correlates of Mothers' Well-Being   157
   Models of Mothers' Well-Being   165
   Summary and Conclusions   174

7. **Family Structure and Children's Well-Being**   **179**
   Measuring Children's Well-Being   181
   Children's Well-Being
       Across Family Types   183
   Factors Influencing Well-Being   188
   Correlates of Children's Well-Being   191
   Models of Children's Well-Being   199
   Summary and Conclusions   213

8. **Beyond Family Structure**   **217**
   Family Structure, Family Processes,
       and Mothers' Well-Being   221
   Family Structure, Family Processes,
       and Children's Well-Being   222
   Theoretical Implications   225
   Implications for Practitioners   228
   Limitations and Strengths of the Study   228

Conclusions   230

Appendix A: Coding and Items Used in Analysis   232
Family Structure in Context   233
Research Design and Profile
  of American Families   236
Marital, Postmarital,
  and Nonmarital Relations   238
Parent-Child Relations   242
Family Structure and Mothers' Well-Being   251
Family Structure and Children's Well-Being   257

Appendix B: Additional Tables   265

References   275

Name Index   289

Subject Index   294

About the Authors   299

Dedicated to
Toni and Leslie
for who they are

Acknowledgments

This book is the product of three years of intense, stimulating, and rewarding collaboration. One of the biggest challenges in writing this book was to present complicated analyses in a language that was understandable to and meaningful for students, some of whom are new to the field of family studies. We thank Mitch Allen, Executive Editor at Sage, and Diane Foster, our Production Editor, for their helpful guidance and thoughtful suggestions in orienting this book to its diverse audiences. We also benefited from thorough reviews provided by anonymous reviewers for Sage.

We want to extend special appreciation to Katherine Allen and Gary Lee, both of whom provided extensive and meticulous commentary on drafts of several chapters. We are indebted to a number of other colleagues for generously sharing their reactions and expertise: Alexis Walker, Marilyn Coleman, Larry Ganong, Mark Fine, Jay Edwards, Jim Michaels, Anisa Zvonkovic, and Karen DeBord.

The data we examined for this project comes from the National Survey of Families and Households. This survey was funded by the Center for Population Research of the National Institute of Child Health and Human Development. It was designed at the Center for Demography and Ecology at the University of Wisconsin, under the direction of Larry Bumpass and Jim Sweet. The interviews were conducted by the Institute for Survey Research at Temple University.

We thank the National Council on Family Relations for allowing us to reprint and adapt material from previously published articles. Specifically, we have adapted material from Demo (1992), Parent-child relations: Assessing recent changes, published in *Journal of Marriage and the Family, 54,* 104-117; and from Demo & Acock (1993), How much have things really changed: Family diversity and the division of domestic labor, published in *Family Relations, 42,* 323-331. We are grateful to Jacqueline Tasch for her careful copyediting of the manuscript, and to Sandy Frye for her assistance in preparing figures.

Most importantly, we thank our partners, Toni Acock and Leslie McHaney Demo, for everything they have done for us and for our families, and for being who they are. We dedicate this book to them.

ONE

Family Structure in Context

In the lives of John and Mary marriage comes first and parenthood follows in due course. In our culture that is the normal order in the development of the individual. This means that for us the primary meaning of marriage is to provide children with what they need for their full development. Marriage has come to have other important purposes, both personal and social. But its organic purpose still remains, for it can be a tragedy for a child if the mother's basic service is neglected or becomes impossible.

In our advanced human culture children need for their proper development the full service and cooperation of the two parents. In fact, they need in addition the services of several outside specialists—teachers and doctors and dentists and counselors. But the major task of guiding them to mature adulthood is the responsibility of their two parents.

David R. Mace,
The Encyclopedia of Child Care and Guidance, 1956 (p. 952)

American marriage and family life have changed dramatically in the past 3 decades. The "traditional" family of the 1950s and 1960s, alluded to above, has been reshaped by high rates of teenage and nonmarital childbearing, sharp increases in the divorce rate, postponed marriage and childbearing, smaller families, single-parent families, stepfamilies, and dual-earner marriages. Many scholars call this diverse array of family types the "postmodern" family (Cheal, 1991; Denzin, 1986; Stacey, 1991). How have these developments influenced marital relationships

1

and parent-child relationships? Were family members better served by the traditional family? Or, are today's diverse arrangements meeting family members' needs just as well, or even better? How important is *family structure* in shaping family relationships? Does family structure have an important influence on the social and psychological well-being of family members?

This book explores these questions. Our central objective is to study the hypothesis that family structure influences family relationships and personal well-being. Throughout the book we discuss four prevalent family structures:

1. Two-parent families where the mother and father are both in their first marriage
2. Single-parent families headed by a mother who is divorced from her children's father
3. Two-parent stepfamilies in which the mother has a biological child (or children) from a previous marriage
4. Single-parent families where the mother has never married.

We are interested in how family relationships are similar and different across these four types of families. Analyzing data from a nationally representative sample, we seek to determine how parents and children are faring in today's diverse families.

Throughout the remainder of this chapter we will highlight some of the most frequently asked and controversial questions about family structure and its importance for children and adults. How are children affected by divorce, by living in single-parent families, or in stepfamilies? How are family relationships in nontraditional families similar to and different from those in traditional families? What do we know about the traditional families of the 1950s and 1960s, and why is this family form the standard against which all other family structures are judged? Have family values really deteriorated? Do parents care less about, and spend less time with, their children than in "the good old days"? How have adults been influenced by changes in family structure? How do women and men adjust psychologically following divorce? What about remarriages and stepfamilies? Are remarried partners as happy, or happier, in these families compared to their counterparts in first-married families? After addressing these questions, we conclude the first chapter by distinguishing between family structure and *family process* and briefly describing the chapters that follow.

Children in Families

Many people, including family scholars, worry that nontraditional living arrangements harm children. The popular literature and media blame nontraditional families for high rates of teenage sexual activity, pregnancy, delinquency, alcohol, and drug use. They blame these problems on parents (and typically blame the mothers) for spending little time with their children and for not instilling the "proper" family values in their children. They point to lax parental control, high levels of family conflict, and "broken homes." Father-absent families were maligned in the 1992 presidential campaign by then-Vice President Dan Quayle because such families were assumed to constitute a deficient family environment for rearing children. Popular news magazines commonly sound the same alarms, describing African American families as struggling and endangered because of high rates of nonmarital childbearing and single-parent families (e.g., *Newsweek*, "A World Without Fathers," 1993). Some social scientists concur that parental commitment is at the heart of the problem: "We suggest that it is an erosion of the bond between parent and child—one characterized by parental commitment and willingness to sacrifice self-interest—that is a significant cause of the declining well-being of [American] adolescents after 1960" (Uhlenberg & Eggebeen, 1986, p. 38).

Hostile attitudes toward children are common in the United States today. Child abuse, sexual abuse, incest, and child pornography are prevalent. Many apartment complexes prohibit families with children. Many nonresidential fathers visit their children irregularly and fail to pay child support. These problems prompted the weekly news magazine *Newsweek* to run a cover story on "Deadbeat Dads" (1992). Airline passengers complain if they are seated near children. Patrons at "family restaurants" are annoyed by children who cry, talk back to their parents, or argue with their siblings. Young married couples view children as expensive luxuries and often opt to delay parenthood or avoid it altogether. Other young couples are ambivalent or indifferent about having children (Neal, Groat, & Wicks, 1989). Prospective parents wonder what the "payoff" is for having children. In his presidential address to the American Sociological Association, James S. Coleman (1993) reasoned that many parents no longer value their children because children have no economic value. In a study of 610 married couples in the early years of marriage, Neal and his colleagues found that both wives and husbands rated personal freedom, leisure time, and women's employment opportunities as more important than having children. They viewed having children as only slightly more valuable than a neat house or pursuing recreational interests.

Are these problems due to today's diverse family experiences? Research indicates that parents in dual-earner families spend less time with their children than their single-earner, traditional counterparts (Nock & Kingston, 1988). Other studies find that parental divorce and remarriage disrupt primary bonds between parents and children, causing short-term emotional and behavioral problems for children. Constraints imposed by wage work and family work make it difficult for single parents to assist and supervise children in their schoolwork (Furstenberg & Nord, 1985). It is also more difficult and more stressful for single parents to monitor, control, and discipline children and adolescents (Dornbusch et al., 1985). These and other family processes lead adolescents in single-parent families to higher rates of deviant and delinquent behavior.

We know very little, however, about how parent-child relations have changed—that is, the nature, scope, and magnitude of change—and we know less about how children's development and well-being have been influenced. Thus it is important to identify the linkages among changing household arrangements, family processes, family resources, and their effects on children.

A fundamental weakness of much prior research on family structure is the absence of a comparative research design. Many studies (especially clinical studies) examine only children of divorced mothers or children living in single-parent families, and then attribute any observed problems to the divorced or single-parent family structure (Demo & Acock, 1988). For example, in a national best-seller, Wallerstein and Blakeslee (1989) describe how parental divorce destroys the lives of many children:

> When Sammy Moore, age seven, learned that his father was leaving for good and that he would be left at home with his mother and two older sisters, he took a marking pen and wrote "Fuck Mom" on the refrigerator.
> His reaction didn't surprise me in the least. Unlike his sisters, Sammy had no clue that his family was about to collapse; when the separation occurred, he was stunned and then intensely angry. I have seen many boys this age express anger at their parents in oblique, unpredictable ways. More-over, they are likely to blame the mother when things go wrong. Some boys refuse to go to bed, do homework, complete chores, or perform a variety of other previously routine tasks, while others displace their anger onto a younger brother or sister. For Sammy, a well-behaved boy from a polite house-hold, the outrageous act of writing on the refrigerator was the opening salvo in a barrage of aggressive behavior. (p. 71)

Although it is clear that for some children parental divorce and the associated life changes are enormously stressful and trou-bling, we think that characterizations such as this one that blame all of children's problems on parental divorce are simplistic and myopic. Such accounts distort children's lives in that they ignore the wide range of events and experiences bearing on children's development and well-being. As one example, studies that focus on children's postdivorce adjustment typically fail to consider the possibility that these children may have had lower levels of social and psychological well-being *prior to the divorce,* stemming in part from unhappiness, lack of attention, persistent conflict, family violence, or alcoholism in two-parent families. Thus many chil-dren may be better off as a result of parental divorce in that they are insulated from any further involvement in unhappy and conflict-ridden families.

A principal shortcoming of previous studies is failure to simul-taneously examine other family types (e.g., two-parent units), precluding assessment of whether children in these other family types also experience adjustment problems. Clearly, children express their anger in "unpredictable ways" in all types of families. Thus we cannot conclude that family structure or family disruption is responsible for children's conduct (positive or negative) until we examine large numbers of children living in different family types and examine other factors (such as economic resources and family relationships) that may affect their development and well-being. One central objective of this book is to examine whether parent-child relations and children's well-being vary across families in which the parents are in their first marriage, families in which the parents are divorced, those in which parents remarried (stepfamilies), and those in which the parents never married.

Adults in Families

The second major objective of this book is to determine how adults are faring in contemporary families. We examine how marital and nonmarital couple relations are similar and different across family types, and we trace the consequences for adult well-being. More than half of contemporary marriages involve two earners. Dual-earner marriages have advantages and disadvantages. On the one hand, economic resources are generally more plentiful, a higher standard of living can be maintained, women's economic vulnerability is reduced, and there is the potential, at least, for sharing power and decision making. On the other hand, when both spouses are employed there is less time for household work, less time to spend with children, and less time for spouses to spend with each other or alone. Of course, traditional single-earner marriages are not immune to these problems. Wives and husbands in both single-earner and dual-earner marriages complain of strained communication, lack of spontaneity, infrequent sexual activity, and low levels of marital satisfaction, especially during the childrearing years. Married women complain that they frequently feel overburdened and distressed by their multiple roles of wives, wage earners, mothers, and homemakers. Compared to full-time homemakers, employed women report slightly better physical and mental health (Spitze, 1988).

An important question is whether the division of domestic labor and child care, nonwage work traditionally performed by women, varies as a function of the wife's employment status and/or her marital status. Some studies have shown that husbands and other family members perform only slightly more household labor when the wife/mother is employed (Dressel & Clark, 1990; Ferree, 1991; Pleck, 1985). The available evidence is limited, however, because most studies of housework involve small samples of white, middle-class families (Spitze, 1988). We will examine this question using data obtained from a representative national sample consisting of families of diverse racial and socioeconomic backgrounds. Previous research is also limited in that variations in family structure have been ignored. How does the proportion of work done by husbands and other family members vary across first-married families, stepfamilies, and single-parent families?

As wives or husbands and as parents, adults face many other challenges in contemporary marriages and families. The sheer expense of raising children is enormous. Economists estimate that for a child born in 1989, it will cost an average of $200,000 for the "typical" expenses involved in feeding, clothing, entertaining, and caring for that child through age 17 (Lino, 1990).[1] It is further estimated, based on current tuition, room, and board expenses (U.S. Department of Education, 1991) and recent inflation rates (Hauptman & Merisotis, 1990), that it will cost an average of $100,000 for that child's 4-year college education at a public university.[2] These numbers are staggering, totaling $300,000, and they pertain only to the expenses of rearing one child! Financial strains and hardship make family life difficult for millions of families. Economic downturns, unemployment, and underemployment contribute to marital conflict, inconsistent and harsh parenting, wife abuse, and divorce (Elder & Caspi, 1988; McLoyd, 1990; Voydanoff, 1990). As difficult as it may be for many two-parent families to afford child-related expenses, imagine the reality for most single parents. Their reality is not middle-class entertainment, quality health care, and college savings accounts. They have more pressing needs, often struggling to survive from one paycheck to the next. Further, whereas the real income of married couples with children increased from 1960 to 1990, that of single-parent families declined (Lino, 1993).

But just as we have argued that all two-parent families cannot be lumped together in one simplistic classification, we think it is equally important to examine variations among different types of single-parent families. In particular, we distinguish between single-parent families formed as the result of divorce, and non-disrupted single-parent families where the biological parents did not marry. The marital and family histories of these two family types are very different, suggesting that there may be interesting differences in family relationships that bear on adult and child well-being. For example, families headed by divorced mothers with long-term cohabiting partners may be very similar to step-families in parenting and work trajectories and in family dynamics, with perhaps the principal distinction between these two family types being one of legal status. In contrast, families consisting of continuously single mothers with long-term cohabiting partners may be more similar to first-married family units, again the primary distinction being a legal one.

Another interesting distinction between the two most prevalent single-parent family types—divorced families and families headed by continuously single mothers—is that divorced mothers may also have ongoing relations with at least one former spouse, relations that are themselves widely variable (Kitson, 1992). In this respect the family dynamics in divorced and step-families may be quite similar. The trajectories of family development in first-married and never-married families, on the other hand, do not involve marital dissolution, family disruption, or relationships with former spouses, although in never-married families there may be ongoing relations with former partners. In the chapters that follow we will seek to describe how relationships with former spouses vary in frequency and quality. How often do women talk with their former spouse? How much conflict do they have with their former spouse? What kind of support, if any, do they receive from the former spouse? How do they feel about the interaction between their former spouse and their children?

In addition to examining postmarital relations, we will examine ongoing marital relationships and their influence on adult well-being. To what degree are the problems confronting adults due to today's diverse family living arrangements? In what ways are marital relationships different in first marriages compared to remarriages? In what ways are they similar? Is the division of household chores different in stepfamilies than in first marriages? Does satisfaction with family roles vary across family types? Are contemporary women satisfied in their roles as mother and wife? How much time do first-married and remarried wives and husbands spend together? Do they enjoy this time? What do wives and husbands argue about, how frequently do they argue, and how does their conflict compare with that between previously married or never-married partners? What accounts for high rates of marital conflict and spousal violence? How are the responsibilities, the joys, and the stresses of parenting similar and different in first-married families, stepfamilies, and single-parent families? How important are marital relationships for adult well-being, and how important are nonmarital relationships, such as relations with a former spouse?

THE TRADITIONAL AMERICAN FAMILY AND RECENT CHANGES

Contemporary family living arrangements are diverse. To appreciate this diversity consider the typical arrangements and experiences of the traditional American family. This family consisted of a husband and wife, both married for the first time, rearing their biological children. The male served as the provider and the female as wife, mother, and homemaker. This "ideal" continues to serve as a glimmering goal against which contemporary families are judged. This is curious for several reasons. First, this traditional family structure of the 1950s was an historical aberration, with families generally characterized by much greater diversity in the years prior to and subsequent to the 1950s (Skolnick,

1991; Stacey, 1991). Following the uncertainties and instabilities of the Great Depression and World War II, a high value was placed on marriage and family life, contributing to a short-term drop in the divorce rate. The postwar economic boom improved the standard of living for many families, and marriage and birthrates rose. For these and other reasons, Cherlin (1988) cautions that "in any consideration of the changes that have occurred since the 1950s, it is important to remember that the 1950s were probably the most unusual decade for family life in this century" (p. 3).

A second reason that the nostalgia surrounding the families of the 1950s is curious is that many traditional marriages were characterized by severe inequities, with women bearing disproportionate responsibilities for unpaid domestic work and parenting. In many cases, women performed these activities in addition to responsibilities associated with wage labor. Women's employment is frequently forgotten or overlooked in all of the nostalgia surrounding traditional families (Coontz, 1992). Yet in 1960, less than half of American families consisted of single-earner married couples, and nearly one fourth were dual-earner couples (Masnick & Bane, 1980). Thus many families did not conform to the monolithic family structure of a male breadwinner and female homemaker, mother, and wife. In addition, traditional marriages tended to be patriarchal, characterized by male dominance, exploitation, and oppression of women, male absorption in work and other nonfamily activities, marital unhappiness, alcoholism, and wife abuse (Coontz, 1992). For many married couples, her marriage was less attractive than his (Bernard, 1972). Contrary to the popular image of the happy housewife, Coontz (1992) documents that

> In 1956, the *Ladies' Home Journal* devoted an issue to "The Plight of the Young Mother." When *McCall's* ran an article entitled "The Mother Who Ran Away" in the same year, the magazine set a record for readership. A former editor commented: "We suddenly realized that all these women at home with three and a half children were miserably unhappy." By 1960, almost every major news journal was using the word *trapped* to describe the feelings of the American housewife. When *Redbook's* editors asked readers to provide them with

examples of "Why Young Mothers Feel Trapped," they received 24,000 replies. (p. 37)

Still, the shape and composition of families have changed profoundly. Compared to children in the 1990s, children in the 1950s were much more likely to live with two parents. As Table 1.1 illustrates, in 1960 the vast majority (87.7%) of children under age 18 lived with two parents, only 9.1% with one parent, and 3.2% with neither parent. Figure 1.1 shows these figures for white children, and Figure 1.2 shows the changes for black children. Among black children in 1960, two out of three (67.0%) lived with two parents and one out of five (19.9%) lived in mother-only households. But the percentage of children living in single-parent (predominantly female-headed) households increased steadily in the second half of the 20th century. From 1960 to 1992 the percentage of children living with one parent increased from less than 1 of every 10 American children (9.1%) to more than one fourth (26.6%) of all children. In 1992, more than half (53.8%) of black children lived in mother-only households.

But the most important changes may have been in the events and processes associated with the *formation* of single-parent families. Table 1.2 shows that in 1959, many of the single-parent families were headed by widows (45.4%), three times the percentage headed by divorced parents. These patterns changed quickly during the ensuing 3 decades. In 1992, the largest percentage of single-parent families, nearly two out of every five (36.6%), were precipitated by divorce. More than one third (34.2%) of single-parent families were headed by never-married parents, one fourth (24.4%) were characterized as spouse absent (usually separated), and only 4.9% were headed by a widowed parent. This is compelling evidence of the ever increasing diversity characterizing American families.

Even more pronounced are the changes in black children's living arrangements. In 1992, never-married parents constituted the largest proportion (55.8%) of black single parents. One in five (21.7%) black single-parent families were spouse absent, one in five (19.1%) were divorced, and only 3.3% were headed by a widowed parent.

(text continued on p. 15)

TABLE 1.1 Living Arrangements of Children Under 18, by Race and Hispanic Origin: 1960 to 1992

Living Arrangement	1960	1970	1980	1992
All races				
Children under 18 (1,000s)	63,727	69,162	63,427	65,965
% Living with two parents	87.7	85.2	76.7	70.7
% Living with one parent	9.1	11.9	19.7	26.6
% Mother only	8.0	10.8	18.0	23.3
% Father only	1.1	1.1	1.7	3.3
% Other relatives	2.5	2.2	3.1	2.0
% Nonrelatives only	0.7	0.7	0.6	0.6
White				
Children under 18 (1,000s)	55,077	58,790	52,242	52,493
% Living with two parents	90.9	89.5	82.7	77.4
% Mother only	6.1	7.8	13.5	17.6
% Father only	1.0	0.9	1.6	3.3
% All others	1.9	1.8	2.2	1.7
Black[a]				
Children under 18 (1,000s)	8,650	9,422	9,375	10,427
% Living with two parents	67.0	58.5	42.2	35.6
% Mother only	19.9	29.5	43.9	53.8
% Father only	2.0	2.3	1.9	3.1
% All others	11.1	9.7	12.0	7.5
Hispanic[b]				
Children under 18 (1,000s)	na[c]	4,006	5,459	7,619
% Living with two parents	na	77.7	75.4	64.8
% Mother only	na	na	19.6	28.5
% Father only	na	na	1.5	3.7
% All others	na	na	3.5	3.1

NOTE: From U.S. Bureau of the Census, "Marital Status and Living Arrangements," *Current Population Reports*, Series P-20. March 1988, No. 433, Table A-4; and March 1992, No. 468, Table G. Excludes persons under 18 years old who were maintaining households or families.
a. Blacks include all nonwhites in 1960.
b. Persons of Hispanic origin may be of any race.
c. na means not available.

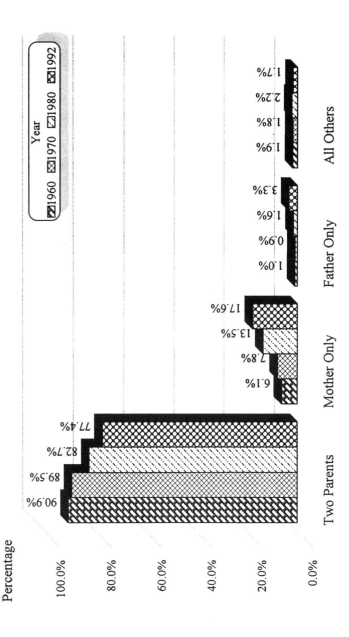

Figure 1.1. Living Arrangements of Children Under 18, Whites, 1960 to 1992

13

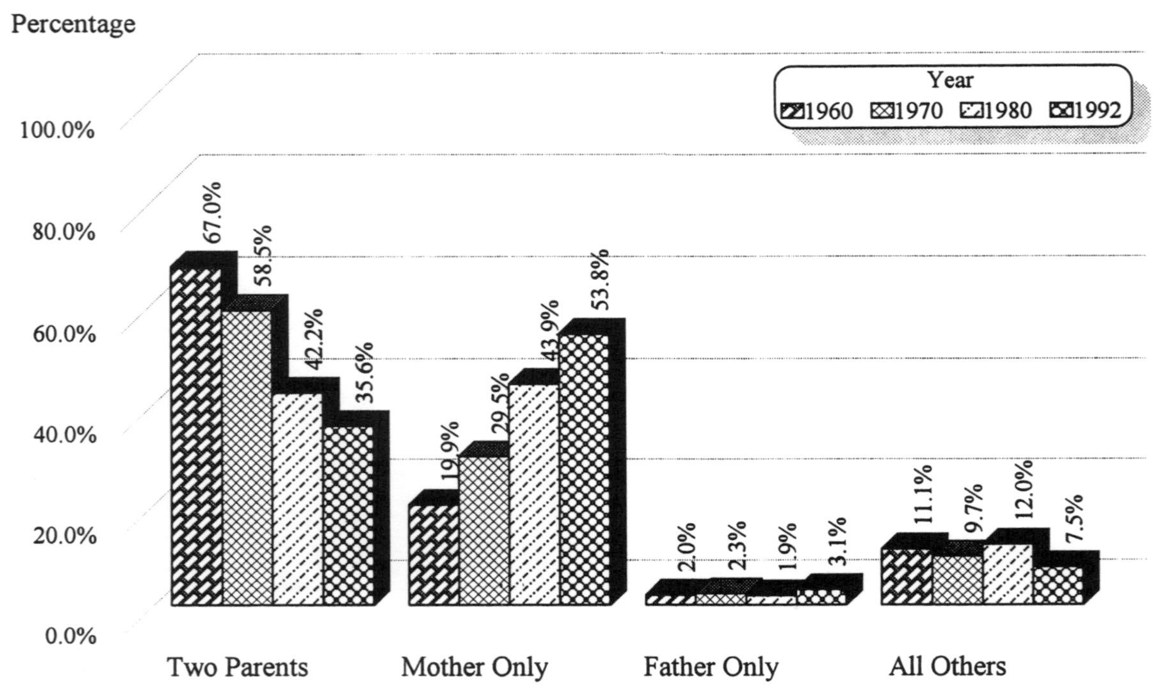

Figure 1.2. Living Arrangements of Children Under 18, Blacks, 1960 to 1992

Table 1.2 Number and Percentage of Children Under 18 Living With Only One Parent by Marital Status, Race, and Hispanic Origin: 1959 and 1992

Family Type	1959	1992
All children		
Living with one parent (1,000s)	9,165	17,578
Percentage living with single parent who is:		
Never married	na	34.2
Spouse absent	38.7	24.4
Widowed	45.4	4.9
Divorced	14.8	36.6
White children		
Living with one parent (1,000s)	6,406	10,971
Percentage living with single parent who is:		
Never married	na	22.3
Spouse absent	30.2	25.9
Widowed	50.7	5.7
Divorced	17.5	46.1
Black children		
Living with one parent (1,000s)[a]	2,699	5,934
Percentage living with single parent who is:		
Never married	na[b]	55.8
Spouse absent	59.0	21.7
Widowed	32.9	3.3
Divorced	8.1	19.1
Hispanic children		
Living with one parent (1,000s)[c]	na	2,447
Percentage living with single parent who is:		
Never married	na	35.6
Spouse absent	na	30.2
Widowed	na	5.6
Divorced	na	28.6

NOTE: From U.S. Bureau of the Census, "Family Characteristics of Persons: March 1959, No 112, Table 2; and "Marital Status and Living Arrangements: March 1992," No. 468, Table 5, *Current Population Reports*, Series P-20.
a. Blacks compiled as nonwhites in 1959.
b. na means not available.
c. Persons of Hispanic origin may be of any race.

Beyond these changes in single-parent families, the structure and dynamics of two-parent families also changed. Many children are living in stepfamilies. By the late 1980s, traditional married couples with an employed father, housewife mother, and two or more school-age children made up only 7% of American households (Otto, 1988). In short, there is now much greater diversity in family structure than 30 years ago. The factors precipitating different family types include changing social values, teenage childbearing, divorce, remarriage, and maternal employment.

As dramatic as these changes in family structure have been, they tell only part of the story. There have been many changes in family dynamics since the 1960s. How traditional were family roles 30 years ago and how have they changed?

The Domestic Division of Labor

In the 1960s, husbands spent an average of 11 hours per week on child care and housework, whereas wives invested 35 to 40 hours weekly. Thus men spent between one third and one fourth of the time on domestic labor that their wives spent. This pattern persisted despite the number or ages of children and regardless of wives' employment status. Of the 11 hours per week men spent in household labor, only 15 minutes per day (or less than 2 hours per week) were devoted to child care, compared to 54 minutes per day (more than 6 hours per week) among women (Coverman & Sheley, 1986). Some modest changes occurred during the 1970s and 1980s. Although men's involvement in housework and child care did not change much during the 1970s, the amount of time women spent on housework decreased significantly (Coverman & Sheley, 1986). By 1985, there were some increases in men's housework (Robinson, 1988). Still, married women continued to spend twice as much time as their husbands on housework and 50% more time on child care (Barnett & Baruch, 1987). However, we do not know how the domestic division of labor varies across different family structures, and we will explore this issue in Chapter 4.

Childrearing Values

We know that there have been substantial changes during the past few decades in the values parents instill in their children. Parents in the 1950s and 1960s stressed the importance of obedience in their children whereas parents in the 1970s and 1980s emphasized greater personal autonomy and responsibility (Alwin, 1986, 1990). These changes occurred across American families of different religious, ethnic, and social class backgrounds. Similar changes in parental values have been observed in other industrialized societies, such as West Germany and Japan (Alwin, 1986; Tromsdorff, 1983). Thus some changes in parent-child relationships may be due to shifting cultural values regarding traits desired in children. For example, one reason parents may be finding it difficult to control or direct their children and adolescents is that parents have placed less importance on obedience and control.

Parent-child relationships are interdependent and reciprocal. As parents' views of children have changed, so have children's views of their parents. Sebald (1986) observed a marked decline between 1963 and 1976 in the importance adolescents placed on parents' opinions, and a corresponding increase over the same period in the importance attached to the opinions of friends.[3] Although parental opinions had regained some respect by 1982, adolescents continued a consistent trend of making decisions independent of parental or peer advice. The declining importance of parental opinions is noteworthy, however, especially when considered together with the trend in childrearing values during this period. As we have established, this is the same period during which parents attributed greater significance to their children's personal autonomy. Considering these social changes, it is understandable that parental advice is sought (and followed) less frequently. This is just one illustration of how children's well-being may be more profoundly influenced by recent changes in parent-child relationships than by changes in family structure.

In sum, the American family is increasingly diverse and complex. Compared to children in 1960, children today are much less likely to live with their two biological parents. In response to changing sexual attitudes and behavior, coupled with men's flight from commitment, many children today are living in single-parent families with a mother who never married. Children are more likely to have experienced family disruption by divorce than to have experienced the death of the absent parent. Children of all ages, whether living in single-parent or two-parent families, are more likely than children 3 or 4 decades ago to have employed mothers and less likely to have employed fathers. Yet across a variety of two-parent family forms, women continue to spend significantly more time than their husbands on housework and child care. The traditional American family, to whatever degree it may have existed in the past, is now conspicuous by its absence.

But how influential have these changes in family *structure* been in changing family *relationships*? Do parents view their children differently across family types? How much time do parents and children spend together, and does this vary by the type of family? What about "quality" time? In families where fathers are present, has their involvement in parenting changed? Are conflict and violence between parents and children more prevalent in one family structure than another? In explaining changes in parent-child relationships, how important is family structure compared to race or socioeconomic status? These questions will be explored in Chapters 5 and 6.

In the next section we consider two of the most important structural changes occurring over the past 3 decades and their influence on family relations. Conventional wisdom and popular opinion hold that both developments have deleterious consequences for marital and parent-child relations. First, we consider some trends associated with increasing levels of maternal employment; then we consider high rates of divorce and single-parent family structure.

MAJOR DEVELOPMENTS IN
RESTRUCTURING FAMILY RELATIONS

Maternal Employment and Dual-Earner Families

A major societal concern is the consequences for the family and for children of increasing maternal employment. Most Americans believe that working mothers are detrimental to aspects of child development and well-being (Greenberger, Goldberg, Crawford, & Granger, 1988). Although employed women spend less total time with their children compared to nonemployed women, research suggests that mother's employment, per se, has very few adverse effects. In fact, there are some important positive effects on child development (e.g., see Bianchi & Spain, 1986; Menaghan & Parcel, 1990; Parcel & Menaghan, 1990; Spitze, 1988). Many adverse effects attributed to mothers' employment may be mediated by other factors, notably children's age, sex, social class, personality characteristics, quality of substitute care, and mothers' occupational status. We will explore how these variables affect parent-child interaction in Chapter 5, and the consequences for mothers' and children's well-being in Chapters 6 and 7.

Single employed mothers, whether divorced or continuously single, generally have much lower family income than employed mothers in dual-earner families. For these single women and their children, it would seem the more relevant question is the consequences of mothers' *not* working. Unfortunately, research on the consequences of maternal employment generally ignores single parents (Spitze, 1988). One objective of our research is to concentrate on different groups of single parents, their family relationships, and their children's well-being.

A related question concerns the short- and long-term consequences of maternal unemployment in two-parent families. A common assumption underlying much research on maternal employment is that for married women, employment is "optional." The importance of her employment for her own well-being and for the support of her family is often overlooked. Yet the wife's income often raises the family's status above poverty or from lower to middle class (Spitze, 1988). Beyond social, psychological, and financial benefits stemming from steady employment, there is the security and income it provides married women in the event they divorce. One question we will examine is how maternal employment influences family relations under varying socioeconomic conditions.

Finally, it may be that lower levels of mother-child interaction are not always detrimental to children of employed mothers. *More* time together is not always *better* time together. The nurturance, warmth, support, and sincerity expressed during the times they are together may be more important than the frequency or level of interaction. Viewed differently, in some cases higher levels of interaction between nonemployed mothers and their children become strenuous for parents and unhealthy for children. There is some evidence for what Gelles (1987) terms *the time at risk hypothesis*: rates of child abuse are higher among women who would normally spend the most time with their children— housewives with preschool children—than among mothers with full-time employment. A more detached style of parental support (Demo, 1992a) may facilitate culturally valued independence and autonomy in children and reduce parental role strain.

In sum, despite the fervor with which Americans cling to traditional notions of maternal responsibility for children, it may be that children of employed mothers fare as well or better than children of nonemployed mothers. These relationships will be examined in Chapter 7.

Divorce and Single-Mother Families

Clearly, children in the 1990s are much more likely to experience the disruption of their parents' marriage and to live with a single parent than children in the 1960s. Three fifths of children in single-parent families are living with a separated or divorced parent, whereas about one third of the children in these families are living with a never-married parent (Table 1.2). For many, living with one parent will be a long-term arrangement. Over half of the children whose parents divorce spend at least 6 years with only one parent. The majority of children in single-parent families will live out their childhood without ever entering a second family (Bumpass & Sweet, 1989). Most black children will spend the majority of their childhood years in a mother-only family (Sweet & Bumpass, 1987).

How are children affected by parental divorce and by living in single-parent families? The answers are not simple or clear-cut. Although popular and clinical impressions suggest that children of divorce suffer harmful and long-lasting effects, research on nonclinical populations suggests that most children experience short-term emotional adjustments. Where there are differences between children in single-parent families and children in continuously intact two-parent families, the differences between groups tend to be small. For example, children living in mother-only families fare worse on measures of intellectual performance and educational attainment (Hetherington, Camara, & Featherman, 1983; Keith & Finlay, 1988; McLanahan, 1985) and exhibit higher rates of sexual and delinquent activity. One explanation for the latter finding is that levels of parental supervision and control are lower in single-parent families, allowing adolescents more opportunities to make decisions independent of parental input (Dornbusch et al., 1985; Newcomer & Udry, 1987). In addition, Nock (1988) proposes that the more peerlike nature of parent-child relationships in single-parent families blurs generational boundaries and obstructs hierarchical authority relations. He views these arrangements as socialization deficits that impair performance in hierarchical educational and occupational structures and result in lower educational and occupational attainment.

Of course, not all children are affected the same way by family disruption. Many variables are important in understanding how children respond. For example, some children may benefit because their postdivorce family is happier and less conflictual than their predivorce family. For these children family change is positive rather than stressful. Older children often have an easier time adjusting than younger children (Hetherington et al., 1983). Children's gender and race, family socioeconomic status, and levels of family conflict also appear to be important in mediating the effects of divorce and family composition (Demo & Acock, 1988; Emery, 1982). Studies show that frequent marital and family conflict in two-parent families may be more detrimental to children's physical health than divorce (Gottman & Katz, 1989; Mechanic & Hansell, 1989). Thus, although divorce and single-parent family structure may have some adverse effects on children, the effects that are directly attributable to these experiences (rather than to other factors) are not nearly as dramatic or as permanent as popularly believed. We will examine in detail the consequences of family structure for children's well-being in Chapter 7.

It is important to recognize that divorce and living in a single-parent family are two different experiences for children and affect them in different ways. Salient events for children when their parents divorce include dramatic declines in the time they spend with nonresidential parents, reduced interaction with grandparents and other kin related to the nonresidential parent, persisting interparental conflict, residential changes involving new neighborhoods, new schools, and new friends, as well as declines in standard of living associated with lowered household income. Children who live in continuous single-parent families, such as children of mothers who never married, often experience economic hardship but do not experience many of the other stressful life changes associated with family disruption.

Many children live in economic hardship, including children whose fathers and/or mothers are unemployed or underemployed. Living in a single-parent family often means severe and long-lasting financial problems. Compared to children living with both parents, those in mother-only families are five times as likely to be living below the poverty threshold (47% versus 9%); for black children, three of every five in mother-child families are living in poverty (Sweet & Bumpass, 1987). Further, since 1967 the economic well-being of mother-only families has worsened vis-à-vis other family types (McLanahan & Booth, 1989). Economic hardship has dire consequences for parents and children. These include lower levels of parental nurturance, inconsistent discipline, and adolescent distress (Lempers, Clark-Lempers, & Simons, 1989). For these reasons, it is essential to examine family socioeconomic conditions when trying to identify correlates and consequences of different family types.

FAMILY STRUCTURE AND FAMILY PROCESS

Whether living with one parent or two, and whether living with biological parents or stepparents, family *processes* are critical to children's development and well-being. One such family process is parental supervision and control. The documented pattern of lower parental supervision in single-parent families is both important and understandable. But how are we to interpret it? Often these findings are interpreted as problems inherent in single-parent families, inevitable consequences of deviation from traditional marriage and family patterns. Viewed from a different perspective, the key to understanding these families may be the participation and support of the nonresidential father. Long-term single parenting, usually performed by employed women, is a chronic stressor (Thompson & Ensminger, 1989). Yet the typical pattern of visitation, involvement, and financial support by nonresidential fathers is one of general neglect and abandonment. Using national survey data, Furstenberg, Morgan, and Allison (1987) report that more than two fifths of absent biological fathers had no contact with their children in the preceding year. Three fifths provided no financial support (also see Seltzer & Bianchi, 1988).[4] Importantly, in families where paternal economic support was provided, the likelihood of adolescent problem behavior was reduced.

The pattern of findings described here suggests that children, although certainly affected by divorce and single-parent family structure, may be more profoundly influenced by diminished socioeconomic resources and by the degree of involvement, support, and discipline provided by their parents. The latter are examples of important family processes that may vary across different family structures. A recurrent theme throughout this volume will be the importance of family structure compared with family processes and relationships.

PREVALENT FAMILY STRUCTURES

There are many types of families in the United States today, and as the number of family types increases, classification becomes more difficult. Consider just a few examples. Roughly 10% of the adult population is homosexual (Voeller, 1990). This population includes lesbian and gay couples who have children from a prior relationship, adoption, or through biosocial innovations such as alternative insemination (see Bozett, 1987; Edwards, 1991). About 10% of single-parent households are headed by a father; he may be the biological parent or stepfather, or he may have adopted the children. A small, but growing number of stepfamilies contain the father's biological children, and the mother is the stepparent. There are an increasing number of families in which neither parent is present and the children live with a grandparent or other relative. Also growing is the number of families with adult children in the household.

It is beyond the scope of this study to examine all possible types of families. Instead, we selected four types of families that form a substantial proportion of all families. Each of these types has been defined to be fairly homogeneous so that we can draw clear distinctions. Identifying homogeneous family types necessarily means eliminating some family forms from our study. This involved a series of difficult decisions. To illustrate, some divorced mothers had all their biological children while they were married. A smaller group of divorced mothers were stepmothers in their former marriage and now are the custodial parent for these stepchildren. Other divorced mothers had all their children since their previous marriage ended. The latter group may have a great deal in common with never-married mothers. We decided we either needed to create a distinct type of family for each of these, or not include some of them in the study. We took the latter course. When we describe divorced mothers, we are referring to women who were previously married and have at least one biological child from that marriage. Because there are almost endless variations, we have narrowed our focus a great deal. Still, the four types we examine represent the majority (roughly 75%) of contemporary American families with children.[5]

Our methods for defining the four types of families are described in Chapter 3. For the present, we give a brief narrative description of each family form:

1. *First-married mothers.* These are mothers who are in their first marriage, whose husbands are also in their first marriage, and who have at least one biological child of the mother under the age of 19 living in the household at the time of the interview. The husband was also living in the household at the time of the interview.
2. *Divorced mothers.* These are single-parent, female-headed families in which the mother has at least one biological child under the age of 19 from her previous marriage living in the household at the time of the interview.
3. *Remarried mothers.* These are mothers who are in their second or subsequent marriage, who have a biological child under the age of 19 from a prior marriage living in the household, and who have a husband (stepfather) who was present at the time of the interview.
4. *Continuously single mothers.* These are mothers who never married and who have at least one resident, biological child under the age of 19.

Together, these four forms represent the vast majority of American families in which children and/or adolescents are present. We should also point out some problems inherent in labeling family types. One problem is the seemingly unavoidable association between marital status and family structure. For example, we use the terms *first-married, divorced, remarried,* and *continuously single* to define family types. These terms reflect the marital status and history of the biological mothers of the children living in these families. For reasons explained in Chapter 3, we have chosen to focus on mothers rather than fathers. In defining family structure according to mothers' marital status and relying on mothers' report of family relations, we do not intend to imply that the mothers' marital status is paramount to children's well-being, nor that deviations from first-marriage family units are harmful to children. However, a substantial body of research has investigated family structure as an important predictor of family relationships and well-being. We have designed our study to test some assumptions, findings, and interpretations of prior work. In doing so, we use conventional terms to describe family types in an effort to enhance comparability of findings across studies. In essence, this book sets out to study the hypothesis that family structure (as defined by marital status) is influential in shaping family relationships and personal well-being.

THE CHAPTERS THAT FOLLOW

In the next chapter we outline theoretical reasons for expecting that family structure is related to family process and individual well-being. Chapter 3 provides an overview of the study, describing the National Survey of Families and Households (NSFH) and the methods we will use for making comparisons across family types. Descriptions of marital, postmarital, and nonmarital couple relations are presented in Chapter 4. This chapter focuses on how marital relationships are similar and different in first marriages compared to remarriages, and how postmarital relations are similar or different for those who remarry compared to those who remain divorced. In Chapter 5 we examine intergenerational relationships and describe variations in childrearing values and family rules across different family types. We also compare parent-child interaction patterns and areas of disagreement, conflict, and violence across family forms. The focus of Chapter 6 is the influence of family structure and family relationships for mothers' well-being, and in Chapter 7 we trace the consequences of family arrangements and dynamics for childrens' well-being. The final chapter discusses some implications for the future of American families and some directions for further research.

NOTES

1. This figure was based on projected expenditures for rearing the younger child in a two-child, middle-income, husband-wife household. Projections for childrearing expenses varied by household income and family structure. For husband-wife families, the projections are $143,690 per child for low-income

families; $199,560 for middle-income families; and $278,780 for high-income families. For single-parent households, the projections are $90,570 per child for lower-income families, and $167,940 for higher-income families (Lino, 1991). On average, projected expenditures are 3% higher on the older child in two-child, husband-wife households (Lino, 1990).

2. These figures assume 4 consecutive years at a public university beginning in 2007-2008 and ending in 2010-2011. Costs at a private college or university would be substantially higher. Costs were estimated based on the average annual cost for tuition, room, and board at a public university ($4,520) in 1989-90 (U.S. Department of Education, 1991). Projections assume a 9% inflation rate in college-related expenses, which was the annual inflation rate for tuition, fees, room, and board from 1980 to 1987 (Hauptman & Merisotis, 1990).

3. Consistent with other studies, Sebald (1986) found that adolescents turn to peers for advice on some matters and turn to parents on other matters. Generally, they rely on peers for advice on social activities and concerns. Parents are typically consulted on more important matters (e.g., financial, educational, and career concerns). This occurred across the three measurement periods.

4. Using the National Survey of Families and Households data, but analyzing a different subsample than the one examined here, Cooney and Uhlenberg (1990) demonstrate that father-child bonds are permanently weakened by re-duced contact stemming from divorce. They found that compared to married men who had never divorced, men who had been divorced at some point in their lives reported less frequent contact with their adult offspring, were much less likely to have an adult child living in their household, and were much less likely to consider their adult children as potential sources of support in times of need.

5. We explain in Chapter 3 how this figure was calculated and which family types are not included in our study.

Theoretical Perspectives Linking Family Structure, Family Relations, and Well-Being

Why examine family structure? How does family structure influence family relationships and personal well-being? Family researchers and other social scientists have debated these issues for decades. In this chapter we explore some of the most influential theories guiding research on family structure, family relationships, and individual well-being. Family structure is understood in a variety of ways; here we describe theories linking marital status and family relationships to adult well-being. In the second part of the chapter we outline theories emphasizing the role of parents and parent-child relationships for children's development and well-being.

THEORIES LINKING FAMILY STRUCTURE, FAMILY RELATIONS, AND ADULT WELL-BEING

How important is marriage to adult well-being? How important is the quality of marriage and family relationships? Do first marriages and remarriages vary in their importance for adult well-being? Compared to married people, do mothers who never marry have lower levels of happiness and life satisfaction? Are they less integrated into family and other social support networks? Are mothers who have never married happier than their counterparts who are divorced? Are single parents happier than mothers in unhappy marriages? How important is parenting to well-being, and does this vary for women and men, or for adults in different family structures? To address such questions, it is important to consider the theoretical underpinnings that shaped the traditional ideology of the U.S. family and that continue to guide research.

Structural-Functional Theory

According to structural-functional theory, society is structured as a complex system of interdependent parts. Essential components of the social structure include norms, roles, and institutions. The family institution, like other institutions in society (e.g., education, religion, economy, polity) can be viewed as an interdependent role network (e.g., roles of wife and husband, mother and father, daughter and son, sister and brother). It also has certain functions, or tasks, it is expected to perform. One function performed by the family institution is that it regulates sexual behavior, providing a context for socially acceptable sexual relations. The family provides role differentiation and a division of labor. The family is also expected to provide a legitimate place for children to be born and a healthy environment in which they are socialized. Thus every society has patterned needs and patterned ways of fulfilling those needs, and the family institution is vital to assuring that individual and societal needs are met.

Role differentiation in marriage and family is important for understanding marital relationships and adult well-being. One popular and influential version of structural-functionalist theory suggests that leadership roles within the nuclear family tend to be differentiated (Parsons & Bales, 1955; Zelditch, 1955). According to this perspective, for both cultural and biological reasons (Pitts, 1964), the "person-oriented" wife plays the social-emotional, expressive role, tending to family members' social and psychological needs, caring for children, supporting her husband, maintaining family solidarity, and doing housework. Because the husband and father is "exempted from (the) biological functions (of) bearing and early nursing of children" (Parsons & Bales, 1955, p. 23), the "task-oriented" man is assigned the responsibility of providing for the family's socioeconomic needs. In Kingsley Davis's (1949) words, "the weak link in the family group is the father-child bond. There is no necessary association and no easy means of identification between these two as there is between mother and child" (p. 400). The husband thus plays the instrumental provider role, supporting the family financially and determining both its standard of living and its status in the social structure (Parsons, 1942). In the modern U.S. family, therefore, the wife's responsibilities are central to daily family activities and relationships, whereas the husband's responsibilities are primarily extrafamilial. Further, Parsonian functionalists argue that adhering to and conforming to these roles ensures family stability and societal order, whereas deviance from these roles leads to family disorganization, instability, divorce, and behavioral problems among children (Kingsbury & Scanzoni, 1993, p. 197).

Using this framework, there are many implications for families headed by single adults. In these families the possibilities for dividing labor are minimized or absent, meaning that one adult must do all or most of the domestic labor, including childrearing if she (or sometimes, he) has dependent-aged children. Role strain results for the single adult parent, whereas married adults can divide labor, have more manageable workloads, and experience less strain. From a structural-functionalist perspective, then, we would expect married adults to have higher well-being.

One criticism of structural-functional theories in general, and Parsonian versions in particular, is the assumption that the traditional nuclear family provided the optimal arrangement for meeting instrumental needs. However successful the traditional family was at meeting those needs, rapid social changes in the family and in the larger society have created many diverse family structures and have made the traditional family less attractive for many people. The structural-functional approach predicts that the father's absence from the household is important because his instrumental role cannot be provided without him. Families with nonresidential fathers tend to be disadvantaged because they have limited economic resources, not because of the absence of the father, per se. The father-child bond is assumed to be weak, so the more important loss to the single parent and children is the loss of the father's economic contribution.

But how important is it that economic resources derive from the father/husband? To the degree that economic resources are important, alternative systems and family structures may be able to meet those needs. For example, families with nonresidential fathers may derive income from mother's employment or from child support paid by the father, or a combination of these. Other and more innovative systems may also enhance single-parent family well-being. One example is a national system of payroll deductions from nonresidential parents, producing economic support that is automatically sent to the residential parent. Another example is a national health care program that provides basic and preventive health care for all individuals regardless of their family income. Single-parent families would also be bolstered by an educational system that ensures opportunities for children irrespective of their parents' economic resources.

There are many criticisms of structural-functionalist theories. For the purposes of this discussion one other weakness of the general paradigm is noteworthy: family work is not divided equitably in most families. As we will see in Chapters 4 and 5, women do most of the housework and most of the child care. This pattern occurs in families where the wife is employed as well as in families where she is not employed. Thus the notion of separate leadership roles and separate spheres of power is not accurate in describing most contemporary U.S. families. Rather, a power imbalance exists under which most women are disadvantaged. Family researchers using other theoretical perspectives would not consider such arrangements to be functional. Nevertheless, structural functionalism has been very influential in family studies and continues to be valuable in that certain of its core assumptions and concerns remain central to the field, perhaps most notably in family stress and neo-functionalist theories (see Kingsbury & Scanzoni, 1993).

Social Exchange Theory

Derived from the work of Thibaut and Kelley (1959), Homans (1961, 1974), and Blau (1964), social exchange theory proposes that individuals in social relationships (e.g., members of a family) provide benefits to each other contingent upon receipt of benefits from the other. Wives and husbands do not act in random ways; instead, their actions are goal-oriented, rational, and purposeful. The theory assumes that people try to maximize rewards and minimize costs. People "profit" from a relationship if their "rewards" exceed their "costs." Like individuals in other social relationships, spouses are motivated to maximize their own rewards and minimize their costs so that they may enjoy their relationship and judge it profitable.

When one spouse provides a benefit for the other, the norm of reciprocity (Gouldner, 1960) dictates that the recipient provides a benefit of equivalent "value" in return. Although exchange theory sounds simple enough, its complexity comes from the many ways people define value. A mother may value her children doing well at school. Her husband may help a child who is having trouble in Spanish. The mother may do the dishes that week if they are usually done by her husband. The norm of reciprocity does not require a one-to-one matching. If one family member does something extra, she or he can expect other family members to do something extra. The more a person contributes to the family's well-being, the more she or he can expect others to do the same. After enjoying a few hours of leisure time while his wife takes care of the children, a husband may feel obligated to reciprocate by spending some time with the children so that his wife may visit with her friends. Reciprocation is important in that it facilitates symmetry for the long term. Reciprocation may be delayed in informal relationships, but should come eventually. When one partner fails to reciprocate, or provides benefits of lesser value, she or he is exploiting the relationship. Such exploitation can persist only if society legitimates it. In the traditional nuclear family, many would say that the husband/father has been allowed by society to exploit his family. Notice, however, that such exploitation weakens the family. Other family members become less likely to make any extra contribution to the family's well-being and eventually the entire family, including the husband/father, suffers.

Two variants of exchange theory are Emerson and Cook's (Cook & Emerson, 1978; Emerson, 1972, 1976) power dependency model and equity theory (Adams, 1965; Walster, Walster, & Berscheid, 1978). They argue that the profits or outcomes from a relationship should be proportional to investments or inputs. A husband who has a high education and earnings has "invested" more in the relationship than his wife who has less education and lower earnings. Following equity theory, this is an unbalanced relationship unless the husband also derives more "profits" from the relationship than does his wife. The wife can balance the relationship in several ways, ranging from getting more education (we see many older-than-average college students doing just this), getting a better-paying job, or doing more household chores. Note that all of these involve increasing her investment in the family. If she cannot balance the relationship, she runs the risk of being exploited because she is more dependent on her husband than he is on her.

Power dependency and equity theories point to the advantages of a balanced relationship in terms of both satisfaction and stability. However, they also clarify the difference between relationship quality and stability. A relationship has quality to the extent that both members find it profitable and view it as better than alternative relationships. A relationship with low quality, however, may remain stable if the exploited person is too dependent. For instance, a mother of five children who has little education and no marketable skills cannot afford a divorce unless the society has strong and effective provisions for child support. She may be forced to stay in a stable but unhappy relationship and suffer the costs. Exchange theorists say that her present relationship is not profitable or satisfying but her "comparison level for alternatives" (divorce) is even worse.

Society can encourage exploitation. This is done when the contributions of certain members are systematically devalued by society. For example, whereas child care is given enormous attention for its national importance, child care providers are among the lowest paid professionals. By defining certain work as "women's work" and then devaluing that work, society places constraints on relationships between wives and husbands. The wife/mother works harder and longer because the work she does is of lower value. Women do a disproportionate share of many activities (household labor, child care) that are of lower value. Because our society puts a high value on the economic contribution of a spouse and a low value on housework and child care by a spouse, one spouse can use his or her power advantage to exploit the other. Typically, this means the husband can use his power advantage to exploit his wife. The wife is especially dependent if she has no source of economic viability and if her only alternative is divorce.

Clearly many exchanges are informal, and rewards exchanged in a particular transaction need not be of the same (or even similar) kind (Edwards, 1969). From a social exchange perspective, however, marriage provides a wide range of resources, costs, and rewards. Marital satisfaction must be viewed in the context of perceived costs and rewards during the course of the relationship. As Lewis and Spanier (1979) observe, "it is most reasonable to assume that the forecast of future rewards, as balanced against future costs, as well as the memory of cumulative rewards and costs throughout the history of the marital relationship, do greatly affect both the quality and the continuance of marital relationships" (p. 285). From a social exchange perspective then, marriage is profitable. Both the rewards and costs defining the profit are highly subjective. The range of rewards includes social status (e.g., newlywed), a steady companion and source of social support, pleasurable marital interaction, emotional gratification, as well as physical property and economic assets. The range of costs include household labor, child care, wage labor, the inconvenience of coordinating activities, and all the rewards that could be obtained by being single, such as freedom and independence. In situations where a marriage ceases to be profitable and where outcomes fall below the level that could be obtained in other relationships, one or both parties may choose to end the marriage. Of course, separation or divorce are more probable outcomes when one or both individuals perceive that being single, dating, and/or remarrying are attractive alternatives to the current relationship. Thus, from a social exchange perspective, a marriage that ceases to be mutually profitable may be ended, or at least will be threatened by low marital quality.

Applied to the study of family structure and adult well-being, a social exchange perspective suggests that the quality of marital (or nonmarital) interaction is more important than marital status in explaining adult well-being. Many dimensions of marital interaction predict marital quality: frequent interaction, effective communication and problem-solving, role complementarity, perceived similarities and rewards, and shared affection, love, and respect (Lewis & Spanier, 1979). Marital quality, in turn, engenders happiness, mental health, and well-being (Campbell, Converse, & Rodgers, 1976; Glenn & Weaver, 1979). Consistent with exchange theory, studies examining dimensions of marital interaction find that the quality of marital relationships is more important than marriage per se for individual well-being, and unhappily married persons tend to have poorer mental health than the divorced, widowed, or single (Gove, Hughes, & Style, 1983; Williams, 1988).

In sum, the research and theory provide a strong justification for further exploration of the familial and extrafamilial exchange processes contributing to adult well-being. Unfortunately, most research on marital quality continues to be atheoretical, although many studies are guided by an implicit social exchange framework (Glenn, 1990). Clearly, social exchange theory is potentially powerful and needs to be extended to exchange processes and well-being among nonmarried, formerly married, and remarried populations.

Social exchange theories also have limitations, and it is important to keep these limitations in mind as we apply social exchange theories to try to understand adult well-being. Social exchange theories assume that people are rational and that they have a considerable amount of control over their own and others' behavior. But people cannot always choose to act in desired or profitable ways, and they often confront obstacles in trying to influence others' actions. Parental, marital, and other social relationships are highly complex and intertwined. In addition, these relationships are often highly emotional, they tend to be hierarchical, and they are embedded in the context of personal and family histories. As a result, individuals are often forced or coerced into situations over which they have little or no control. A young woman may be divorced, or may never have married, because she never had any alternative. Viewed in these terms, it is simplistic, if not insensitive, to assert that women "choose" the lifestyles and relationships that they deem most profitable. Life is much more complex than simply making rational choices. We cannot always do what makes sense or what minimizes our personal costs.

Family Development and Family Life-Cycle Approach

Many family researchers rely on developmental and life cycle considerations to explain family transitions and trajectories over the life span (Aldous, 1978; Mattessich & Hill, 1987; Rodgers & White, 1993). Just as children and adults progress through stages of individual development, marriages and families typically progress through a series of clearly identifiable stages. The ordering and arrangement of these stages are similar for families in different cultures and different historical periods (Hareven, 1974). At each stage there are social, emotional, and developmental tasks that must be negotiated for individuals and families to proceed developmentally. As a family enters or exits a particular stage, the transition is marked by changes in the role structure of the family.

The Duvall eight-stage family life cycle is based on the assumption that a family's interaction patterns are strongly influenced by the age, developmental needs, and school placement of the oldest child (Duvall & Miller, 1985). Each time the first-born child enters a new phase in life (walking, talking, entering school, dating, or leaving home), new experiences are created for the whole family, and family relationships must be realigned and renegotiated. As subsequent children enter the family, grow, and develop, the family experiences familiar events and processes in child and adolescent development. Carter and McGoldrick (1989) maintain that, at least for intact, middle-class families, "the central underlying process to be negotiated is the expansion, contraction, and realignment of the relationship system to support the entry, exit, and development of family members in a functional way" (p. 12). Duvall and Miller (1985) define eight stages:

1. Married couples (without children)
2. Childbearing families (oldest child birth-30 months)
3. Families with preschool children (oldest child 2 ½-6 years)
4. Families with school children (oldest child 6-13 years)
5. Families with teenagers (oldest child 13-20 years)
6. Families launching young adults (first child gone to last child's leaving home)
7. Middle-aged parents (empty nest to retirement)
8. Aging family members (retirement to death of both spouses)

A family development or life-cycle approach is useful because it directs attention to the changing nature of family relationships and activities during the life course. For example, there are countless ways in which the marital dynamics of newlywed couples are different from those of couples with teenagers or couples in retirement. Changes in parental responsibilities, work status, financial well-being, and physical health cause marital partners to spend more time together and to communicate more effectively with each other at some stages in their marriage than at others. A shared marriage and family history accumulates as the couple moves through each stage of family development, and this history provides guidelines and routines for family communication, decision making, division of labor, and conflict resolution. A developmental approach also recognizes that age norms dictate appropriate behavior for children and adult of all ages and that normative timetables prescribe which activities (e.g., marriage) should precede others (e.g., parenthood). Life events have different meaning when they occur "off-schedule" than if they occur "on time."

Developmental and life-cycle theories have stimulated considerable research during the past 2 decades, and clearly the framework is useful for *describing* the development of many families, particularly intact families, which are more likely to follow normative sequences of activities and stages.[1] However, there has been little development toward a systematic and comprehensive theory for *explaining* changes in marital and family relationships during the life cycle. One limitation of this framework is that it is less useful for explaining subcultural variations in family development, that is, black, Hispanic, or Asian-American family experiences. For example, it does not explain why blacks, when compared to whites, are more likely to live in three-generation households (Beck & Beck, 1989), or why black grandparents are more actively involved in their grandchildren's lives (Cherlin & Furstenberg, 1986). A second limitation of family development/life-cycle approaches is inattention to nonnormative family experiences (e.g., family development patterns where parenthood precedes marriage, or where adult children return home), nonintact families, family disruptions (e.g., divorce), and the consequences of these nontraditional family forms and experiences for individual and family functioning. Where life-cycle stages of nontraditional family forms are described, they are often characterized as "deviations" from the normative family trajectory rather than as adaptive (cf. Carter & McGoldrick, 1989). Thus the dynamics of single-parent families and stepfamilies are blurred because they tend to be viewed from a problem-oriented perspective and as inherently stressful, rather than from a normative-adaptive perspective that directs attention to their benefits, strengths, complexity, and resilience (M. Coleman & Ganong, 1990).

Our analysis of family processes and well-being across diverse family structures is guided by a number of important developmental considerations. Perhaps most important, our examination of parent-child relationships (Chapter 5) and children's well-being (Chapter 7) distinguishes clearly between families in three distinct developmental stages: families with preschoolers (ages 0-4), families with school-age children (ages 5-11), and families with adolescents (ages 12-18). To be sure, the developmental tasks for children as well as those for parents are different across these family stages, and there are important changes in parent-child and marital relationships as families progress through these stages. In cases where the data allow, we make finer distinctions by controlling for the age (and gender) of the youngest child in the family. In addition, throughout the book we control for mother's age. Where appropriate, such as in comparisons of first-married families and stepfamilies, we control for length of current marriage and/or length of time since divorce. The specific reasons for including these and other variables in particular analyses are explained in greater detail in the chapters that follow.

Feminist Perspectives

Women and men experience marriage, even the same marriage, in different ways. Jessie Bernard (1972) may have described this pattern best by stating that in every marriage there are two marriages: hers and his. Women and men hold different expectations of marital and family roles, and they receive very different and unequal benefits from marriage, with women typically disadvantaged and oppressed (Delphy, 1984). Although women do most of the household labor and child care, their power is minimized by hierarchically structured, patriarchal arrangements within the family and other social institutions (Brown, 1981; Walby, 1990). Marriage can be an oppressive institution in which women are routinely controlled and dominated by men, men's interests, and an ideology of male supremacy (O'Brien, 1981). From a feminist perspective, "families, particularly those based on traditional ideologies and practices, are tension-filled arenas, loci of struggle and domination between genders and across generations" (Baber & Allen, 1992, p. 1).

The social control of women affects other dimensions of family life as women are socialized to nurture and be responsible for children's socioemotional development and mental health. Whether engaged in wage labor or not, traditional family ideology dictates that women are responsible for countless everyday family activities, a phenomenon historians call the cult of domesticity (Cott, 1977). Thus women invest substantial time and energy in the execution of tasks that are both identifiable and repetitive, but also tend to be devalued, unappreciated, and unpaid. These activities include caring for children, cooking, cleaning, shopping, and doing laundry. In addition, they routinely do family work that is even less visible and less frequently acknowledged, tasks that often go unnoticed even in research on household labor. For example, women spend considerable time planning and managing meals (DeVault, 1987, 1991); arranging and coordinating family members' schedules and activities; doing emotional work traditionally associated with femininity and motherhood, such as providing family members with a constant source of love, nurturance, companionship, and support; caring for aging parents; kinkeeping; and doing volunteer work. Although most women both resent and cherish family work (Thompson & Walker, 1989), it is gendered labor, simultaneously symbolic of women's subordination and their love and affection for their families (Ferree, 1990). Further, acceptance of and successful performance in these culturally defined roles signifies, to both women and men, that women are "good" wives and mothers (Berk, 1985; Ferree, 1991; Glenn, 1987).

A feminist perspective illustrates that it is important to move beyond simplistic dichotomies that suggest separate spheres of life for women and men. In particular, the distinction between work as the public sphere and family as the private sphere has led many to falsely assume that men historically have been the sole providers for their families and that family work has always been women's responsibility. In fact, married women contributed 25% of household income at the beginning of the century (Rainwater, 1979) and earned 31% of family income by the mid-1980s (Spitze, 1988). Thus women's wage labor has always been important to the family's standard of living, particularly in single-parent families, whose very existence is often dependent on the mother's earnings.

A central theme in feminist thinking on the family is that marital and family experiences are widely variable. Despite the pervasive ideology of the monolithic nuclear family (Thorne, 1982), diversity exists across many axes. There are important variations by social structural location (especially gender, race, and social class), household structure, sexual arrangements, and the nature of marital, nonmarital, and family interaction. Feminists emphasize that conflict is a persistent element in many families, that families are not always or uniformly cohesive, that some men are more dominant than others in controlling women, and that the extent of male involvement in family labor is widely variable (Ferree, 1991). Despite this diversity, however, the lingering ideology of the monolithic family and "women's proper place" operates to oppress women (Thorne, 1982).

Our expectations for adult well-being are thus very different when viewed from a feminist perspective. Whereas marriage typically provides many benefits for men, it provides fewer benefits for most women. Men's occupational attainment is helped by marriage and by their wives' direct and indirect support. In contrast, women's occupational progress is slowed by work-family role conflict; women advance faster occupationally and earn more if they remain single, delay marriage or, if divorced, delay remarriage (Menaghan & Parcel, 1990; Porter, 1984). There also may be psychological benefits for women who remain single or divorce, at least in comparison to unhappily married women. Women and men in inequitable marriages suffer higher rates of depression than their counterparts in relationships characterized by equity and a balanced division of decision-making power (Mirowsky, 1985), and unhappily married spouses report more distress than single women and men (Gove et al., 1983). There is also evidence that the reported happiness of married females declined significantly from 1972-1986 (Glenn & Weaver, 1988) and that the psychological well-being and happiness of formerly married women (and men) improves significantly in the first few years postdivorce (Booth & Amato, 1991).

In sum, a feminist perspective poses many new questions. It forces us to question the insidious ideology of the nuclear family, and it focuses our attention on how family relations are gendered and contentious. Viewed from this perspective, we would expect greater social and psychological benefits of marriage and family life for men than for women, especially for the large group of women living in inequitable and male-dominated marriages. Other groups of women have different experiences, however. Women with meaningful and rewarding employment often have happier marriages and higher well-being (Baruch, Barnett, & Rivers, 1983; Mirowsky & Ross, 1986; Rosenfield, 1989). Further diversity exists along other dimensions of socioeconomic status (e.g., education and income), and along other axes such as race, ethnicity, and sexual orientation.

To date, most studies applying feminist theories to the study of family structure and individual well-being have relied on small and nonrepresentative samples. As a result, the generalizability of many important and provocative findings has been questioned. To our knowledge, this is the first study employing a nationally representative sample and applying a feminist perspective to examine the complex relationships between family structure, family relationships, and individual well-being.

THEORIES LINKING FAMILY STRUCTURE, FAMILY RELATIONS, AND CHILD WELL-BEING

Family scholars using diverse theoretical perspectives maintain that parent-child relationships are critical to children's development. This proposition is central to anthropological, developmental, structural-functional, symbolic interactionist, feminist, social exchange, social learning, social role, family systems, and psychoanalytic theories. These orientations vary widely, however, in the importance they assign to biological ties as compared to environmental circumstances in shaping children's development and well-being. In this section, we trace the linkages among changing household arrangements, family processes, and child outcomes.

Research relating family structure to the well-being of youth of different ages can be summarized by four approaches: (a) family composition, (b) economic deprivation, (c) family conflict, and (d) life stress.

Family Composition

The traditional approach to well-being emphasizes family composition and posits that two parental role models are essential for the normal development and well-being of children. Consistent with the Freudian assumption that a two-parent group is the essential unit for appropriate sex-typed identification, social psychological, developmental, sociological, and anthropological theories have long maintained the necessity of such a group for normal child development. Nuclear families serve as "factories" in which children's personalities are formed (Slater, 1961). It follows that departures from the nuclear family are problematic. For example, it has been shown that parental absence is associated with decreases in parent-child contact and parental supervision, support, and control, and that these processes, in turn, are associated with behavioral problems among children (Dornbusch et al., 1985; Furstenberg et al., 1987). Further, Nock (1988) proposes that the absence of generational boundaries and hierarchical authority relations in single-parent families represents a socialization deficit that results in lower educational and occupational attainment as adults. The literature thus suggests what we call *the family composition hypothesis*: Children reared in households where the two biological parents are not present exhibit lower levels of well-being than children in intact, first-married family units. Specifically, this hypothesis suggests that children in divorced families, stepfamilies, and continuously single-parent families experience lower levels of well-being than children in first-married families.

There is reason to question the veracity of the family composition hypothesis, however. Methodologically, research in support of the family composition hypothesis has been seriously flawed (Blechman, 1982; Demo & Acock, 1988). Most studies:

1. Neglect antecedent variables such as race, gender, and social class
2. Overlook potentially mediating factors such as children's age at the time of disruption, and length of time since disruption
3. Use small and nonrepresentative samples
4. Examine limited dimensions of social and psychological well-being
5. Fail to assess possible beneficial effects deriving from different family structures

Equally critical, no dominant theoretical perspective recognizes that structural effects may be short-lived or otherwise mitigated by compensatory mechanisms. For example, the father's absence from the household often is not a discrete event. Many children in families with nonresidential fathers, especially black children, continue to have significant contact with their fathers, partly due to father absence being temporary or intermittent and partly due to frequent visitation (Mott, 1990). In addition, new father figures and alternative role models are often available and influential in children's lives (Allen, 1978; Oshman & Manosevitz, 1976). Children may not need both biological parents as models if they can select models from stepparents, other relatives, teachers, coaches, or the media (Lamb, 1977). In short, "traditional definitions of family structure may be inadequate for defining all forms of American families" (Mott, 1990, p. 507).

Economic Deprivation

A second approach emphasizes that economic deprivation in single-parent families is the critical variable in explaining children's well-being. Compared to children living with both parents, those in mother-only families are five times as likely to be living below the poverty threshold (47% versus 9%); for black children, three of every five in mother-child families are living in poverty (Sweet & Bumpass, 1987). Further, since 1967 the economic well-being of mother-only families has worsened vis-à-vis other family types (McLanahan & Booth, 1989). Economic hardship has dire consequences for parents and children. Parents become depressed, irritable, hostile, and punitive. Children and adolescents suffer distress because their parents are less nurturant, supportive, responsive, and consistent in disciplining (Lempers et al., 1989; McLoyd, 1990). The *economic deprivation perspective* thus suggests that because family income is much higher in two-parent households than in one-parent households, children in two-parent families (first-married and step-families) experience higher levels of well-being than children in single-parent (continuously single-parent and divorced) families.

An inconsistency in this argument, however, is that parents do not have to be married or living with each other to support their children. This is important in that many children in single-parent families are likely to be disadvantaged because parental income, particularly income earned by nonresidential parents, is frequently distributed in other ways and not invested in their children's well-being. Further, although family income and family structure are related, the correlation is far from perfect. Some single-parent families have substantially higher household income than some two-parent families. A more careful analysis of the economic deprivation perspective involves examination of two hypotheses:

1. That children in higher income two-parent families have higher levels of well-being than children in lower income two-parent families
2. That children in higher income single-parent families have higher levels of well-being than children in lower income single-parent families (Demo, 1993).

Family Conflict

A third perspective posits that rather than family structure being the most influential factor, the experience of family conflict is detrimental to children's well-being. Whether living with one parent or two, and whether living with biological parents or stepparents, family processes are critical to children's development and well-being. Numerous studies show that levels of marital and family conflict are associated with children's adjustment, self-esteem, and other measures of psychological well-being (Berg & Kelly, 1979; Emery, 1982; Grych & Fincham, 1990; Raschke & Raschke, 1979). Other studies show that children's physical well-being is unaffected by divorce, that frequent marital and family conflict in two-parent families is detrimental to children's physical health, and that divorce may, in fact, insulate some children and adolescents from prolonged exposure to health-threatening family interactions (Gottman & Katz, 1989; Mechanic & Hansell, 1989). Indeed, reviews of the literature demonstrate that it is precisely these experiences—conflict in marital and parent-child relationships—that mediate the effect of family structure on children's well-being (Demo & Acock, 1988; Emery, 1982; also see Booth & Edwards, 1989, for an empirical illustration). Thus *the family conflict hypothesis* predicts that regardless of family structure, children exposed to high levels of interparental conflict and parent-child conflict experience lower levels of well-being than children in families with less conflict.

Life Stress

An alternative approach may be described as the life stress perspective: children experience adjustment problems as the result of a combination of stressful life events and experiences rather than because of any single factor, such as family composition. For children who have experienced parental divorce, stressors may include several factors mentioned above: reduced contact with nonresidential parents, grandparents, and other relatives; parental depression or other postdivorce adjustment problems; parental conflict before and during separation; parent-child conflict; and dramatic declines in standard of living (Demo & Acock, 1988). Further, when parents divorce or remarry, children may experience additional stress if they have to move, change schools, make new friends, and adjust to new siblings and the new expectations and sanctions of stepparents (Theis, 1977; Visher & Visher, 1983; Wolchik, Sandler, Braver, & Fogas, 1985). For children who have played a confidant and coparental role in a single-parent family, the addition of a stepfather may be a serious threat. A growing number of children experience a series of family transitions during their childhood, with the cumulative disadvantage of these stressors having long-term, adverse effects on children, even into adulthood (Amato & Booth, 1991).

It is important to note that children who live in single-parent families, such as children of mothers who never married, often experience economic hardship but do not experience many of the other stressful life changes associated with family disruption. By definition, they have always lived in single-parent families and may not have experienced a parent leaving home or a stepparent joining the family and household. Thus the most important factors for predicting child well-being may vary depending on family type. For example, economic circumstances may have a greater effect on well-being in first-married and continuously single-parent families, whereas stressful life changes are stronger predictors of well-being in divorced families and stepfamilies. Although this perspective is inherently more general and more complex than the other three perspectives, *the life stress hypothesis* predicts that because more life stress is generally experienced by children in divorced and remarried families, these children experience lower levels of well-being than those in first-married or continuously single-parent families.

Like the other perspectives, the life stress perspective has limitations associated with valuation of traditional nuclear family ideology. Specifically, it is assumed that parental divorce and remarriage are stressors in the child's life. Although for many children parental divorce is stressful (at least in the short term), and although some children experience stepfamilies as stressful, the broader picture is that these events are only part of children's and adolescents' lives. The central conceptual and empirical question must be which stressors are most salient and deleterious to children—the stresses in high-conflict (even violent) two-parent families prior to divorce, or the stresses of their new families post-divorce? Many life changes, rather than being stressful, are positive and growth-inducing. Rather than relying on assumptions regarding family types, the life stress perspective could be tested by examining hypotheses that focus on the actual stressors. For example, we could hypothesize that the well-being of children of divorce (a) is lower in high-stress stepfamilies than in low-stress stepfamilies, and (b) is lower in high-stress single-parent families than in low-stress single-parent families (Demo, 1993).

It should be clear that there are commonalities and differences among these four approaches and their predictions. In general, they suggest that children in first-married family units are advantaged in terms of social and psychological well-being and that children of divorce and children in single-parent families are disadvantaged. The family conflict perspective, however, stipulates that family process is more important than family type. The economic deprivation perspective suggests that differences across family types are an artifact of differences in family income, and the life stress perspective suggests that children in divorced and stepfamilies are vulnerable.

There is ample evidence that the four family structures we propose to study are different in many ways beyond parents' marital status. Divorced parents who remarry may not represent the population of divorced parents generally. Those who remarry tend to be white, younger, better off financially, and more active in the community. Indeed, as a group, remarried mothers may enjoy greater resources than the first-marrieds, and substantially more than the divorced who do not remarry. Thus it may be that successful adjustment of children in remarriages is due to abundant financial resources. For these reasons, it is important to keep in mind many background characteristics, mediating processes, and control variables, such as children's age, race, and gender, as discussed in the next chapter.

HOW IMPORTANT IS FAMILY STRUCTURE?

We believe that family structure provides a "social address" (Bronfenbrenner, 1979). That is, it tells us something about the social environment in which family members live, such as whether they live in a family formed by a first marriage, a divorce, or a remarriage. But knowing family structure alone tells us very little about the proximate social experiences bearing on parents and children. Knowing family structure tells us little about the dynamics of family relationships, the time family members spend together, their relationships with other relatives, family communication patterns, childrearing practices and values, and other important elements of the immediate family and broader social context. As Bronfenbrenner and Crouter (1983) demonstrate, reliance on social background has serious limitations in explaining developmental outcomes:

> No explicit consideration is given . . . to intervening structures or processes through which the environment might affect the course of development. One looks only at the social address—that is, the environmental label—with no attention to what the environment is like, what people are living there, what they are doing, or how the activities taking place could affect the child. (pp. 361-362)

Yet despite their limitations, social address models remain very popular among researchers interested in explaining human development. This approach is commonly used by researchers trying to understand the consequences of what Bronfenbrenner and Crouter (1983) call the "new demography" (single-parent families, stepfamilies, maternal employment, and day care). Typically the developmental characteristics of children in one environment are compared and contrasted with those of children in a different environment, and any differences between groups are then interpreted to be direct consequences of environmental differences. Thus one possibility that this type of research ignores is that family relationships (and other social processes) may vary for children across different social environments, and these differences (rather than family structure or other social addresses) may account for differences in children's development and well-being.

This is not to suggest that family structure is unimportant. For adults and children alike, family structure influences family relationships. Living with a spouse is fundamentally different from living alone, and living with one parent is different from living with two. Our interest is in identifying the ways in which family structure is important and the ways in which family resources, relationships, and processes are important. We view family processes as intervening links. That is, we believe that family type influences family relationships and, therefore, family type indirectly influences personal well-being. A central objective of this book is to describe how family relationships are similar and different across four prevalent family types. A second objective is to disentangle the separate effects that family structure, family relationships, and other variables (e.g., socioeconomic status, race, and social support) have on family members' well-being. In Chapter 3 we explain our research design and the data we have used to examine these questions.

NOTE

1. Advocating a life-course perspective, Elder (1984, 1985, 1991) and others contend that the notion of a normative family life cycle may have been reasonable in the 1950s, but that the increasing plurality and diversity of postmodern families render useless a family life-cycle framework. Instead, Elder suggests that the focus of analysis be shifted to individuals, whose multidimensional life trajectories (principally involving marriage, parenthood, and work) can be observed and studied over time.

THREE

Research Design and Profile of American Families

Although there are several data sets available with pertinent information on family background and family relationships, we chose to analyze data collected in the National Survey of Families and Households (NSFH). This is the first survey using a large, nationally representative probability sample designed to describe American households and families in their full breadth and scope. The survey was completed in 1987 and 1988. It solicited information on more than 4,000 variables for 13,017 households. Respondents were asked to provide information on their family history and their current living arrangements. Detailed information was collected on marital and nonmarital relationships, including marital communication, marital quality and conflict, division of household chores, and relations with former spouses. Information was also collected on parent-child relationships—relationships that both biological parents and stepparents have with their children, as well as their parenting rules and values. Also of interest to us were many questions asked for information on family members' social and psychological well-being.

The survey was funded by the National Institute for Child Health and Human Development, and it was designed by the Center for Demography and Ecology, University of Wisconsin

(Sweet, Bumpass, & Call, 1988). The survey included a main interview completed by the primary respondent, a series of self-administered questionnaires answered by selected primary respondents (e.g., parents of young children, those in stepfamilies), and a self-administered questionnaire completed by a spouse or cohabiting partner when present.[1] The NSFH represents all ages, races, and socioeconomic levels in the United States—an impressive cross-section of the U.S. population. We can now replace speculations about family life with answers.

The size of the sample and scope of the variables are crucial to understanding differences between types of families. The size of the sample allows us to have enough families to make definitive statements about the adjustment of children and adults in families that have experienced a divorce, those in stepfamilies, and in families where the mother never married. The scope allows us to disentangle the effects of family type from other factors such as poverty, education, and race.

While maintaining a probability sample, the researchers over-sampled some groups. Blacks, single-parent families, and families with stepchildren were among the oversampled. This oversampling ensures sufficient cases in each type of family to establish meaningful statistical relationships. Having sufficient cases is critical to our efforts to disentangle the effects of family type from those of other variables such as family income, education, race, or quality of family relationships.

IDENTIFYING TYPES OF FAMILIES

The study that forms the basis for this book relies on the reports of 2,457 mothers living in one of four types of families:

1. *First marriages* ($N = 1,085$). These are families in which both the mother and the father are in their first marriage, and the couple has one or more biological children under 19 living at home.[2]
2. *Divorced* ($N = 677$). A second family type consists of a mother who has divorced and has at least one biological child under 19 from a previous marriage living at home.

3. *Stepfamilies* ($N = 277$). The third group includes families in which the mother is remarried (that is, married for at least the second time) and has at least one biological child under 19 from a prior marriage living with her and her current husband.

4. *Continuously single* ($N = 418$). The fourth family type consists of a mother who has never married and has one or more biological children under 19 living at home.

The number beside each family type refers to the actual number of families in the sample. These numbers do not represent the prevalence of these family types for the United States. This is because some groups were deliberately oversampled. In the U.S. population there are proportionally fewer divorced and continuously single-parent families and somewhat fewer stepfamilies than the percentages in the sample. But the researchers who designed the survey were interested in these and other less-common family types, so they purposely included more of them in the NSFH sample. This oversampling permits us to conduct meaningful statistical comparisons across family types. Without the oversampling, we would have had too few remarried mothers and too few continuously single mothers to make statistically meaningful comparisons. The prevalence of these different family types, as we have defined them, can be estimated for the U.S. population by weighting the NSFH data. When we weight the data we are compensating for the oversampling. When this is done, 66.0% of the families that fall into one of these four types are in their first marriage, 14.3% are divorced, 9.5% are stepfamilies, and 10.2% are continuously single. These percentages are based on the total number of families in the four types we have defined and excludes the families that do not fit our definitions.

Although our final sample is large compared to earlier studies of family types, we need to clarify how the 13,017 households in the NSFH were reduced to 2,457 families for our study. This involved a series of decisions, and the specific details are provided in Appendix A. We wanted to study prevalent family types, families that represent the experiences of most children growing up in the United States today. This argues for using broad definitions of family forms. But we also wanted family types that are sufficiently homogeneous within each type to make comparison meaningful. To balance these conflicting goals, we eliminated family types that, while important, are beyond the scope of this book.

We focus on mothers and their perceptions rather than fathers and their perceptions. This makes comparisons between families more valid. For example, in describing the adjustment of a child we have the mother's description for all families rather than having the mother's for some families and the father's for other families. This method also simplifies comparing married families to single-parent families. That is, we are not comparing a husband's perception of his wife's well-being to a single-parent mother's perception of her own well-being. In addition, research shows that compared to fathers, mothers tend to be more involved in childrearing, more closely attached to their children, and are better sources of information about their children (LaRossa, 1988; Rossi, 1984). We still use some information from the husbands, which is obtained from a separate questionnaire that husbands completed. By eliminating households in which the primary respondent is male, we reduce the sample size from 13,017 to 7,790. We excluded all households that did not have at least one child age 0-18 living in the household. To ensure that the first-married families and stepfamilies had a husband living in the household at the time of the survey, we deleted households in which the mother reported separation. This was necessary because we wanted to have reasonable homogeneity within each type of family. Families in which the husband and wife are separated due to marital problems are likely to have very different family dynamics than families in which this is not the case. Also, in some families separation may be short-term and in others it may be a permanent condition. Where separation is permanent, the family dynamics may be more similar to divorced families than to other first-married families. The decision to eliminate these families may result in our married families having less conflict than is typical of married families. We also eliminated families in which the mother was a widow or she refused to report her marital status.

The next step was to define the four family types. We identified 1,085 families in which both the mother and the father reported being in their *first marriage* and there was at least one biological child under age 19 living in the household.

We identified 677 families in which the mother was *divorced* and had at least one biological child from a previous marriage. A small number of these women ($N = 70$) reported that they were cohabiting at the time of the interview. We did not examine whether they had cohabited at some time prior to the survey. But, because the presence of a cohabiting partner at the time of the interview can change family dynamics dramatically, we control for this variable in our analyses. In defining divorced families we also excluded 30 families in which all of the children were born more than 10 months after the last marriage ended. This ensures that the divorced mothers we are studying had at least one child from a previous marriage.

We identified 277 *stepfamilies* in which the mother is married for at least the second time, she is the biological parent of at least one of the children living in the household, and that child was born before the current marriage. These households may contain other children who were born after the marriage or for whom the mother is the stepmother. Although we call these stepfamilies, the critical factor is the presence of a stepfather.

Finally, we identified 418 *continuously single-parent* families in which the mother has never been married and has a biological child under 19 living in the household. As with divorced mothers, we included those families ($N = 72$) in which the mother had a cohabiting partner living in the household at the time of the interview, and we control for cohabitation in our analyses.

How well do the family types we have identified represent the full range and diversity of American families with children? This is a more difficult question to answer than it might appear. What is the reference for our comparison? We can compare our families to all families that meet certain requirements. Using our criteria for defining family types eliminates many families who responded to the NSFH. For example, the NSFH data set includes households for which the primary respondent is male and households for which there are no children ages 0-18. Our analysis does not include families in which all the children live elsewhere, nor do we examine male-headed single-parent families. We restrict our attention to families with a child under 19 who have a mother present.

The next question is, how representative of mother-present families with children are the families included in our analysis? The procedures we have described exclude four types of families: those in which the mother (a) did not identify her marital status, (b) is in her first marriage but her husband reports this is not his first marriage, (c) is married but her spouse is absent, and (d) is widowed. If all these families were included in our analysis, we would have 3,397 families.[3] The four family types we examine account for 2,457, or 72.3% of these families.

Families often have adult children living in the household. We include such families only when they also have a child under 19 living at home. Although important, issues of family dynamics and well-being related to adult children living at home are beyond the scope of this book. There are many married couples and single parents whose children are all adults, and the dynamics of these families would be different from the families described here. Our central objective is to examine the influences of family structure and family relations on the well-being of parents and dependent children age 19 and younger. But as increasing proportions of young adults remain at home or return home to live with their parents, the examination of such families becomes increasingly important for family researchers (cf. White & Edwards, 1990).

Having outlined the types of families we eliminated, we should note that other family types cannot be discussed due to the design of the NSFH. In particular, we are unable to describe the characteristics of lesbian families. When we talk about the spouse or cohabiting partner of the mothers in our survey, all of these partners are males. Where such partners are female, the survey did not ask the appropriate questions.

We hope this book can fill many gaps in our understanding of four important family types in the United States. At the same time, the book will provide findings and raise issues that are important to understanding family types that we are unable to cover.

SOCIOECONOMIC CHARACTERISTICS
OF FAMILY TYPES

The four family types vary widely in many ways that make it difficult to isolate the effects of family structure on well-being. To the extent that children in divorced or continuously single-parent families fare worse at school, we do not know the cause. Is the cause of the poor performance the family structure, which has an "absent" father, or is it the economic disadvantage of children living in divorced or continuously single-parent families? This section compares the four family types in terms of a series of socioeconomic factors that distinguish family types.

In this section we present data for the weighted sample. Weighting is a procedure that counts the observations of some families more than other families for statistical purposes. Later in the chapter we compare the merits of using weighted data and using data that are not weighted. Our objective here is to estimate the socioeconomic condition of the four family types in the United States. Because some groups were oversampled in the NSFH, a weighted mean or proportion adjusts to represent all individuals in the United States.

Family income. Much has been written of the link between family status and poverty (e.g., McLanahan, 1985; Weitzman, 1985). The results of the NSFH confirm the strong relationship between family type and family income (see Table 3.1). The average total family income for first-married families is $49,491, and this is similar to the average for stepfamilies, $46,417. Divorced families, by contrast, have a dramatically reduced income level, $20,262. This demonstrates the strong association between being divorced and living in poverty. However, when we consider the average income of continuously single-parent families, the income difference is even more dramatic. The average income of U.S. families headed by a continuously single mother is only $10,512. Compared to married mothers, and even compared to divorced mothers, this is a tragic inequity.

Childrearing practices in single-parent families with low income are similar to two-parent families with the same income,

Table 3.1 Socioeconomic and Demographic Characteristics of Family Types: Weighted Data

Socioeconomic Variables	First-Married	Divorced	Stepfamily	Continuously Single	Significant Differences[a]
Income					
Family income	$49,491	$20,262	$46,417	$10,512	acdef
Family income above poverty level	38,133	10,711	34,608	410	acdef
Mother's income	9,048	15,948	12,827	7,393	abcdef
Mother's income above poverty level	−2,232	6,610	1,018	−2,599	abdef
Other characteristics of mother/other adults					
Hours mother employed/week	20.2	29.5	23.4	16.9	abcdef
Mother's education (in years)	13.1	12.5	12.6	11.6	abcef
Mother's age	34.5	35.8	35.0	27.5	acef
% cohabiting at time of interview	na[b]	15.3	na	27.5	
% with adult relatives in household	2.2	3.0	0.5	8.8	cef
% with maternal grandmother in household	0.9	3.0	0.3	6.8	acdef
% with adult nonrelative in household	0.6	4.5	0.0	4.2	acdf
Sample size	1,085	677	277	418	
Characteristics of children					
Age of youngest child	9.20	8.86	7.88	4.00	cef
Number of children 0-4	.62	.33	.46	.90	abcdef
Number of children 5-18	1.39	1.52	1.78	1.07	abcdef

NOTE: The computed variable called *weight* was used as the weighting factor. There are 1,085 first-married mothers, 677 divorced mothers, 277 stepfamily mothers, and 418 continuously single mothers, except for the estimates of family income above poverty and mothers' income above poverty (in which N is 1,076, 662, 277, and 393, respectively).
a. The letters indicate which means are significantly different at the $p < .05$ level: a = first-married compared to divorced; b = first-married compared to stepfamily; c = first-married compared to continuously single; d = divorced compared to stepfamily; e = divorced compared to continuously single; f = stepfamily compared to continuously single.
b. na means not available.

but these differ from the practices of single-parent and two-parent families with higher income (Colletta, 1979). Because income varies so much by family type, it is necessary to control for household income in all comparisons of well-being and family relations.

On the chance that some differences in household income are mitigated by family size, we compared family income to the poverty level for each of the family types. The difference between a family's income and the poverty threshold for that family (based on size and composition of household) is a good measure of the economic resources that are available to invest in the well-being of family members. As Table 3.1 and Figure 3.1 show, the average first-married family has $38,133 available for this investment because their incomes, on average, exceed the poverty threshold by this much. Stepfamilies have similar economic resources, with their family income exceeding the poverty level by $34,608. The economic resources available to divorced families, by contrast, are extremely limited, just $10,711. The economic tragedy of continuously single-parent families is poignant when we see that their economic resources are $410.

What does this mean? A family's income that is above the poverty level can be invested in better quality of life (e.g., housing or recreation) or in providing greater opportunity for the parent(s) and child(ren) to maximize their individual development (e.g., education or quality child care). Whereas married families have tens of thousands of dollars for such investments, the continuously single-parent family has $410 per year to invest in all these things. This means that, on average, continuously single women and their children live on the threshold of poverty. Poverty is the norm for continuously single-parent families, and economic resources to invest in the well-being of the mother or the children are nil.

Mother's income. An interesting pattern emerges when we compare the family types in terms of the income earned by mothers. The average income for first-married mothers is $9,048. In sharp contrast, divorced mothers make half again as much, $15,948. This is consistent with research indicating that divorce has a positive effect on the earnings of women (Porter, 1984). Some of this gain also appears among divorced mothers who remarry, as

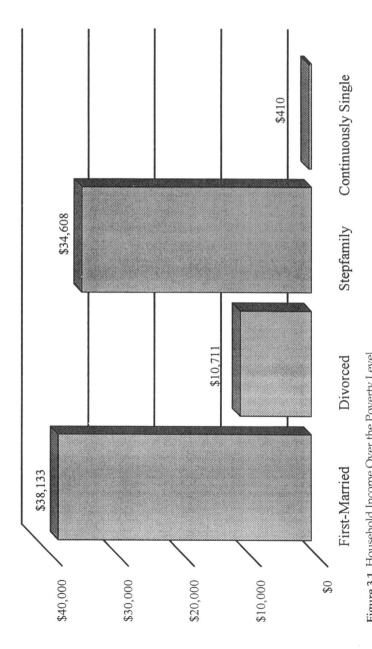

Figure 3.1. Household Income Over the Poverty Level
NOTE: Poverty level shown as zero dollars. Other values indicate how far family is above poverty level.

the average income of mothers in stepfamilies is $12,827. A note-worthy point is that continuously single mothers have the lowest average earnings, $7,393.

The difference in mothers' earnings in divorced and continu-ously single-parent families demonstrates the folly of lumping single-parent mothers into one category that is presumed to be monolithic. Whereas being divorced appears to enhance the earn-ings of mothers, and perhaps facilitate their performance as providers, being continuously single has the opposite effect. With an average income of just $7,393, continuously single mothers as a group are not only poor, but they are handicapped in their capacity to provide an adaptive role model to their children. Further, the income earned by the divorced mother, in general, provides a more stable and nonstigmatized income than the income available to the continuously single mother, who is more likely to be dependent on welfare (Bould, 1977).

Another way of considering income is in terms of the mother's economic dependency. Any mother is economically dependent when her family income is below the poverty level. A divorced or continuously single mother is dependent on a social welfare system when her family is in poverty. What about a married mother? Consider a family in which the husband earns $35,000 per year and the wife earns $11,000 per year. Although the family is not economically dependent on the social welfare system, the wife or mother is economically dependent on her husband. Table 3.1 shows the extent to which married mothers are economically dependent on their spouses. This is evident in the row of numbers that compare the mothers' own income to the poverty level. On average, mothers in stepfamilies earn just $1,018 more than the poverty level. Without their husbands' income these mothers would be close to poverty. Mothers in their first marriage earn less than the poverty level by $2,232. This means that these mothers would be below the poverty level without the earnings of their husbands. The average first-married family has $38,133 to invest in the well-being of family members, but with just the mother's income they would be living in poverty. Atkinson, Blackwelder, and Risman (1992) describe wives' economic de-pendency in two-parent families as "perhaps the most hidden dimension of inequality in contemporary society" (p. 1). When the husband "owns" the extrafamilial resources, he controls the power structure and the rules of exchange, and the mother is in an impossible bargaining position (Curtis, 1986). Thus, although married women have more family resources to invest in family members, they may be just as economically dependent as non-married mothers, only in a different way.

Hours employed per week. Closely paralleling mothers' income differences are the hours mothers spend in wage labor each week. Table 3.1 shows that continuously single mothers are employed the fewest hours per week (16.9). In contrast, divorced mothers are employed the most hours per week (29.5). These two groups of mothers have the lowest and highest incomes, respectively. As a practical matter, the alternative to employment for single-parent mothers is poverty or, at best, economic uncertainty. Any effect of mother's employment on child and adolescent well-being thus needs to be compared to the effects of her nonemployment and subsequent level of income, and this will be considered in our analyses in Chapter 7.

Education. There are significant differences in the educational levels of mothers in the four types of families.[4] The sharpest contrast appears in comparing the continuously single mothers, who have a mean education of under 12 years (11.6), with each of the other groups. Whereas the average for continuously single mothers is less than a high school degree, the average for each of the other groups is some education beyond high school, or about one additional year of education compared to continuously single mothers.

It is important to control for education because mothers' education is related to many aspects of children's well-being. Conditions of employment also vary by education. Flexible working hours, community respect, and visibility are examples of such benefits that depend on education and may improve the quality of life (Blechman, 1982).

Age. There are significant, but not surprising age differences. On average, mothers in their first marriage are younger than the divorced or stepfamily mothers (this is not surprising because being first-married precedes being divorced or being remarried). But by far the youngest group is the continuously single mothers, with an average age of 27.5 years. Because the age of the mother is highly related to marital status, it is critical to control for this whenever we compare adjustment of family members across types of families.

Cohabitation. Among the single parents in our sample, divorced mothers are significantly less likely than continuously single mothers to live in cohabiting relationships. Less than one in six (15.3%) divorced mothers, compared with more than one in four (27.5%) continuously single mothers, reported cohabiting partners at the time of the survey. It is important to note that these figures refer to those mothers who were cohabiting at the time of the interview. These are reasonable estimates of the percentage of single-parent mothers who have a cohabiting partner at any particular time. However, it is likely that a much higher percentage of these women had earlier cohabitation experiences but were not cohabiting at the time of the interview. Thus the figures we report are the lower limit on the true percentage of single-mother families with cohabitation experiences.

Other adults in household. Families headed by continuously single mothers also are significantly more likely to include other adult relatives living in the household. Whereas 8.8% of continuously single mothers report such arrangements, only 3% or fewer of mothers in other family types report other adults living in the household. In most cases the other adults are grandparents, usually the maternal grandmother. In addition, a small percentage (roughly 4%) of divorced and continuously single-parent families report adult nonrelatives living in the household. The presence of other adults, related or unrelated, is virtually nonexistent in two-parent households.

Number and age characteristics of children. There are significant differences among the four types of families in the number and age distribution of children. Divorced mothers have the fewest children age 4 or younger, and continuously single mothers have the most young children. In fact, the average age of the youngest child is 4 years in continuously single-parent families, compared with nearly 8 in stepfamilies, nearly 9 in divorced families, and slightly more than 9 years in first-married families.

There are also differences in the number of older children, ages 5-18. Older children are least common in continuously single-parent families (with an average of 1.07) and most common in stepfamilies (with an average of 1.78 older children). The fact that continuously single mothers have fewer children between ages 5 and 18 may be attributed to the relative youth of these mothers.

Race and ethnicity. Although many black children live in two-parent families, black children experience a disproportionately large percentage of single-parent households. Table 3.2 and Figure 3.2 show that more than two in five black families (42.7%) in our data set are continuously single-parent families, compared to only 3.9% of white families. Hispanic families are intermediate in this classification, with 18.0% consisting of continuously single-parent families. Corresponding differences occur for the other family types. More than four in five white families with children present include married mothers (70.8% in their first marriage and 11.1% in a stepfamily). In sharp contrast, less than one in three black families (31.8%) with children present are first-married families, and only 5.1% are stepfamilies. It is clear from Table 3.2 that black mothers are much less likely than white mothers to be married or remarried.

It must be emphasized that the percentages we report refer to mothers' marital status at the time of the interview. It is estimated that 94% of black youth currently under age 19, and 70% of white youth, will experience some family structure other than a two-parent household before they reach age 18 (Hofferth, 1985).

Residential distribution. Table 3.2 shows the proportion of metropolitan and nonmetropolitan families that are in each family type. The differences are statistically significant but not as large as might be expected. Metropolitan families are less likely than nonmetropolitan families to be first-married families (63.1% vs.

Table 3.2 Racial and Residential Characteristics of Family Types: Weighted Data

Category on Dependent Variable	First-Married	Divorced	Stepfamily	Continuously Single	Total
Race/ethnicity: $x^2(9) = 381.74; p < .05$					
Black	81	52	13	109	255
	31.8%	20.4%	5.1%	42.7%	100.0%
White	969	194	152	52	1,367
	70.8%	14.2%	11.1%	3.9%	100.0%
Hispanic	92	21	10	27	150
	61.2%	13.9%	6.9%	18.0%	100.0%
Other	20	2	2	2	26
	77.2%	6.2%	7.3%	9.3%	100.0%
Metro versus nonmetro: $x^2(3) = 11.26; p < .05$					
Metro	863	208	136	162	1,369
	63.1%	15.2%	9.9%	11.8%	100.0%
Nonmetro	302	61	42	28	433
	69.6%	14.1%	9.8%	6.5%	100.0%
Region of the United States: $x^2(9) = 10.57; ns$					
Northeast	246	45	27	50	368
	66.7%	12.3%	7.4%	13.6%	100.0%
North Central	320	77	52	50	499
	64.1%	15.3%	10.5%	10.1%	100.0%
South	383	97	62	62	604
	63.4%	16.1%	10.2%	10.2%	100.0%
West	216	50	37	28	331
	65.2%	15.1%	11.2%	8.5%	100.0%

69.6%), and metropolitan families are more likely to be continuously single-parent families. There is little difference in divorce or remarriage figures.

These comparisons may obscure real differences in residential patterns. Metropolitan areas include entire counties. Large areas of some metropolitan areas are clearly rural in terms of land use. Also, metropolitan areas include both inner cities and suburbs. It might be the case that continuously single-parent families and

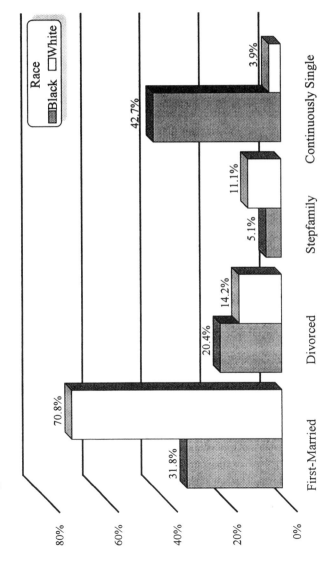

Figure 3.2. Percentage of Black Families and White Families in Each Family Type

divorced families are concentrated in the inner city areas and in the less affluent suburbs. In contrast, first-married families and stepfamilies may be concentrated in the more affluent suburbs. The metro versus nonmetro distinction we have discussed here does not address this issue.

Table 3.2 also compares four regions: the Northeast, North Central, South, and West. The differences are not statistically significant.

WEIGHTING VERSUS CONTROLLING
FOR RELEVANT VARIABLES

Although our socioeconomic comparison of family types used weighted data, for the remainder of this book we will not use the case weight variable. Certain groups were deliberately oversampled to ensure enough cases to make meaningful generalizations. The case weight factor has the effect of reducing the weight of our smallest groups while increasing the weight of our largest groups. The average value of the weight for our first-married mothers is 1.07. This means that each case, on average, counts as slightly more than one case in computing statistical information because this group was not oversampled. In contrast, the average value of the weight for continuously single mothers is .46, meaning that each continuously single mother, on average, counts as only .46 of a case. For the divorced mothers the average is only .40, and for the stepfamilies it is .64. These results would be appropriate if we were generalizing to all people in the United States. If we did not weight these mothers the overall estimates would over-represent the opinions of the oversampled mothers. However, the families within each family type can be thought of as representative of their particular family type. For example, each of the 277 stepfamily mothers is useful for estimating the response of this type of family.

The effect of weighting can be understood by comparing what the sample size is when we weight and when we do not weight. Without weighting, as mentioned above, we have 1,085 women in the first-married group, 677 women in the divorced group, 277 women in the stepfamily group, and 418 continuously single women. Because the researchers made special efforts to oversample less-common family types, these are the actual cases. Thus, for instance, there are 418 completed interviews of continuously single mothers.

When weighting is used, the computed number of cases is not actual respondents but an estimate of what the numbers would be if no oversampling had been done. Using the weighting, we estimate there would be 1,165 women in their first marriage, 269 divorced mothers, only 178 stepfamilies, and just 190 continuously single mothers. This would give us too few cases for some groups, substantially fewer than the actual number of respondents in these groups, and would nullify the advantages of the oversampling.

Including Variables as Controls

An alternative to weighting that avoids discounting the very cases the researchers spent extra effort to obtain is to control for relevant variables, especially those critical to the sample design. Although there are many possible controls, we will use only a few particularly important variables.

When we use statistical control we are using a procedure called analysis of covariance. This procedure allows us to estimate what the score on the dependent variable would be if all the control variables were held constant. For example, if we are trying to estimate the health of mothers who are in their first marriage compared to those who are continuously single, we would want to control for such variables as the mother's age and household income. Analysis of covariance allows us to do this by holding the control variables at their mean value. Thus we are comparing the health of a continuously single mother and a first-married mother who are both average on age and household income.

The selection of variables was based on the differences on socioeconomic factors across the four types of families. In the remainder of the book, analyses by family type will control for the following variables:[5]

1. Whether the respondent was in the primary sample or an over-sampled group
2. The total family income
3. The mother's education
4. The mother's race
5. The mother's age
6. The hours the mother is employed each week
7. The number of people living in the household at the time of the interview

We try to use this set of control variables throughout the book to provide a consistent presentation. However, in some cases other variables need to be controlled. For example, in divorced and continuously single-mother families, we need to control for whether there is a cohabiting partner present. For other analyses, having young children may be a critical variable, and we will control for the age of the youngest child. Some questions concern a particular child and it is possible to control for the child's age and gender. Although a reader may identify any number of variables that might be controlled in a particular analysis, our main objective is to identify the effects of family structure, and thus we control for variables that are closely linked to family structure.

Controlling for whether the respondent is in the primary or oversampled group is a general control that incorporates the sum of all the factors the researchers used in their sample design. It is an attempt to incorporate possible effects of variables that we have not included as explicit controls. The total family income differs dramatically by family type, and we need to control for this to determine whether family type or economic resources is the more proximate cause of the well-being of family members.

Education also differs by family type, and there is extensive research showing that education is related to many aspects of well-being. We control for race because it is related to well-being, and it is highly confounded with family type. Specifically, we control for race to separate out the effect of race from the effect of being in a continuously single-parent family, because blacks are much more likely than other groups to live in this type of family.

The average age of mothers varies by family type and will also be controlled. We need to allow age to explain any differences in well-being before we attribute differences to family structure. We control for hours the mother is employed each week. This is important because it is highly correlated with her income, which varies dramatically by family type. Finally, we control for cohabitation status of divorced and continuously single mothers because the presence of a cohabiting partner alters family dynamics and family resources in so many ways.

SUMMARY

Our socioeconomic and demographic description of American families illustrates incredible diversity within and across family types. We have documented the importance of distinguishing between different types of one- and two-parent households. First-married and remarried mothers, although similar on several socioeconomic characteristics, have different marital, family, and work trajectories. Remarried mothers, perhaps partly because they have experienced divorce, are employed more hours and earn more income than first-married mothers. Mothers in stepfamilies also are less likely than their first-married counterparts to have young children and more likely to have children ages 5 through 18.

For many years family researchers have been aware of the socioeconomic disparities between two-parent and one-parent families. But the dramatic distinctions *within* single-parent families have gone largely unnoticed. Families headed by continuously single mothers live on roughly half the income of divorced families, and barely more than one fifth the income of first-married families. For continuously single mothers and their families, life is a day-to-day economic struggle. As providers, continuously single mothers are handicapped by their youth, their lack of high school degrees, and by part-time low-wage employment. Divorced mothers, by contrast, are significantly older, better educated, and are employed nearly twice as many hours per week.

There are also interesting differences in the household composition of divorced and continuously single-parent families. More than one fourth of continuously single mothers report cohabiting partners, thus providing family environments that in many ways resemble first-married, two-parent families. Families headed by continuously single mothers also are three times more likely than those headed by divorced mothers to include other adult relatives such as grandparents. These dissimilarities in household composition are partly due to other sociodemographic features of these families. As we have discussed, continuously single-parent families are more likely to be black, to be young, and to be poor, requiring the assistance of other kin, such as grandparents, for social and economic support. Throughout the remaining chapters we explore the consequences of these and other distinctions in family structure for family relationships and personal well-being.

NOTES

1. The main interview was 161 pages long. Certain groups also completed sections of a self-administered questionnaire. The complete set of self-administered questionnaires was 64 pages long.

2. For each family type there are some questions that include children who are 18. These children are included in our sample only when there is at least one sibling living in the household who is the biological child of the mother and who is under 18. Appendix A includes a detailed definition of each of the family types.

3. The weighted number of families in each type provides an estimate for the United States population.

4. Throughout the book, when we refer to statistically significant findings, we are referring to differences that are significant at the .05 level, unless indicated otherwise.

5. To minimize problems of missing data on some of the control variables, we substituted the mean value by family type. This was done for household income, the hours the mother is employed each week, mother's education, and mother's age. The weighted means reported in Table 3.1 were used for this purpose. For example, a first-married mother who did not report family income was assigned a value of $49,491. A continuously single mother who did not report family income was assigned a value of $10,512.

F O U R

Marital, Postmarital, and Nonmarital Relations

An important question in trying to understand contemporary families is how couple relations are similar and different across diverse family structures. In this chapter we examine the division of household labor across family types, and we describe the typical contributions of wives, husbands, cohabiting partners, children, and other family members.[1] We also examine similarities and differences in marital relations across first marriages and remarriages, including discussion of marital quality, role strain, and areas of disagreement. In the final section we examine postmarital relations between former spouses, relationships that are integral to understanding family dynamics in divorced and stepfamilies.

DIVISION OF HOUSEHOLD LABOR

Any mother knows how much time it takes to run a household. Some major chores are cooking, washing dishes, cleaning, outdoor maintenance, shopping, laundry, paying the bills, repairing the car, and endless chauffeuring of children. Child care is another time-consuming aspect of family labor, and it is examined in detail in Chapter 5. Previous research demonstrates that the most important factor influencing the division of domestic labor is gender, with women typically performing three fourths of all housework (Berk, 1985; Huber & Spitze, 1983). Although many studies have examined how married couples divide housework in single-earner and two-earner arrangements, very few studies have examined the distribution of housework in single-parent families (Voydanoff, 1987) or compared first marriages with re-marriages. Ferree (1991) has demonstrated that there is consider-able variability in the arrangements of two-earner couples and that it is important to examine subgroups of women who are more likely to be forced into a "second shift" (Hochschild, 1989). How is family structure related to the time mothers spend on household labor? The time fathers spend? The time children spend? Many people think of some of these chores as traditionally the responsibility of women (e.g., cooking, washing dishes, clean-ing) and others as the responsibility of men (e.g., car maintenance and outdoor work). Is this the way the jobs are actually divided? Is the allocation similar across family types?

A feminist perspective provides a useful conceptual founda-tion for studying the division of household labor. One of the central themes in feminist thinking on the family is that marital and family experiences are widely variable. Despite the perva-sive ideology of the monolithic nuclear family (Demo, 1993; Thorne, 1992), diversity exists across many axes. There are impor-tant variations by social structural location, especially gender, race, and social class; household structure; sexual arrangements; and the nature of marital, nonmarital, and family interaction. Feminists emphasize that families are not always or uniformly cohesive, that some men are more dominant than others in con-trolling women, and that the extent of male involvement in family labor is widely variable (Ferree, 1991). Despite this diversity, however, the lingering ideology of the monolithic family and "women's proper place" operates to oppress women (Thorne, 1992). Thus we would expect that, despite recent changes in gender ideology, women's employment, and family structure, gender inequality remains and women continue to perform a disproportionate share of domestic labor. One objective of this chapter is to assess whether the division of household labor is more egalitarian (or less oppressive for women) in some family structures than others.

By comparing our data with earlier studies we can also address another question: How much has the division of household labor really changed during the past 30 years? As discussed in Chapter 1, studies show that in the 1960s, men spent between one third and one fourth of the time on housework as their wives, regardless of the number or ages of children in the family and regardless of the wife/mother's employment status (Coverman & Sheley, 1986). Considerable popular and scholarly attention has focused on changes occurring during the past few decades in gender role ideology, women's employment, and family living arrangements. Have these changes had a significant impact on the division of housework? If marriages and cohabiting relationships have become more egalitarian in recent decades, and if changes in gender attitudes are indeed translated into behavioral change, we would expect a more egalitarian division of household labor in the late 1980s.

Comparison of how domestic labor is divided across family types is complicated because husbands are present in two of our family types (first-married and stepfamilies), but not in the other two types (divorced and continuously single-parent families). Still, all of the households in which mothers are divorced or continuously single have children and possibly nonfamily members who may offset demands on the mothers' time.

Another complication is that the presence of a spouse or partner may increase or decrease the time the mother spends on household labor. Spouses or partners provide a potential source of labor, but they also contribute to the amount of work needed. Families that do not have a father present lose both the labor he contributes to household chores and the burden he adds to the total labor required to run the household. When a father does not reside in the household, he does not leave shoes in the living room, ask that breakfast be prepared for him, or pile clothes in the corner of the bedroom. Whether the husband's labor exceeds the work he creates for others is an empirical question we can answer with our data.

This section begins with a comparison of the division of household labor across the four family types. The analyses extend previous work in a number of ways. First, most studies of household labor examine two-parent families, ignoring how single-parent families divide domestic responsibilities. Second, there is an over-reliance on small convenience samples of white, middle-class families (Spitze, 1988). A large nationally representative sample affords us the ability to compare the division of household work across families of different social classes, races, family structures, and other social categories. Finally, our data (collected in 1987-1988) provide a more recent benchmark for understanding household labor than data collected in the 1970s (and earlier), which are typically analyzed in studies of housework and family relations (Spitze, 1988; for exceptions, see Brayfield, 1992; Coltrane & Ishi-Kuntz, 1992).

DIVISION OF HOUSEHOLD LABOR
ACROSS FAMILY TYPES

We examine both the percentage of different chores done by the mother and the hours she and other household members spend on chores. We present data both on percentages and actual hours because the two types of data produce different findings and interpretations. For example, one mother may average 28 hours per week doing housework, whereas her husband typically spends 14 hours on housework. She thus performs two thirds of the household's necessary labor (assuming that no one else in the household does any housework). By contrast, imagine a household in which the mother typically spends 25 hours per week on housework and her husband averages 5 hours per week. In the latter case, the mother performs a much higher proportion (five sixths) of all the domestic labor performed in the household, yet she spends less time on housework than the mother in the first illustration.

Comparing percentages and data on actual time investments has other virtues. The central focus of this book is the role of family structure in shaping family relationships and well-being. Because family structures vary in the number of adult household members (e.g., one-parent or two-parent families), the percentage of housework done by mothers is likely to vary considerably by family structure. Yet the *amount* of time mothers spend on housework may be relatively constant across family structures. Further, many previous studies have relied on percentages to draw conclusions about recent changes in women's and men's housework. Although the proportion of housework done by women decreased (and the proportion done by men increased) in the 1970s and 1980s, this change was primarily the result of women spending less time on housework (Coverman & Sheley, 1986). Men's housework changed very little during this period, but because women's housework decreased, the *proportion* of housework done by men increased. We thus present and interpret both types of data.

The Percentage of the
Total Time Spent by the Mother

Table 4.1 presents percentages showing how much of all housework, and how much of each specific chore, is done by mothers in each family type. These figures reflect the depth of the household burden women have in the United States. As with all the tables in this chapter, the percentages reported in Table 4.1 adjust for effects of our control variables: whether the respondent was in the oversampled population or not, the household's total income, mother's education, mother's race, mother's age, hours per week the mother is employed, the number of people living in the household, and age of the youngest child. The figures represent the mothers' perceptions. Some mothers may overestimate and some may underestimate the actual time they spend on household labor. For information on the significance of the control variables and the direction of the effects, see Appendix B.

Table 4.1 shows that mothers report they devote the bulk of time on most household chores, corroborating earlier studies (Berk, 1985; Kamo, 1988; Mederer, 1993; Warner, 1986). The exceptions are outdoor work and car repairs, neither of which entails a substantial amount of actual labor. In addition, neither outdoor work nor car repairs tend to be done routinely or regularly

(Mederer, 1993), unlike most jobs women do (Berk, 1985; Pleck, 1985). Data on actual time investments (discussed in more detail below) show that husbands and male cohabiting partners average between 3 and 4 hours per week doing outdoor work, and between 1 and 2 hours per week doing car maintenance. When we exclude these two occasional tasks and consider only the routine tasks, across all family types mothers perform between 69% and 94% of the work. This means that, on average, women are doing at least two thirds, and usually three fourths or more, of the most time-consuming household labor.

The last row of Table 4.1 presents the percentage of time the wife spends on all chores combined. The total includes time spent by the husband or partner (if present), children, and others living in the household. Even including all of these alternative sources of labor, mothers report they are the primary household laborers. This is not because mothers work fewer hours for pay than their husbands, because we adjusted for covariates including the hours per week the mother is employed. We will consider the case of mothers who are not employed in a section below.

Without diminishing the uniformly high percentage of house-hold work done by mothers, regardless of family type, Table 4.1 shows there are still significant differences in mothers' household labor across family types. For most tasks, mothers do a greater percentage of housework when the father does not reside in the home. For example, compared to married mothers, single moth-ers do a greater percentage of preparing meals, washing dishes, shopping, and paying bills. For some chores, such as driving or paying bills, it simply is not possible for children or other house-hold members to replace the work that might be done by the father in other family structures. Hence the differences are espe-cially dramatic in these areas.

At first glance it is tempting to conclude that men are doing many of the household chores and that when they are absent from the household the mother has an added burden. Yet any notions that recent changes in family structure, female employment, or gender roles have produced many egalitarian two-parent fami-lies are dismissed by the numbers in Tables 4.1 and 4.2. Planning and preparing meals, washing dishes, and general cleaning are

Table 4.1 Percentage of Housework Done by Mothers

Household Task	First-Married	Divorced	Stepfamily	Continuously Single	Significance[a]
Preparing meals	84.5 (1,045)	88.1 (652)	81.0 (264)	87.3 (393)	abcdf
Washing dishes	79.5 (1,012)	79.8 (618)	70.7 (259)	83.1 (387)	bcdf
Cleaning house	83.3 (1,028)	81.3 (634)	78.5 (266)	83.1 (392)	bf
Outdoor work[b]	33.4 (719)	71.5 (418)	32.5 (207)	72.1 (183)	acdf
Shopping	80.8 (1,021)	92.6 (649)	77.7 (263)	92.8 (396)	abcdf
Laundry	89.9 (1,039)	89.7 (645)	84.9 (270)	88.6 (394)	bdf
Paying bills	72.3 (942)	93.5 (646)	73.1 (252)	91.8 (377)	acdf
Car maintenance[b]	13.0 (539)	75.4 (284)	15.6 (146)	65.3 (90)	acdef
Driving	69.2 (745)	91.0 (470)	69.5 (224)	87.4 (163)	acdf
TOTAL	71.6 (676)	85.7 (526)	69.4 (177)	84.4 (324)	acdf

NOTE: The numbers appearing in parentheses are the sample sizes on which each percentage is based. The row for the total reflects an average of the responses where mothers gave an answer for at least eight of the nine items.
a. The letters indicate which means are significantly different at the $p < .05$ level: a = first-married compared to divorced; b = first-married compared to stepfamily; c = first-married compared to continuously single; d = divorced compared to stepfamily; e = divorced compared to continuously single; f = stepfamily compared to continuously single.
b. The number of mothers for these items is unusually low. It is possible that mothers who spend no time on these activities skipped the items. Such cases would constitute missing data and are dropped from the analysis.

three of the most time-consuming activities in our list. Mothers alone report spending an average of 26 hours per week, or nearly 4 hours per day, on these three tasks (Table 4.2). They involve endless effort and an absence of closure. There are few conditions less permanent than clean dishes or a clean house. Before the last room is finished the first room is waiting to be redone. As one meal is finished the next must be planned, and then prepared.

What happens on these three time-intensive chores? Mothers report they devote from 71% to 88% of the total time family members spend on these chores. Even if other household members share some responsibility for these tasks, the fact that mothers in all four family types perform 71% to 88% of the labor shows that the responsibility primarily falls on mothers. What makes matters even less equitable is that these percentages are not comparing the women directly to their husbands or partners. They are comparing mothers to all other family members combined. The total contribution of all individuals excluding the mother is a modest 12% to 29% of household labor.

The general pattern in Table 4.1 is that married women—whether they are in their first marriage or in a stepfamily—are similar in the percentage of time they spend (about 70% for most chores). Divorced and continuously single mothers are similar to each other in the percentage of time they spend (roughly 85% for most chores). Thus, when compared to women in single-parent families, married women spend a significantly lower percentage of the total time on most tasks. This suggests that children and other household members in single-parent families do not compensate for the "lost labor" of a nonresidential father. Next we consider the actual hours each family member spends on family labor.

Hours Spent on Household Labor

Table 4.2 presents the mothers' estimates of the hours per week they spend on each task. Combining all activities, mothers report spending between 40 and 44 hours per week on the household chores we have included, depending on the family type.[2] As noted earlier, these estimates are adjusted for differences in the covariates (family income, mother's education, race, age, the hours per week she is employed, household size, and age of the youngest child).

It is likely that the numbers presented here underestimate women's domestic labor. Women invest substantial amounts of time to ensure that their family's needs are met, much of which is devoted to invisible labor. In addition to time spent in the actual execution of tasks, such as dishwashing and doing laundry, they also spend substantial and immeasurable amounts of time thinking about and planning to do various household tasks (DeVault, 1987, 1991). For example, they need to plan ahead what foods they need to buy or defrost in order to put balanced meals on the table day after day. Much of this invisible labor devoted to planning activities and family caregiving is not reflected in these data.

Family type has a much less significant effect on the *number of hours* the mother spends on tasks than it does on the *percentage* of time the mother contributes. When the hours are summed for all

Table 4.2 Hours of Housework Performed Per Week by Mothers

Household Task	First-Married	Divorced	Stepfamily	Continuously Single	Significance[a]
Preparing meals	10.6 (1,047)	10.4 (655)	10.2 (265)	10.2 (394)	ns
Washing dishes	6.8 (1,015)	6.9 (620)	6.3 (259)	7.0 (389)	ns
Cleaning house	9.7 (1,035)	9.9 (639)	9.6 (267)	8.6 (392)	e
Outdoor work[b]	1.9 (832)	2.3 (608)	1.9 (225)	2.1 (369)	a
Shopping	3.1 (1,024)	3.4 (650)	3.3 (263)	3.3 (398)	a
Laundry	4.9 (1,049)	4.9 (652)	5.0 (271)	4.8 (400)	ns
Paying bills	1.9 (954)	2.2 (654)	2.2 (253)	2.2 (395)	ns
Car Maintenance[b]	.2 (750)	.6 (622)	.3 (198)	.6 (363)	acdf
Driving	2.3 (977)	3.2 (645)	2.4 (258)	2.2 (372)	ade
TOTAL	41.8 (677)	43.6 (529)	40.8 (178)	40.0 (325)	ns

NOTE: The numbers appearing in parentheses are the sample sizes on which each calculation is based. The row for the total reflects an average of the responses where mothers gave an answer for at least eight of the nine items.
a. The letters indicate which means are significantly different at the $p < .05$ level: a = first-married compared to divorced; b = first-married compared to stepfamily; c = first-married compared to continuously single; d = divorced compared to stepfamily; e = divorced compared to continuously single; f = stepfamily compared to continuously single.
b. The number of mothers for these items is unusually low. It is possible that mothers who spend no time on these activities skipped the items. Such cases would constitute missing data and are dropped from the analysis.

the activities, there is no statistically significant difference across the four family types. For our sample, the average divorced mother is spending two to three extra hours per week on household labor compared to married mothers. The total household labor of the average continuously single mother is virtually identical to that of remarried mothers, and the totals for all four family types are remarkably similar. Thus our findings suggest that the absence of a husband or partner does not significantly increase the time the mother spends on most tasks. One important reason for this is that women perform most household work. A second reason is that each household member is not only a source of labor but also creates work for others (by wanting meals prepared, producing dirty clothes, dirty dishes, etc.). The answer to the question of whether husbands do more work than they create appears to be that husbands produce about the same amount of *additional* work for their wives as they provide in return.

Children's household labor. It is also possible that other family members contribute in ways that compensate for the nonresidential father. First, we consider children's housework. Although some studies have examined children's participation in housework (Goldscheider & Waite, 1991; Huber & Spitze, 1983; White & Brinkerhoff, 1981), we know very little about variation in children's involvement across family types. Having children do chores is a way of ensuring the family completes necessary functions. Housework is also a way of developing responsibility in children, of teaching them how families work, and of socializing them for families they later form (Goldscheider & Waite, 1991).

The data show that, on average, children do little housework, but there is variation by family structure. Table 4.3a shows the hours contributed by husbands (where present) and children who are under 19 years old. Children under 19 average 3 to 6 hours per week doing household chores (compared to roughly 13 for their fathers, when present, and 40 for their mothers). Across family types, children of divorced mothers spend the most time, nearly 6 hours per week. This contribution is significantly greater than that of children in stepfamilies or continuously single-parent families, who average between 4 and 5 hours per week. But the children doing significantly less household labor than any of their counterparts in other family types are those in first-married families, who average 3 hours per week.

The data provide some evidence for the argument that, in single-parent families, children's labor partially compensates for the work not being done by the nonresidential father. This appears to occur in divorced families, where children do significantly more housework than their counterparts in other family types. On the other hand, children in stepfamilies spend more time on housework than children in continuously single-parent families. In all cases, children's housework amounts to less than 1 hour per day, a small fraction of what mothers do. It is noteworthy, however, that children in single-parent households and children in stepfather households (most of whom lived in single-parent households for some time) perform more housework than children in first-married, two-parent households. Children in the latter group average less than half an hour per day doing household chores. One explanation for these findings is that single-parent family arrangements necessitate greater housework contributions by children (Weiss, 1979). It may be that single mothers have higher expectations for children's housework. These expectations and family routines then carry over to their stepfamilies. Importantly, these results control for the covariates, including the age of the youngest child, so these findings cannot be attributed to children in first-married families being too young to make substantial contributions to household chores.

The limited research that has examined children's contributions to household labor suggests that, as with adults, gender is a critical variable. The evidence suggests that daughters, especially teenage daughters, perform substantially more household chores than other children (Berk, 1985; Goldscheider & Waite, 1991). The responsibilities of daughters may be greatest in single-parent families (Michelson, 1985). Unfortunately, the limitations of our data prevent us from exploring these and other distinctions in the housework of children.

At least for families with dependent-aged children then, mothers' domestic labor is extensive and the father's presence or absence has little net effect on the amount of time mothers spend on housework. Judging from the percentages alone, it would seem that married mothers do less housework than single mothers. But when we examine the hours spent by each family member, it is clear that married women spend virtually the same amount of time on family labor as single women, partly because married women have the added responsibilities of another household member. Still, there are specific chores where the father's absence from the household significantly influences the mother's workload. Compared to first-married mothers, divorced mothers spend slightly more time shopping, doing outdoor work and car repairs, and chauffeuring family members.

Cohabiting partners and other household members. Other potential sources of labor are cohabiting partners and other adult house-

Table 4.3a   Hours of Housework Performed Per Week by Husbands and Children

Household Task	First-Married Husband	First-Married Child <19	Divorced Child <19	Stepfamily Husband	Stepfamily Child <19	Continuously Single Child <19	Significance[a] Husband	Significance[a] Child <19
Preparing meals	1.7	.4	.9	1.9	.7	.8	ns	abcd
Washing dishes	1.1	.9	1.6	1.2	1.6	1.0	ns	abef
Cleaning house	1.2	.8	1.7	1.1	1.3	1.1	ns	abde
Outdoor work	3.7	.5	.8	3.6	.7	.7	ns	a
Shopping	.9	.1	.2	1.1	.1	.1	b	ade
Laundry	.4	.2	.4	.5	.4	.4	ns	abc
Pay bills	.9	.0	.0	1.0	.0	.0	ns	ns
Car maintenance	1.6	.0	.0	1.5	.0	.1	ns	ns
Driving	1.2	.1	.1	1.2	.1	.1	e	a
TOTAL	12.7 (1,083)	3.0 (1,153)	5.8 (677)	13.3 (275)	4.8 (275)	4.2 (418)	ns	abcde

NOTE: Sample sizes for individual items (tasks) varied due to missing data.
a. The letters indicate which means are significantly different at the $p < .05$ level: a = first-married compared to divorced; b = first-married compared to stepfamily; c = first-married compared to continuously single; d = divorced compared to stepfamily; e = divorced compared to continuously single; f = stepfamily compared to continuously single.

hold members. As shown in Table 4.3b, the cohabiting partners of mothers in divorced and continuously single-parent families provide nontrivial contributions, roughly 13 hours per week of household work. These numbers are virtually indistinguishable from the household work of husbands in first-married and remarried families. The point remains, however, that the total domestic labor of husbands and male cohabiting partners represents one third of the effort expended by mothers across all family types. Gender, not family type or statutory relationship, is the critical variable explaining domestic labor.[3] Other people age 19 and older invest very little time in family work, averaging 2 hours per week or less in single-parent families and half an hour per week in first-married families, and providing no assistance at all in stepfamilies. This substantiates the old adage that "A mother's work is never done."[4]

Table 4.3b Hours of Housework Performed Per Week by Cohabiting Partners and Others Over 19 Years Old

Household Task	First-Married Others > 19	Divorced Cohabitating Partner	Divorced Others > 19	Stepfamily Others > 19	Continuously Single Cohabitating Partner	Continuously Single Others >19	Significance[a] Cohabitating Others > 19	Significance[a] Partner
Preparing meals	.1	2.0	.4	.0	2.1	.4	acdf	ns
Washing dishes	.1	1.0	.3	.0	1.1	.3	acdf	ns
Cleaning house	.1	.8	.4	.0	1.5	.4	acdf	ns
Outdoor work	.1	3.6	.1	.0	2.5	.2	abcdf	ns
Shopping	.0	.6	.1	.0	1.0	.2	abcdef	ns
Laundry	.0	.3	.2	.0	.5	.2	acdf	ns
Paying bills	.0	.9	.0	.0	1.0	.1	acdef	ns
Car maintenance	.0	2.3	.0	.0	1.7	.1	cdf	ns
Driving	.0	1.8	.1	.0	1.1	.1	acf	ns
TOTAL	.5 (1,083)	13.3 (70)	1.6 (677)	.1 (275)	12.5 (72)	1.9 (418)	acdf	ns

NOTE: Sample sizes for individual items (tasks) varied due to missing data.
a. The letters indicate which means are significantly different at the $p < .05$ level: a = first-married compared to divorced; b = first-married compared to stepfamily; c = first-married compared to continuously single; d = divorced compared to stepfamily; e = divorced compared to continuously single; f = stepfamily compared to continuously single.

Perceptions of Equity in Housework

We also consider married women's perceptions of equity in the division of household labor. There are reasons we would not expect women to report equity. Previous research documents that wives do substantially more family work than their husbands (Berk, 1985; Kamo, 1988; Warner, 1986). In addition, most of the work women do is invisible, unrelenting, repetitive, stressful, and devalued (Berk, 1985; Shaw, 1988). Yet traditional cultural norms suggest it is fair and just for women to carry the burden of household responsibilities. Many women and men continue to define family work as women's responsibility (Szinovacz, 1984; Thompson & Walker, 1989). Women also tend to compare themselves to other women rather than to men (Major, 1987), and to compare their husbands to other men (Hochschild, 1989). Within-gender rather than between-gender comparisons tend to evoke greater perceptions of equity (Thompson, 1991). Further, many women do not recognize or appreciate the variety or volume of the family labor they do (DeVault, 1987, 1991). These processes may facilitate women's perceptions that the division of house-work is equitable.

A single item asked married mothers whether they thought the division of household labor was unfair to them or to their hus-band. A score of 1 indicates it was very unfair to them, a score of 3 indicates it was fair to both, and a score of 5 indicates it was very unfair to their husband. For this question then, an answer of 3 indicates the relationship is perceived as equitable by the wife/mother.

Our data indicate that mothers in their first marriage are no different from mothers in stepfamilies in their perceptions of equity.[5] First-married mothers had a mean of 2.6 and stepfamily mothers had a mean of 2.7. It is provocative that with such a disproportionate share of the effort, mothers typically respond that the division of housework is fair to both. The average re-sponse shows some awareness of the inequity, because the two means are slightly below 3.0, but is not a clear statement that the results are unfair.

Because women who are not engaged in paid work may see things quite differently in terms of equity, we selected two groups of women. The first group worked for pay 30 or more hours per week, and the second group worked for pay zero hours. With these extreme differences we anticipated that those employed 30 or more hours per week would experience much greater inequity. However, the results showed no differences. Mothers who were not working for pay reported average responses of 2.7 in first-married families and 2.8 in stepfamilies. Mothers who were em-ployed 30 or more hours per week had an average response of 2.6, regardless of family type.

Another factor that can influence the mothers' perceptions of equity is the amount of time they spend relative to the amount of time their husbands spend on household chores. Such compari-sons also may be related to the number of hours the mother works for pay. To explore this possibility, we ran a regression of the mother's perceived equity on the hours she spends on all chores, the hours the husband spends on all chores, the hours the mother is employed per week, and the control variables.[6] The model, including the control variables, had an R^2 of .07 ($p < .05$). The major predictors were consistent with our expectations. It is possible to gauge the relative importance of different predictors using Beta Weights, β. These range from −1.0 to +1.0. The larger the absolute value, the more important the predictor. The more hours per week the mother worked for pay, the lower her sense of equity ($\beta = -.14$, $p < .05$). The more hours the mother spent on household chores, the lower her sense of equity ($\beta = -.14$, $p < .05$). The strongest effect, however, was the number of hours the husband spent on household chores ($\beta = .27$, $p < .05$). None of the control variables had a beta of .10 or more. Thus, when relevant variables are controlled, although mothers report a surprisingly high level of satisfaction with an objectively unfair situation, the mother's perception is responsive to her husband's effort, the hours she is employed for pay, and the hours she spends on household labor. Even though husbands typically do far less housework than their wives, doing more than the average husband facilitates the wife's perception of an equitable relationship.

WHEN MOTHERS DO NOT WORK FOR PAY

How is household labor divided when the mother is a full-time homemaker? What about when she works outside the home full-time? Because female labor force participation is such an important issue in its own right, we will briefly discuss the division of household labor in families where mothers were employed and where mothers were not employed.

We isolated mothers who do not work for pay outside the household ($N = 649$) and found that, across family types, they perform an even higher percentage of household labor than employed mothers. Among nonemployed mothers, those who are married report they devote three fourths of the total time the family spends on housework (78.2% for first-married mothers and 76.2% for mothers in stepfamilies). Nonemployed single mothers do about 90% of housework (90.8% for divorced mothers and 89.7% for continuously single mothers). When we isolate mothers who work at least 30 hours per week outside the home ($N = 853$), we find that married mothers still contribute nearly two thirds of the total time the family spends on housework (66.5% for first-married mothers and 65.1% for mothers in step-families). Employed single mothers perform higher percentages of housework: 81.1% for divorced mothers and 80.7% for continuously single mothers. Thus employed mothers contribute a lower percentage of the total family time spent on housework than nonemployed mothers, and this finding holds across family types. Viewed differently, these findings illustrate that the effects of family type are identical for both employed and nonemployed mothers. That is, whether employed or not, divorced and continuously single mothers assume a greater percentage of household labor than married mothers.

Recall that in the previous section we showed that the hours mothers spend on household chores do not vary as widely across family types as the percentage of time mothers spend on chores. We observe the same pattern when we compare employed and nonemployed mothers. Figure 4.1 shows the total number of hours mothers spend on household labor for each family type by whether they are employed or not. Those mothers who are not employed spend between 38 and 52 hours per week on household labor. Mothers who are employed at least 30 hours per week spend from 32 to 38 hours per week on household labor. Thus time and energy devoted to employment reduces the hours mothers spend on household labor, regardless of family type.

Some of the reduction in time spent on housework by employed mothers may be offset by their husbands, when they are present. Figure 4.2 shows the number of hours husbands spend on household chores when their wife is not employed compared to when she is employed at least 30 hours per week. The figure shows that husbands of employed wives contribute more hours per week than husbands of nonemployed wives. On a proportional basis, the difference is substantial. Husbands spend about 40% more time on household chores when their wives are employed 30 or

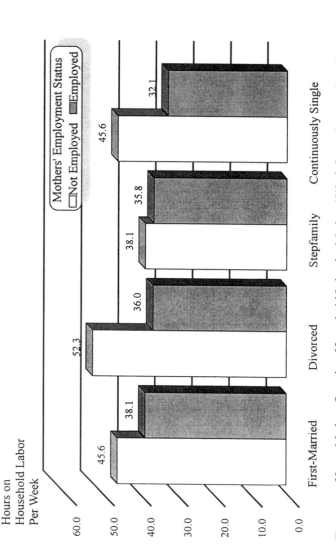

Figure 4.1. Hours Mothers Spend on Household Labor by Mothers' Work Status (not employed vs. 30+ hours/week)

more hours per week. Still, husbands' efforts are a small proportion of the total responsibility. When a mother takes on employment of 30 or more hours per week, it appears the father adds
about 4 hours per week to the housework he contributes. Thus,
although the difference between the amount of housework done
by husbands of employed mothers and those of nonemployed
mothers is statistically significant, the difference (4 hours) is
substantively small. Expressed in terms of workweek days, when
the mother works for pay at least 6 hours per day, the father works
on housework an additional 30 minutes per day. A more substantively (and statistically) significant difference is the greater amount
of housework performed by mothers (employed or not) in all
family types compared to that of their husbands.

ROLE STRAIN REGARDING HOUSEHOLD LABOR

We have seen how a father's absence from the household
increases the proportion of housework done by the mother but
has little effect on the actual time she spends on housework. The
next question is how mothers view their household work. Do
they think it is simple? Do they view their domestic workload as
manageable? Do they find housework boring? Do they feel appreciated for doing it? Is it lonely doing housework? Do they
perceive the work as well done?

Clearly, the popular culture portrays unmarried mothers as
having serious disadvantages. As we discussed in Chapter 1,
structural-functional theory also suggests that single mothers are
vulnerable because their opportunities for dividing family labor
are compromised. In the absence of clearly differentiated roles
between husband and wife, a single mother must perform most of
the housework, paid work, parenting, caring for aging parents, and
other forms of family labor. Although a number of theories would
predict role strain for overworked mothers regardless of family
type, it is important to recognize that a structural-functional perspective emphasizes the necessity of role-differentiation. According to
this perspective, single mothers should experience greater role strain
than mothers living in two-parent households. Table 4.4 presents

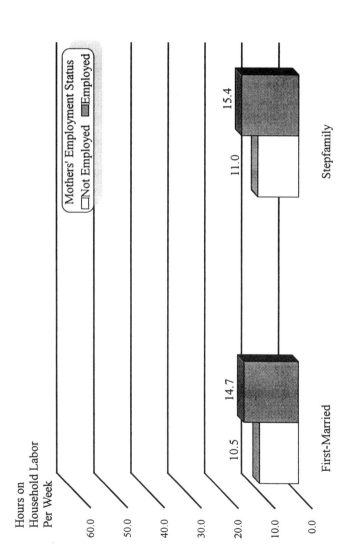

Figure 4.2. Hours Fathers Spend on Household Labor by Mothers' Work Status (not employed vs. 30+ hours/week)

the results for six items. These items are scored so a higher number signifies more strain. A score of 1 means that mothers rated chores positively (e.g., interesting, manageable, simple), a score of 4 means that chores were rated neutrally, and a score of 7 means that chores were regarded negatively (boring, unmanageable, or complicated). From Table 4.4 we see that continuously single mothers are most likely to report that their chores are boring. Still, the average for all groups on this item is fairly close to the neutral response (4).

Marital status has an important influence on whether mothers feel their work is appreciated or not. When mothers are asked if their housework is appreciated, single-parent mothers are more likely to say no; married mothers report significantly more appreciation. Whether the married mother is in her first marriage or a stepfamily does not make a difference, nor does whether the single parent is divorced or continuously single. It is interesting that although our previous findings show that husbands create as much additional work as they perform, married mothers report their household work is more appreciated than divorced or continuously single mothers report. This suggests that although husbands fail to share equally, or even near equally, in doing housework, they provide a source of social approval for their wives' labor. We must caution, however, that much housework is invisible, unnoticed, and unappreciated by husbands or other household members (Berheide, 1984; Shaw, 1988). At the very least, husbands do not have enough appreciation for the importance of household labor to become more involved themselves.

Contrary to structural-functional theory, Table 4.4 shows that divorced and continuously single mothers see their chores as being relatively manageable; their ratings are virtually identical to those of married mothers. The scores concentrate around 3, which indicates that mothers, regardless of family type, feel their housework is fairly manageable. It is important that the father's absence from the household has little effect on women's ratings of their performance or of how manageable their housework is. In fact, the only significant difference on these items is that, compared to divorced mothers, mothers in stepfamilies—who

Table 4.4 Role Strain Regarding Housework

Variable	First-Married Mean	Divorced Mean	Stepfamily Mean	Continuously Single Mean	Significance[a]
Chores are interesting	4.10	4.21	4.06	4.35	cf
(1) to boring (7)	(1,047)	(636)	(267)	(382)	
Housework is appreciated	3.22	3.67	3.28	3.70	acdf
(1) to unappreciated (7)	(1,040)	(636)	(266)	(383)	
Chores are manageable	2.88	2.74	3.02	2.84	d
(1) to overwhelming (7)	(1,034)	(630)	(265)	(377)	
Chores are simple (1)	2.36	2.37	2.38	2.43	ns
to complicated (7)	(1,029)	(633)	(264)	(382)	
Chores are sociable	3.68	3.84	3.62	3.67	ns
(1) to lonely (7)	(1,027)	(630)	(263)	(378)	
Chores are well done	2.47	2.51	2.34	2.51	ns
(1) to poorly done (7)	(1,032)	(633)	(266)	(381)	

NOTE: The number of cases is in parentheses.
a. The letters indicate which means are significantly different at the $p < .05$ level: a = first-married compared to divorced; b = first-married compared to stepfamily; c = first-married compared to continuously single; d = divorced compared to stepfamily; e = divorced compared to continuously single; f = stepfamily compared to continuously single.

have husbands present—rate their household responsibilities as less manageable. Thus, although the husband may be a source of social approval, his presence (and modest contributions) do not make household labor any easier to manage, partly because his presence contributes to the workload. This is important because a key assumption in structural-functional theory is that the absence of role differentiation creates a greater workload and greater stress for the single parent. Our data show, however, that mothers perform substantial and virtually indistinguishable amounts of domestic labor across diverse family structures.

Three other items asked mothers to rate the degree to which their household work is simple, sociable, and well done. There are no differences by family type on these three items. On average, mothers feel household work is relatively simple, that sometimes it can be sociable but other times it is lonely doing housework, and that most of their work is very well done.

WIFE-HUSBAND RELATIONS:
INTERACTION, QUALITY, AND STRAIN

In this section we examine the quality and stability of contemporary American marriages. Specifically, we describe and compare marital interaction and marital adjustment in first marriages and remarriages. Although many studies have compared first marriages and remarriages, previous studies have had important limitations. Specifically, most studies have relied on small, white, middle-class samples; they have implicitly adopted the standards and values of nuclear families to judge stepfamilies; they have focused on stepfamily problems rather than strengths; and they have failed to examine processes in stepfamilies (Coleman & Ganong, 1990).

Remarriages and stepfamilies are increasingly common. Stepfamilies are necessarily more complex in structure for a variety of reasons. One factor is the father's absence from the household, and another is the presence of a stepfather. Interviews with stepfamily mothers suggest that they have special problems because of these complex relationships (White & Booth, 1985). It is also clear that societal attitudes toward stepfamilies, as well as widely shared stereotypes regarding stepfamily members, tend to be negative (Ganong, Coleman, & Mapes, 1990). Thus, although conflicts exist in most families and across all family types, when problems arise in stepfamilies they may be blamed on the stepfamily structure. Lost in this view is the reality that some of the same problems, as well as other kinds of problems, occur in other types of families. In short, the structure of stepfamilies is viewed as inherently problematic. When a stepfather argues about child care, household chores, or in-law relations, these problems may not be objectively worse than such arguments in first marriages. However, stepfamily members may attribute the problem to the complexity of the family structure. Complaints such as, "You're not my real father," attest to the ambiguity of stepfamily norms.

Representing the view that remarriages and stepfamilies have unique problems, ambiguities, and stresses, Cherlin (1978) characterized remarriage as an "incomplete institution." A number of studies substantiate this view, demonstrating that stepfamily members lack clear guidelines for their relationships (Bray, 1988;

Furstenberg & Spanier, 1984). Parents, stepparents, stepgrandparents, stepchildren, stepsiblings and half-siblings struggle to define their relationships and to determine which relatives are part of their family. The term *quasi-kin* has been used to describe relations across households that lack any formal ties (Bohannon, 1970). In short, the absence of social support and of institutionalized ways of defining relationships and resolving conflicts strain marital, parent-child, and stepparent-stepchild relations in stepfather families.

Although there is much impressionistic literature on problems mothers have in stepfamilies,[7] little is known from national probability samples about the actual level of conflict and adjustment. The NSFH allows us to make an objective comparison of mothers in first marriages and in stepfamilies. We can assess whether first marriages or remarriages have greater adjustment problems. Comparing mothers in first marriages and in stepfamilies, how happy are they with their marital relationships? Do they feel appreciated? Are they bored? How much do they argue? Is there evidence of violence? Do mothers in stepfamilies have more or fewer marital problems than those in their first marriage?

Table 4.5 presents the relevant data on these questions and includes the range of possible answers. Some items report the frequency of an event, some report perceived strain, and others focus on conflict. In addition to the control variables described earlier, we control for length of the current marriage. This is important because, when viewed in cross-section, first-married mothers have been married longer than remarried mothers, and there is considerable evidence that aspects of marital quality decline with length of marriage (N. D. Glenn, 1990). The incomplete institution hypothesis predicts that stepfamilies, because of their greater complexity and unclear norms for guiding relationships, should have more problems in wife-husband relationships (Cherlin, 1978; Clingempeel, 1981; White & Booth, 1985).

Interaction

We use two items to evaluate the interaction of wives and husbands. The first is the frequency of direct interaction. For

Table 4.5   Interaction, Satisfaction, and Role Strain Regarding
Wife-Husband Relations

Item Being Compared	First-Married	Stepfamily	Significance[a]
Interaction			
Frequency of interaction (0) rarely to (6) daily	4.59 (1,056)	4.93 (258)	*
Frequency of intercourse last month	8.05 (876)	10.93 (234)	*
Adjustment			
Marital happiness (1) very unhappy to (7) very happy	5.84 (1,032)	6.03 (256)	ns
Marriage in trouble during last year, percentage yes	28.3 (944)	32.7 (250)	ns
Chance of divorce (1) very low to (5) very high	1.43 (988)	1.37 (249)	ns
Role strain			
Role as wife is (1) interesting to (7) boring	2.71 (991)	2.51 (245)	ns
Role as wife is (1) appreciated to (7) unappreciated	2.67 (988)	2.43 (243)	ns
Role as wife is (1) manageable to (7) overwhelming	2.86 (985)	2.77 (242)	ns
Role as wife is (1) sociable to (7) lonely	2.65 (986)	2.51 (241)	ns
Role as wife is (1) well done to (7) poorly done	2.37 (988)	2.19 (242)	ns

some couples this type of interaction is a rare event and for others it is a daily occurrence. Table 4.5 shows that mothers in stepfamilies report a significantly higher frequency of interaction with their husbands than mothers in their first marriage. Some would expect a lower level of interaction for stepfamilies because of their complexity (e.g., involvement with former spouses, children from prior marriages, in-laws, etc.), but it is possible that the complexity requires more frequent interaction. Our data do not allow us to evaluate this alternative explanation.

Table 4.5   Continued

Item Being Compared	First-Married	Stepfamily	Significance[a]
Conflict			
Argue about household tasks	2.16	1.81	*
(1) never to (6) daily	(1,015)	(253)	
Argue about money	2.24	1.98	*
(1) never to (6) daily	(1,017)	(253)	
Argue about time together	2.13	1.68	*
(1) never to (6) daily	(1,013)	(251)	
Argue about sexual relationship	1.78	1.47	*
(1) never to (6) daily	(1,006)	(251)	
Argue about in-laws	1.60	1.39	*
(1) never to (6) daily	(1,010)	(253)	
Argue about children	2.26	2.49	ns
(1) never to (6) daily	(1,014)	(253)	
When we argue we are calm	2.66	2.46	*
(1) never to (5) always	(1,014)	(253)	
When we argue we are heated	2.14	2.10	ns
(1) never to (5) always	(1,013)	(251)	
Hit or throw things	1.12	1.10	ns
(1) never to (5) always	(1,013)	(251)	
Arguments get physical,	9.0	10.0	ns
percentage yes	(978)	(245)	

NOTE: The number of cases is in parentheses.
a. An * is used to show which comparisons are significant at the .05 level.

The second interaction item concerns frequency of sexual inter-course. On average, mothers in stepfamilies report having had intercourse with their husband nearly 11 times in the 30 days preceding the interview (10.9). In comparison, first-married moth-ers report significantly less frequent intercourse, 8 times in the past month (8.0). These figures suggest that sexual relationships occur on an average of two to three times per week for married couples. It is interesting that mothers in stepfather families report having intercourse much more frequently. Unfortunately, we do not have more comprehensive questions measuring other important as-pects of sexual interaction.

Adjustment

We know that remarriages have a higher divorce rate than first marriages (Martin & Bumpass, 1989; Teachman, 1986). We also know that there is not a perfect relationship between marital adjustment and divorce. Many couples continue to live together even though their marriages are unhappy. The comparison of first-married and remarried mothers on three adjustment items is provocative. The average responses are nearly identical for all three items. The average first-married mother has a mean of 5.8 on Marital Happiness, compared to 6.0 for mothers in stepfamilies. On this scale a score of 6 signifies the marriage is *happy* (7 signifies *very happy*). Thus both types of mothers are generally happy with their marriage. This is consistent with many previous studies showing small differences in marital satisfaction between first-married and remarried couples (for a review, see Vemer, Coleman, Ganong, & Cooper, 1989).

Popular attitudes and stereotypes might lead some to expect that individuals in remarriages would be more likely than their counterparts in first marriages to report that their marriage was in trouble at some point in the 12 months preceding the interview. Yet when simply asked to indicate yes or no, the two groups reported nearly identical responses (28.3% answering yes in first marriages and 32.7% aswering yes in stepfamilies). The clearest interpretation of these average responses is that about 70% of mothers in both family types report they had no marital trouble during the last year. That 30% of both types report significant trouble, however, shows that *current* marital happiness does not mean the marriage is free of difficulty. Many mothers who reported having trouble during the last year also reported that they are happy in their marriage.

The third item concerning adjustment is the subjective chance the mother sees of getting divorced. The answers ranged from 1 for *very low* to 5 for *very high*. The modal response among both groups of married mothers was 1.

Together, these results have interesting implications for adjustment in American marriages. A substantial percentage (30%) of marriages have had trouble at some point in the last year. This is true regardless of whether it is a first marriage or a remarriage in a stepfather family. In spite of this, most mothers are happy or very happy in their marriage and have a very low expectation that they will get a divorce. Differences in marital adjustment are far greater *within* family types than *between* family types.

Role Strain

How much strain do mothers report in their role as wife? Are mothers in stepfamilies more likely to have high role strain in trying to perform their role and manage its demands? Are they frustrated in their role performance? Table 4.5 shows the average answers to five items. These have been scaled so the most strain has a score of 7 and the least strain has a score of 1. Importantly, there is no significant difference between first-married and re-married mothers on any aspect of strain in their role as wives. In general, mothers in both types of married families describe their activities and experiences as wives in positive terms—interesting, appreciated, manageable, sociable, and well done.

Conflict

Wives and husbands can fight about many things. In this chapter we focus on marital conflict involving the division of household labor, money, spending time together, their sexual relationship, in-laws, and children. The incomplete institution hypothesis suggests that because of the added complexity and ambiguous norms characterizing stepfamilies, they should exhibit greater conflict in wife-husband relationships.

Table 4.5 reports the mean responses for 10 items that involve conflict, and there are several significant differences. Mothers in stepfamilies are significantly different from mothers in their first marriage on 6 of the 10 items. What is interesting here is that the differences are in the opposite direction of what is predicted by the incomplete institution hypothesis. Mothers in stepfamilies report fewer arguments about household tasks, money, time spent together, their sexual relationship, and in-laws. When there are arguments, remarried mothers are more likely to stay calm. None of the other differences are statistically significant. It is noteworthy that mothers in first marriages and remarriages report that arguments rarely get physical or involve wives or husbands hitting each other or throwing things at one another. Evidence from other studies, however, would suggest that these reports underestimate the amount of spousal violence, particularly wife abuse (Straus, Gelles, & Steinmetz, 1980; Yllo & Bograd, 1988). It is also important to consider that many of our female respondents in male-dominant families may not have felt free or comfortable answering such questions.

POSTMARITAL RELATIONS WITH NONRESIDENTIAL PARENT

For divorced mothers and mothers in stepfather families, relationships with former spouses are an integral part of family life, particularly where the interaction involves their continuing role as parents. In Table 4.6 we present information on the frequency of interaction and the nature of conflict with nonresidential parents. In addition to the control variables we have used throughout the chapter, we also control for the age and gender of the focal child.

Interaction

Nonresidential parents (exclusively fathers in our analysis) tend to live a long distance from their children, an average of more than 400 miles.[8] This is true for both divorced families and stepfamilies. There are a number of significant differences between family types, however, in the frequency and nature of interaction with former spouses and coparents. Compared to mothers in stepfamilies, mothers in divorced families report significantly more interaction and communication with nonresidential fathers. Mothers were asked, "During the past year, how often have you had any contact with your former husband (by phone,

Table 4.6 Postmarital Relations With Former Spouse and Children's Nonresidential Parent for Mothers in Divorced and Stepfamilies

Item Being Compared	Divorced	Stepfamily	Significance[a]
Interaction			
Number of miles nonresident parent lives away from child	402.00 (564)	426.00 (171)	ns
Frequency parents talk with each other about child (1) never to (6) often	3.10 (607)	2.27 (195)	*
Frequency of mother's contact with nonresident parent (1) not at all to (6) more than once a week	3.64 (444)	2.50 (111)	*
Conflict with former spouse			
Conflict about where child lives (1) none to (3) a great deal	1.16 (600)	1.10 (192)	ns
Conflict about how a child is raised (1) none to (3) a great deal	1.27 (600)	1.09 (192)	*
Conflict about how mother spends money on child (1) none to (3) a great deal	1.16 (600)	1.07 (191)	*
Conflict about how nonresident parent spends money on child (1) none to (3) a great deal	1.33 (600)	1.95 (192)	*
Conflict about nonresident parent's visits with child (1) none to (3) a great deal	1.38 (598)	1.22 (192)	*
Conflict about nonresident parent's child support (1) none to (3) a great deal	1.62 (598)	1.38 (192)	*
Dissatisfaction with relation to nonresident parent			
About where child lives (1) very satisfied to (4) very dissatisfied	1.20 (602)	1.07 (193)	*
About nonresident parent's contact with child (1) very satisfied to (4) very dissatisfied	2.14 (602)	1.90 (192)	*
About nonresident parent's contribution to child support (1) very satisfied to (4) very dissatisfied	2.63 (602)	2.36 (191)	*
Relation with former spouse (1) very unfriendly to (5) very friendly	2.92 (462)	3.19 (113)	ns

NOTE: The number of cases is in parentheses.
a. An asterisk is used to show which comparisons are significant at the .05 level.

mail, visits, etc.)?" Most mothers in stepfamilies report that they rarely talk with or have contact with their former spouse. On average, contact occurs between once and several times per year. Divorced mothers report more frequent contact with their former husband but still only averaging once per month.

One important reason for continued contact is children. Research indicates that contact between ex-spouses is much less frequent where there are no children (Kitson, 1992). Yet *any* communication between residential mothers and nonresidential fathers occurs so infrequently that they rarely make the time to discuss their children. Nearly half (48.7%) of mothers in stepfamilies report that they talk about the child with the nonresidential father once a year or less. Although divorced mothers are more likely to report continued involvement of the nonresidential father, more than one third (36.9%) of divorced mothers report they talk about the child with the nonresidential father once a year or less.

Conflict With Former Spouse

Considering that divorced mothers interact more frequently with their former spouses than remarried mothers do, it is not surprising that divorced mothers also report significantly more conflict with their former spouses concerning how the child is raised, how the mother spends money on the child, the father's visits with the child, and the father's child support. One area where mothers in stepfamilies report a higher frequency of disagreement with their former spouses concerns how the nonresidential father spends money on the child. In general, very little or no conflict is reported concerning where the child lives, how the child is raised, or how the mother spends money on the child. On the other hand, former spouses have more frequent disagreements regarding the nature and frequency of the nonresidential parent's visits with the child. Conflicts about the nonresidential parent's child support are also common, particularly for children living with divorced mothers who have not remarried. Mothers in stepfather families report high levels of disagreement concerning how the nonresidential parent spends money on the child. Such conflicts may arise partly because of nonresidential parents (exclusively fathers in our analysis) refusing to pay childrearing expenses that they think could be paid by residential mothers and stepfathers.

Dissatisfaction With Relationship With Nonresidential Parent

In evaluating the overall relationship between the child and the nonresidential father, mothers express a high level of satisfaction, particularly in stepfamilies. However, compared to mothers in stepfamilies, those in divorced families report significantly greater dissatisfaction with where the child lives, the father's contact with the child, and the father's level of child support. It is important to keep in mind that in these comparisons we controlled for a series of socioeoconomic and family composition variables. Thus these differences cannot be attributed to such factors as stepfamilies having greater financial resources or having older children. Finally, there are no significant differences by family type in mothers' overall assessments of their own relationships with their former spouses.

Collectively, these findings are interesting in that they paint a picture of divorced and stepfamilies in which nonresidential fathers live a day's drive away, but many are not really "absent" from the picture. Of course, some nonresidential fathers do not maintain contact with their former spouses, even to discuss their own children. The frequency and nature of nonresidential fathers' contacts with their children vary substantially (Mott, 1990). We also know that contact between ex-spouses diminishes with time since the divorce (Ambert, 1989; Kitson, 1992). But relying on mothers' reports, which could underestimate paternal involvement, the interaction and communication between parents is described at intermediate levels in divorced families. Most divorced fathers and their former spouses maintain contact with each other. But the frequency of interaction and communication is much lower in families where the mother has remarried. Further, coparenting is not always harmonious. The greater level of parental interaction in divorced families is associated with greater conflict between parents. Divorced mothers also are less satisfied with fathers' involvement with, and support of, their children.

Our primary focus in this chapter has been on couple relations. In the next chapter we examine in more detail the nature of children's relationships with residential and nonresidential parents.

SUMMARY AND CONCLUSIONS

In this chapter we explored many aspects of marital relationships, marital adjustment, and the division of household labor. Corroborating previous studies, we found that mothers devote the vast proportion of time and labor on most household chores (Berk, 1985; Kamo, 1988; Mederer, 1993; Warner, 1986). This finding holds across family types. Excluding two tasks that are done infrequently and require little time, mothers in all family types provide 69% to 94% of the time needed for household tasks. Further, the proportion of family work done by mothers is even greater in single-parent families.

Domestic work by husbands (when present) or male cohabiting partners is modest, and household work by children is negligible. Mothers spend between 40 and 44 hours per week on household labor across family types, husbands (or male partners) average 13 hours per week, and children under 19 average 3 to 6 hours per week doing household chores. The absence of a father/husband does not significantly increase the time the mother spends on most tasks, although it does increase the *proportion* of the total household labor she performs. It appears that husbands produce about the same amount of additional work for their wives as they provide in return. At least for families with dependent-age children, then, mothers' domestic labor is extensive and the father's presence or absence has little net effect on the time mothers spend on household labor.

These findings highlight an important and seemingly unrelenting pattern of family life—women's family labor. In the face of enormous social change during the past 3 decades, and with the accompanying popular interest in how families have been reshaped by changing gender roles, by steady increases in female labor force involvement, and by substantial diversity in family structure, women's domestic labor has remained at a constant and substantial level. Previous research shows that husbands averaged 11 hours per week of housework in the 1960s, and wives devoted 35 to 40 hours weekly (Coverman & Sheley, 1986). Our data, collected in the late 1980s, indicate very modest increases in men's household labor (from 11 to 13 hours per week), as well as modest increases in women's housework (varying from 40 to 44 hours weekly depending on family type). That women continue to do three times as much nonwage family labor as their husbands or partners is compelling evidence that popular descriptions of changes in marital, family, and gender roles are overstated, that family labor remains gendered, and that women are disadvantaged and vulnerable.

Yet even when women provide such a disproportionate share of the effort, they typically respond that the work is fairly divided and manageable. Women report greater equity when married to men who do a larger share of housework than most men, even though most of these men are doing far less housework than their wives. These findings support the conclusion that women and men continue to devalue housework, to view it as "women's work" (Szinovacz, 1984; Thompson & Walker, 1989), and to make within-gender comparisons that serve to undermine women's sense of fairness and entitlement (Thompson, 1991). Further evidence for this conclusion is provided by comparing families with employed and nonemployed mothers. This comparison shows that, across family types, employment reduces the hours mothers spend on household labor. But even when their wives are employed, husbands' efforts are still a small proportion of the total responsibility. When a mother takes on employment of 30 or more hours per week, the father adds 4 to 5 hours per week to the household chores he performs. It appears that many husbands lack sufficient appreciation for the importance of household labor to become more involved themselves. The clear and consistent pattern is that, across all family types, mothers (whether employed or not) perform two to three times more housework than their husbands or cohabiting partners.

Comparing marital relations in first marriages and remarriages yields a number of findings that refute the view of remarriage as an "incomplete institution" (Cherlin, 1978), riddled by its complexity and ambiguous norms (Clingempeel, 1981; White & Booth, 1985). Stepfamily mothers report significantly higher frequencies of marital interaction and sexual intercourse than mothers in their first marriage report. In addition, mothers in stepfamilies report arguing less frequently about a variety of concerns including household tasks, money, time spent together, their sexual relationship, and in-laws. When there are arguments, mothers in stepfamilies are more likely to stay calm. In first marriages or remarriages, most mothers report they are happy or very happy in their marriage and have a very low expectation that they will get a divorce. In short, subjectively perceived marital quality is high for first marriages and even higher for remarriages in stepfather families.

In the next chapter we consider intergenerational relations across different family structures. Recognizing that children are minimally involved in domestic work across family types, what types of values, expectations, and family rules do parents have for children in different family types? Does the level of involvement, support, conflict, or violence in parent-child relationships vary by family type?

NOTES

1. This section of the chapter is a revised version of an earlier article we published (Demo & Acock, 1993). The analyses presented here involve slightly different subsamples from those used in the original article, causing some minor changes in the number of hours and percentage of time invested by family members. In all cases, the changes are trivial and the conclusions are unaffected.

2. In some cases mothers reported a very large number of hours spent on individual chores. Extreme responses, those beyond the third standard deviation, were treated as outliers, and each of them was recoded to the value corresponding to the third standard deviation above the mean number of hours.

3. In an unknown number of cases involving cohabiting partners, the mother may have a lesbian partner. Although we do not have the necessary data to identify and examine these cases, it is noteworthy that such families are exceptional in that the division of labor is not gender-based.

4. It should be pointed out that relatively few households include other members age 19 and older, and that most people in this category are older (i.e., young adult) children. But there is also variation by family type. For example, more than 5% of continuously single mothers report other adult relatives living

in the household. Unfortunately, there are too few cases to conduct finer analyses of these household members and their contributions across family types.

5. In addition to the controls used early in this chapter, this analysis also controls for the length of the current marriage.

6. Control variables include whether the respondent was in the oversampled population or not, the household's total income, mother's education, mother's race, mother's age, number of people living in the household, age of the youngest child, and marriage length.

7. It is important to note that all of the remarried mothers in our sample have a biological child from a previous marriage living in the household, but some may also be a stepmother for other children in the household.

8. Some of these nonresident fathers may have other children (biological children or stepchildren) living with them, including children who were born in previous and/or current families. Our focus, however, is on these men as nonresident fathers and as former spouses of the mothers in our sample.

Parent-Child Relations

Popular commentary and political debate concerning the "decline of the American family" often focus on how nontraditional types of families, especially those where the mother is divorced or continuously single, provide a "second-class" socialization experience. During the 1992 presidential campaign, then-Vice President Dan Quayle announced his opposition to a fictional television character, Murphy Brown, for having a child without being married. The implications are many and serious: children need their fathers, single parents (most often mothers) are inadequate, single parents do not have the "proper" values, they have lower expectations for their children, and they do not spend enough time with their children. One nationally syndicated columnist describes it very simply: "The two-parent household as the ideal arrangement for rearing children has been universal across both time and geography" (Raspberry, 1993).

Popular wisdom holds that the breakdown of the traditional family somehow leads to a breakdown in traditional values and expectations. It is further assumed that the values identified with traditional families were superior. We are told by social and political commentators that poverty perpetuates itself because these families have poor values and expectations (Moynihan, 1965; Whitehead, 1993). In this chapter we evaluate the credibility of the argument that family values and parent-child interaction are "deficient" in nontraditional families.

One reason that these ideas are so widely held and firmly entrenched in our culture is that family researchers have provided support for some of these beliefs. One prominent and influential paradigm, outlined in Chapter 2, is the family composition model. It emphasizes that two parental role models are essential for the normal development and well-being of children. Alternative family environments are viewed as socialization deficits. For example, Nock (1988) argues that single-parent families blur generational boundaries, that children in these families do not successfully learn hierarchical authority relations, and, consequently, they do not do as well educationally or occupationally. Other studies attribute behavioral problems among children in single-parent families to reduced parental contact, supervision, support, and control (Dornbusch et al., 1985; Furstenberg et al., 1987; Newcomer & Udry, 1987). From this perspective, we would expect single parents to have lower expectations for their children, to be less supportive, to spend less time with them, and to be less effective in maintaining control.

In contrast, an economic deprivation argument suggests that family resources and family processes are more important than family composition. Economic hardship distresses parents and causes them to be less nurturant, less supportive, and less consistent in disciplining (Lempers et al., 1989; McLoyd, 1990). From this perspective, there is no reason to expect different family values across family types. Parents want and expect the same of their children, but resources are widely discrepant across family types. The main idea here is that economic and structural constraints block opportunities for children in some families to fulfill their goals and values.

In the first part of this chapter we examine whether mothers in different family types have different rules, expectations, and values for their children. Should children follow their parents' rules or should they be independent? What values are emphasized by mothers in different family types? How important is it that children carry out responsibilities on their own, or get along well with other children? Is it important to do well at sports? In the second part of the chapter we examine mothers' and fathers' actual involvement with their children and the types of relationships that nonresidential parents have with children. How much time do parents and children spend together, and how does parental involvement vary across family types? In what ways do childrearing values and behaviors change as children grow older, develop, and mature?

FAMILY VALUES, RULES, AND EXPECTATIONS

Families With All Children Under 5

This section focuses on mothers who have at least one child under age 5. Mothers were asked to describe their childrearing values regarding 12 aspects of children's behavior. Each aspect of behavior reflects a culturally valued trait in children. Specifically, they were asked how important it is that their children follow rules, do well in school, be independent, be kind and considerate, control their temper, do what you ask, carry out responsibilities on their own, keep busy by themselves, get along well with other kids, do well in athletics, try new things, and do well in creative activities such as music, art, or drama. Contrary to popular stereotypes, parenting values held by mothers do not vary across family types. The responses of first-married, divorced, and continuously single mothers are contained in Table 5.1. As with all the tables in this chapter, the data reported in Table 5.1 adjust for effects of our control variables: whether the respondent was in the oversampled population or not, the household's total income, mother's education, mother's race, mother's age, hours per week the mother is employed, the number of people living in the household, and age of the youngest child. There are too few mothers in stepfamilies who have children age 4 or younger for them to be considered in our analysis.[1]

The complete scale (an average of the 12 items) provides clear and consistent results. Divorced mothers place the greatest importance on their young children's behavior across the 12 culturally valued areas. Their average score (5.83 on a 7-point scale) reveals they consider most of these behaviors quite important.

Table 5.1 Mothers' Childrearing Values, Child Age 0-4

Item Being Compared	First-Married	Divorced	Continuously Single	Significance[a]
Overall values—(1) not at all important to (7) extremely important				
Scale of values	5.63	5.83	5.59	ns
Values in specific areas—(1) not at all important to (7) extremely important				
Follow the rules	5.76	5.99	5.34	bc
Do well at school	5.88	6.16	5.88	ns
Be independent	5.91	6.01	5.88	ns
Be kind	6.60	6.53	6.53	ns
Control temper	6.03	6.25	6.11	ns
Do what you ask	5.56	5.76	5.38	ns
Do responsibilities	6.00	6.08	5.69	c
Do creative activities	4.75	5.02	4.75	ns
Keep self busy	4.84	5.26	4.94	a
Get along well	6.16	6.38	6.18	ns
Do well at sports	4.08	4.52	4.26	ns
Try new things	5.93	6.00	5.93	ns

NOTE: Stepfamilies are excluded because we had only 12 respondents reporting who had a child 0-4 years of age. The number of mothers in their first marriage varies from 315 to 318, the number of divorced mothers varies from 62 to 64, and the number of continuously single mothers varies from 115 to 120.

a. The letters indicate which means are significantly different at the $p < .05$ level: a = first-married compared to divorced; b = first-married compared to continuously single; c = divorced compared to continuously single.

Continuously single mothers (5.59) and mothers in their first marriage (5.63) place slightly less importance on these behaviors. However, the differences are not statistically significant. That the average responses of mothers in all three family types fall slightly below 6 on a 7-point scale provides evidence that, across family types, mothers consider it important that their children learn to act in culturally valued ways.

When we examine the individual items, there are few statistically significant differences by family type for the individual parenting values. One exception is the value attached to children keeping busy by themselves, which divorced mothers value more strongly than first-married mothers. Also, divorced mothers place the highest value on following rules, followed by first-married mothers, with continuously single mothers having the lowest scores. For the remaining values, however, mothers' values concerning their children's behavior do not vary by family type. These findings seriously challenge those who attribute weak values to single parents. Most mothers attribute considerable importance to children conforming to cultural expectations. The greatest importance is assigned to children being kind and considerate, and less importance is assigned to children keeping busy by themselves, being creative, and doing well athletically.

Families With Children 5-18

What happens when children grow older? Some might argue that although single mothers share culturally prescribed values for young children, the stresses of single parenting and the difficulties of single-parent families work to erode parents' expectations as children get older. We examine the same set of 12 values, and the results for the complete scale are shown in Figure 5.1. The average responses for each of the individual values are shown in Table 5.2. The analysis includes all four family types and is based on much larger samples than when we focused on families with children under age 5.

The results show no differences in childrearing values across the four family types. Mothers in various family structures report they assign considerable importance to their children learning culturally valued behaviors. As with mothers of younger children, mothers of children aged 5-18 attribute the most importance to children being kind and considerate, and the least importance to creativity, keeping oneself busy, and athletic ability.

When we examine the respective values individually, there are no statistically significant differences across family types in the importance assigned to children following rules, doing well at school, being kind, or doing well at sports. For the other items, there are small, but statistically significant differences. Importantly, however, the scores are not consistently higher (or lower) for any one family type. For example, first-married mothers

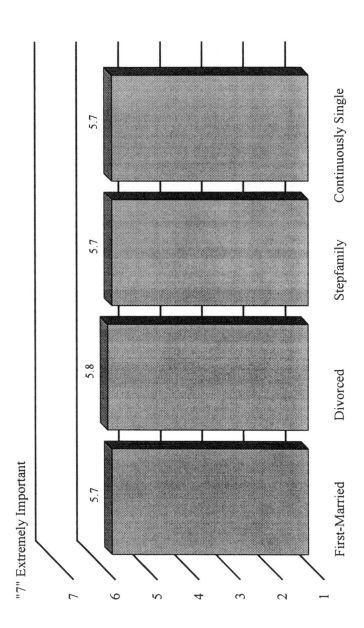

Figure 5.1. Mothers' Childrearing Values: Importance of Culturally Prescribed Values Across Family Types

Table 5.2 Mothers' Childrearing Values, Child Age 5-18

Item Being Compared	First-Married	Divorced	Stepfamily	Continuously Single	Significance[a]
Overall values—(1) not at all important to (7) extremely important					
Scale of values	5.72	5.77	5.68	5.69	ns
Values in specific areas—(1) not at all important to (7) extremely important					
Follow rules	6.08	5.92	5.95	5.91	ns
Do well at school	6.20	6.27	6.16	6.25	ns
Be independent	5.98	6.13	6.00	6.10	a
Be kind	6.58	6.62	6.65	6.57	ns
Control temper	6.10	6.10	6.17	5.94	f
Do what you ask	5.78	5.66	5.76	5.57	c
Do responsibilities	6.17	6.17	6.16	5.95	cef
Do creative activities	4.87	4.87	4.63	4.86	b
Keep self busy	4.94	5.05	4.76	5.12	df
Get along well	6.16	6.22	6.21	6.05	e
Do well at sports	4.24	4.43	4.24	4.33	ns
Try new things	5.57	5.76	5.51	5.71	ad

NOTE: The number of first-married mothers varies from 686 to 690; the number of divorced mothers varies from 564 to 566; stepfamily mothers range from 240 to 242, and continuously single mothers vary from 235 to 241.
a. The letters indicate which means are significantly different at the $p < .05$ level: a = first-married compared to divorced; b = first-married compared to stepfamily; c = first-married compared to continuously single; d = divorced compared to stepfamily; e = divorced compared to continuously single; f = stepfamily compared to continuously single.

attribute less importance than other mothers to children being independent, continuously single mothers attribute less importance to children doing responsibilities on their own, and mothers in stepfamilies attribute the least importance to children's creativity and ability to keep themselves busy. Compared to mothers in other family types, divorced mothers place the highest value on children's independence and trying new things. It is worth reiterating, however, that these differences across family types are small. The data make it abundantly clear that any disadvantages associated with nontraditional families are not attributable to differences in family values or expectations for child outcomes. Mothers of young children, older children, and adolescents consider it quite important that their children learn many socially acceptable and culturally valued behaviors.

Parental Rules and Control

Although the above data show that mothers' expectations for their children do not vary by family type, some argue that expectations are not enough, and that single parents do not or cannot control their children. The lack of control and direction attributed to single-parent families is viewed as a root cause of delinquent behavior, teen pregnancy, and other social problems (Dornbusch et al., 1985; Newcomer & Udry, 1987). We can address some aspects of this argument by examining data on various strategies and techniques mothers use to control children in different family types. Setting rules and imposing restrictions on children's activities represent one dimension of parental control.

For very young children we have only two questions that focus on control specifically, but a broad set of questions on that subject were asked of mothers with children ages 5-11 and 12-18. Different questions were asked because different issues are important in parenting children of different ages.

For the comparison of mothers with children under age 5, we exclude stepfamilies because there were too few of them with very young children. The first question asked if mothers restrict the amount of time their children spend watching television. Continuously single mothers (63.2%) are significantly more likely than first-married mothers (44.8%) to restrict television time. Divorced mothers are intermediate in this respect, with more than half (53.6%) reporting they restrict television time.

Whereas continuously single mothers are most likely to restrict the amount of time their young children watch television, they are least likely to restrict the programs. Fully 87.6% of the first-married mothers and 91.6% of the divorced mothers restrict the programs their young children watch. By contrast, only 72.0% of the continuously single mothers restrict programming. The percentage for continuously single mothers is significantly lower than the percentage for mothers in either of the other family types. Although these data are very limited, they suggest that continuously single mothers find it easier or more important to regulate the *amount* of television their children watch rather than controlling the *content* of what they watch.

The survey included nine questions focusing on parental rules for children ages 5-11 (see Table 5.3). Mothers were asked if they would allow their school-age child to be at home alone at various times: before or after school, all day when there is no school, at night, or overnight if parents were away on a trip. Across family types, mothers are generally opposed to leaving a child alone at home before or after school. For the before- and after-school periods, first-married mothers are least likely to leave their school-age child at home alone. Mothers in all family types are strongly opposed to leaving their child alone all day, at night, or overnight. Mothers also are in general agreement that they insist on knowing where their child is when the child is not at home. These findings reflect strengths of many single-parent families in that mothers in these families find ways to monitor and supervise their school-age children despite the difficulties many of them have trying to arrange and coordinate their wage work and family work.

We saw in Chapter 4 that children in first-married families are less involved than other children in household labor. One reason for this is that first-married mothers are least likely to require school-age children to do regular chores (although this difference is statistically significant only in comparison to divorced mothers). Across family types, there are some attempts to restrict the amount of time children spend watching television, and mothers in continuously single-parent families are somewhat less likely to impose these restrictions on their children. Continuously single mothers also are significantly less likely than either first-married or stepfamily mothers to control the kinds of television programs their children watch.

The NSFH contains 12 questions concerning parental rules for adolescents (ages 12-18). The data are presented in Table 5.4. There are no differences by family type on any aspects of parental willingness to leave adolescents alone at home during the day or night. In general, mothers allow adolescents to be alone at home during the day and at night, but do not allow them to be alone

Table 5.3 Mothers' Rules for Children Ages 5-11

Item Being Compared	First-Married	Divorced	Stepfamily	Continuously Single	Significance[a]
Leave child alone before school, (1) yes, (2) depends, (3) no	2.70	2.51	2.50	2.40	abc
Leave child alone after school, (1) yes, (2) depends, (3) no	2.61	2.44	2.35	2.26	abc
Leave child alone all day, (1) yes, (2) depends, (3) no	2.90	2.83	2.83	2.77	c
Leave child alone at night, (1) yes, (2) depends, (3) no	2.96	2.95	2.97	2.89	ns
Leave child alone all night, (1) yes, (2) depends, (3) no	2.98	2.99	3.00	2.99	ns
Able to locate child, (1) always to (4) rarely	1.11	1.08	1.08	1.08	ns
Require regular chores, percentage yes	75.9	82.1	85.3	80.2	b
Restrict TV time, (1) no, (2) try, (3) yes	2.19	2.26	2.26	2.05	e
Restrict TV programs, (1) no, (2) try, (3) yes	2.77	2.67	2.80	2.60	cf

NOTE: There are from 303 to 328 mothers in their first marriage, from 244 to 255 divorced mothers, from 95 to 99 stepfamily mothers, and from 154 to 157 continuously single mothers.
a. The letters indicate which means are significantly different at the $p < .05$ level: a = first-married compared to divorced; b = first-married compared to stepfamily; c = first-married compared to continuously single; d = divorced compared to stepfamily; e = divorced compared to continuously single; f = stepfamily compared to continuously single.

overnight. There is one difference, however, in terms of allowing adolescents to be alone all night, with first-married mothers less likely than divorced mothers to allow adolescents this privilege. Across family types, mothers always want to know where their teenage children are.

Mothers place fewer restrictions on television time for adolescents than for younger children, but there are no differences across family types. However, first-married mothers are significantly more likely than mothers in any other family type to restrict the programs their teenage children watch. About 90% of the mothers report their teenage child has regular chores, except in continuously single-parent families, where 75% have regular

Table 5.4   Mothers' Rules for Children Ages 12-18

Item Being Compared	First-Married	Divorced	Continuously Stepfamily	Single	Significance[a]
Leave child alone before school, (1) yes, (2) depends, (3) no	1.39	1.28	1.33	1.35	ns
Leave child alone after school, (1) yes, (2) depends, (3) no	1.28	1.21	1.19	1.21	ns
Leave child alone all day, (1) yes, (2) depends, (3) no	1.54	1.40	1.41	1.35	ns
Leave child alone at night, (1) yes, (2) depends, (3) no	1.75	1.60	1.58	1.59	ns
Leave child alone all night, (1) yes, (2) depends, (3) no	2.43	2.26	2.38	2.33	a
Able to locate child (1) never to (4) always	3.76	3.76	3.85	3.70	ns
Restrict TV time (1) no, (2) try, (3) yes	1.67	1.61	1.50	1.59	ns
Restrict TV programs (1) no, (2) try, (3) yes	2.22	1.91	1.83	1.79	abc
Child has regular chores, percentage yes	88.6	89.5	90.0	74.5	cef
Allow child to earn dollars, percentage yes	63.1	63.1	54.8	62.8	ns
Number of dates last month	2.02	2.46	2.70	2.85	ns
Sex under 18 OK with strong affection (1) strongly agree to (5) strongly disagree	3.65	3.34	3.48	3.09	abcef

NOTE: There are from 303 to 314 mothers in their first marriage, from 297 to 303 divorced mothers, from 125 to 129 stepfamily mothers, and from 62 to 65 continuously single mothers for all but the last item. The last item has 1,043 mothers in their first marriage, 649 divorced mothers, 269 stepfamily mothers, and 387 continuously single mothers.
a. The letters indicate which means are significantly different at the $p < .05$ level: a = first-married compared to divorced; b = first-married compared to stepfamily; c = first-married compared to continuously single; d = divorced compared to stepfamily; e = divorced compared to continuously single; f = stepfamily compared to continuously single.

chores. Other ways that parents might control their adolescent's behavior and lifestyle include controlling part-time or occasional work and dating. There are no differences by family type in these areas. About three out of five families allow adolescents to earn money through part-time work, baby sitting, or other activities. Across family types, adolescents average between two and three dates per month, and between 20% and 25% of adolescents have a steady boy or girlfriend. One area where there are strong differences, however, is in the mothers' views on adolescents having sexual intercourse. Compared to mothers in other family types, first-married mothers are more strongly opposed to the view that sexual intercourse is acceptable when there is strong affection. Continuously single mothers express the least opposition to this view. It should be pointed out, however, that this question measures a maternal value which may or may not correspond with mothers' attempts to control adolescent sexual behavior.

In general, the data on families with children ages 18 and younger refute the argument that single parents have less control over their children. Sometimes and regarding certain activities, first-married mothers are more restrictive, but for most of the domains we studied, parental control does not vary by family type.

Educational Expectations

Two questions were asked about educational expectations. The first question concerns how much education mothers expect their children to complete. The second concerns whether parents should help pay for college. The results reveal that first-married mothers have significantly higher educational expectations for their children and are more willing to help pay college expenses. However, we do not want to exaggerate the difference. For all four groups, the average expectation is between a junior college degree and some education at a four-year college. Mothers generally agree that parents should help with expenses.

Our findings regarding family values, rules, and expectations provide very little support for the family composition argument. Using a nationally representative sample of families and using measures of a variety of childrearing values, the evidence suggests that mothers in first-married, divorced, stepfamily, and continuously single-parent families have very similar rules and expectations for their children. To be sure, there is considerable variation within family types, but most mothers consider it very important that their children ascribe to cultural standards for proper behavior. Where differences occur across family types, they tend to be modest. Further, each of the four family structures appears to have identifiable strengths. No one family type is consistently higher or stronger on family values or parental rules and restrictions. If any one family structure, such as a unit headed by two first-married parents, provides a better environment in which to rear children, this distinction is not attributable to differences in family values. The next question is whether there are important differences in parents' interaction and involvement with their children.

PARENT-CHILD INTERACTION: SUPPORT, CONTROL, AND CONFLICT

There is much more to parenting than setting rules, having values, and defining expectations. In this part of the chapter we examine the actual involvement of parents with their children—the time they spend together, the activities they share, the physical affection and emotional support that are expressed, the control that is exercised, as well as areas of disagreement, strain, aggression, and violence.

Parental Involvement

Researchers distinguish between three components of parental involvement: responsibility, accessibility, and engagement (Lamb, Pleck, Charnov, & Levine, 1987; LaRossa, 1988). Parents often invest considerable amounts of time, energy, and financial resources to fulfill their responsibilities as parents. Providing financially for the family and keeping track of children's extracurricular activities, social calendar, medical, and dental appointments are examples of the responsibility dimension. Accessibility refers to situations in which parents have to do things in or around the home while their children are doing something else. For example, a mother may be accessible for her child while she is preparing a meal or doing laundry, although she is not directly interacting with her child. Beyond being responsible for children or being accessible for them, an important aspect of parent-child relationships is time spent in direct, face-to-face interaction. This more intense form of parental involvement is termed *engagement*. Children develop a variety of skills through firsthand observation of parental behavior, and they get a sense that they matter to parents when the parents invest time with them. Participation in shared activities is a valuable tool for transmitting affection, nurturance, and support. Eating meals together, reading with children or helping them with homework, playing with them or working on a family project together, are examples of parental engagement.

Important aspects of parent-child relationships include the frequency or regularity of interaction, the degree to which the relationships are enjoyable, and the range of activities in which parents and children participate. A series of questions asked mothers how regularly they have an especially enjoyable time with their children, have a lot of arguments or difficulty dealing with them, and participate with their children in school, religious, community, or athletic activities. A separate series of questions asked mothers to assess their spouses' (or partners') involvement with the children.

The data presented in Table 5.5 show that, compared to mothers in other family types, mothers in first-married families report a significantly higher frequency of enjoyable times with their children. Mothers in stepfamilies have significantly fewer enjoyable times with their focal child. The differences are small, however, showing that across family types, mothers frequently engage in enjoyable activities with their children. Compared to mothers in stepfamilies, first-married mothers report their spouses have more enjoyable times with the children. Thus, at least according to the perceptions of biological mothers, the frequency of enjoyable interaction with children is greater for biological fathers than for stepfathers.

The absence of clear cultural norms defining *appropriate* stepfather involvement may partially explain why stepfather-stepchild relationships are less enjoyable. Children's expectations for stepfathers vary considerably, as do children's responses:

Table 5.5   Overall Involvement of Mother with Children

Item Being Compared	First-Married	Divorced	Stepfamily	Continuously Single	Significance[a]
Enjoyable times with focal child 0-18, (1) never to (6) daily	5.34	5.03	4.85	5.18	abcdf
Arguments or difficult times with focal child 0-18, (1) never to (6) daily	3.11	3.31	3.33	3.24	ab
Spouse's enjoyable times with focal child 0-18, (1) never to (6) daily	5.01	na	4.25	na	b
Spouse's difficult times with focal child 0-18, (1) never to (6) daily	2.71	na	2.99	na	b
Involvement in school, religious, community, and sports activities (hours per week)	3.98	3.30	3.48	2.08	c

NOTE: For the first four items there are 1,050 to 1,076 first-married, 669 to 675 divorced, 269 to 274 stepfamilies, and 413 to 414 continuously single-parent families. For the last item there are 611 first-married, 520 divorced, 221 stepfamilies, and 208 continuously single respondents. The last item is a scale summed over individual items (see Appendix A).
a. The letters indicate which means are significantly different at the $p < .05$ level: a = first-married compared to divorced; b = first-married compared to stepfamily; c = first-married compared to continuously single; d = divorced compared to stepfamily; e = divorced compared to continuously single; f = stepfamily compared to continuously single.

The children's hidden agenda usually involves the extent to which they will allow the stepfather to assume all the trappings of the father role. Children seem to have four different kinds of responses, which may also be stages. The first type is the child who is adamant in his distaste for the stepfather. Sometimes the child genuinely dislikes him as a person. But, just as often, he is still close to the natural father, feels the stepfather does not compare favorably with him, or fears that the mother's relationship with another will deprive him of love and attention. There is also the child who is initially aloof but somewhat willing to interact with the stepfather; he will ultimately be won over if the stepfather proves worthy. The third reaction—or stage—is one in which the child is ready to accept the stepfather as father. Most children who welcome the stepfather right away are young and have never experienced a father figure. Finally, there are the children who are old enough and mature enough to think of the new addition to the family as mother's husband, rather than a stepfather. (Bohannon & Erickson, 1978, p. 54)

Stepfather-stepchild relations may be less enjoyable than biological father-child relations, but they may not be any more difficult or combative. In fact, our data show no differences across any of the family types in the frequency of mothers' or spouses' difficult times with children.

Another dimension of parenting is mothers' involvement in various school-related, religious, community, and youth sports activities. Figure 5.2 illustrates the total hours per week that mothers in the four family structures spend on these four types of activities (also shown in Table 5.5). The total level of involvement is highest among first-married mothers and lowest among continuously single mothers. Mothers in first-married families spend roughly 4 hours per week in all these activities combined—more in some, less in others. This is roughly twice the time spent by mothers in continuously single-parent families. The contrast of first-married mothers and continuously single mothers is stark. Analyzing the activities one by one (results not shown in the table), first-married mothers spend two to four times as much time as continuously single mothers on these activities. For example, continuously single mothers stand out clearly in community youth activities, on which they spend an average of just 7 minutes per week. It is also important to keep in mind that in these analyses we have controlled for relevant covariates, so these findings cannot be attributed to such factors as continuously single mothers being younger or having lower levels of education.

In Table 5.6 we present information separately on mothers' direct interaction with children younger than age 5 and with children 5-18. For mothers of younger children, our comparisons exclude stepfamilies because the NSFH had too few cases. Across the other family types, there are no differences in the frequency of mothers' outings or play with children or in time spent reading with them. On average, mothers report they play with their children almost every day, read with them several times a week, and go on outings about once a week.

(text continues on p. 124)

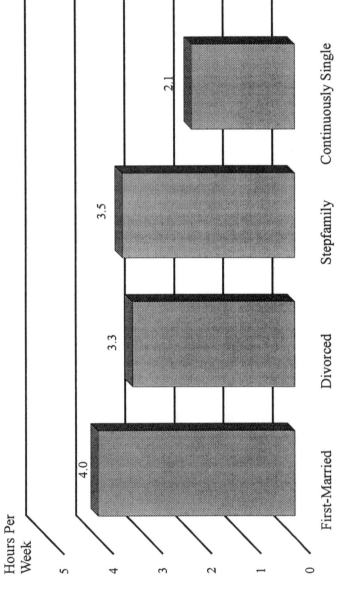

Hours Per
Week

5

4

3

2

1

0

First-Married   Divorced   Stepfamily   Continuously Single

4.0   3.3   3.5   2.1

Figure 5.2. Mothers' Involvement in School, Religious, Community, Youth, and Sports Activities

Table 5.6   Mothers' Interaction With Child 0-4 and 5-18

Item Being Compared	First-Married	Divorced	Continuously Stepfamily	Single	Significance[a]
Child 0-4					
Have outings with child (1) never to (6) almost every day	3.60	3.70	na	3.80	ns
Play with child (1) never to (6) almost every day	5.73	5.57	na	5.72	ns
Read with child (1) never to (6) almost every day	4.63	4.89	na	5.09	ns
Hours spent caring for child in a typical day	6.70	6.19	na	5.79	c
Child 1-4 attends a nursery school, percentage yes	22.2	35.6	na	33.8	ac
Child 1-4 spent how many days in nursery school last week (0-7)	.83	1.49	na	1.48	ac
Child 5-18					
Number of days had breakfast with child last week	3.90	3.61	2.77	3.63	bdf
Number of days had dinner with child last week	6.06	5.62	5.70	5.49	abc
Leisure activity away from home (1) never to (6) daily	3.75	3.75	3.55	3.79	ns
Work on project or play with child at home (1) never to (6) daily	4.51	4.64	4.24	4.44	bd
Private talks (1) never to (6) daily	4.43	4.74	4.48	4.54	ad
Help with reading or homework (1) never to (6) daily	4.52	4.70	4.49	4.58	ns

NOTE: For items about children 0-4, the number of first-married mothers varies from 320 to 430, and the number of divorced mothers varies from 64 to 101. Stepfamilies are excluded because there were only 12 stepfamily mothers. The continuously single mothers varied from 130 to 157. For items about children 5-18, the number for first-married mothers varies from 689 to 717; the number of divorced mothers varies from 565 to 590; the number of stepfamily mothers varies from 238 to 249, and the number of continuously single mothers varies from 237 to 261.

a. The letters indicate which means are significantly different at the $p < .05$ level: a = first-married compared to divorced; b = first-married compared to stepfamily; c = first-married compared to continuously single; d = divorced compared to stepfamily; e = divorced compared to continuously single; f = stepfamily compared to continuously single.

Mothers in their first marriage report spending the most hours per day in caring for their young children (just under 7 hours). This is significantly more time than continuously single mothers report. Still, these numbers indicate that across family types, mothers devote substantial time on a daily basis caring for their infants, toddlers, and preschoolers. Children in first-married families also are significantly less likely than their counterparts in single-parent families to attend nursery school, and those who attend spend fewer days per week in nursery school.

Examining mothers' relationships with older children and adolescents, mothers in first-married families eat meals with their children more regularly than do mothers in other family types. On average, first-married mothers eat breakfast with their children 4 days per week and eat dinner with them 6 days per week. Mothers in stepfamilies eat breakfast with their children fewer than 3 days per week, which is significantly less than mothers in any of the other family types. The frequency of mothers' leisure activities with children ages 5-18 does not vary across family types. Other studies have examined time spent together in social and recreational activities and found few differences across family types (Furstenberg & Nord, 1985). However, Furstenberg and Nord suggest that family routines and demands in single-parent and stepfamilies lead residential parents in these families to be less involved in homework than parents in nondisrupted two-parent families. Our findings show no significant differences across four diverse family structures, with mothers in all family types helping their children with homework regularly, an average of several days per week. It should be noted that our items assess only the frequency of activities such as helping with homework. We do not have more precise measures of the actual duration of time mothers invest in these activities. We examine fathers' involvement in homework and other activities in a section below.

Two aspects of parental involvement with older children and adolescents that vary across family types are how often they play or work on a project together and how often they have private talks. Mothers in stepfamilies spend less time working on projects with their children, whereas mothers in divorced families report the most time spent in this activity. Mothers in divorced families also have private talks with their children more frequently than married mothers. The differences are small, however, with most mothers reporting they work on a project, play with their child, and have private discussions with their child at least once per week.

In sum, parent-child interaction varies by family type to a greater degree than parental rules, values, and expectations. Still, the differences tend to be small, with mothers in first-married families exhibiting greater involvement with their children and having enjoyable times with them more regularly than mothers in other family types.

Mothers in all family types want the best for their children and try to instill what they consider to be important values, but the constraints imposed by particular family and work arrangements, schedules, and demands restrict the ability of some mothers to be as involved as they might like to be in the everyday lives of their children. To be sure, the absolute levels of interaction we have observed suggest that although most parents and children engage regularly in many different activities with each other, in other families parents and children spend very little time together.

Maternal Support

Three indicators of mothers' support for their children are how often they praise their children or hug their children, and whether they allow children to help set rules (Table 5.7). The data show few and small differences across family types in maternal support. Across family types, mothers of children ages 0-4 report that they praise and hug their children very often. For mothers of older children, mothers in continuously single-parent families are significantly less likely to praise and hug their school-age and adolescent children. Mothers in all family types report they occasionally allow children to help set rules. Mothers in their first marriage do this significantly less frequently than mothers who are divorced. The clear pattern here is high levels of maternal support across family types.

Table 5.7 Maternal Support and Control

Item Being Compared	First-Married	Divorced	Continuously Stepfamily	Single	Significance[a]
Support					
How often praise child 0-4, (1) never to (4) very often	3.81 (326)	3.72 (64)	na	3.68 (131)	ns
How often hug child 0-4, (1) never to (4) very often	3.97 (326)	3.94 (65)	na	3.95 (131)	ns
How often praise child 5-18, (1) never to (4) very often	3.65 (718)	3.71 (591)	3.69 (248)	3.48 (258)	cef
How often hug child 5-18, (1) never to (4) very often	3.77 (713)	3.78 (590)	3.80 (246)	3.65 (258)	cef
Allow child 5-18 to help set rules, (1) never to (4) very often	2.78 (708)	2.89 (578)	2.88 (243)	2.82 (243)	a
Control					
Remind child 5-11 to do chores, (1) rarely to (4) all the time	2.73 (251)	2.83 (208)	2.70 (85)	2.62 (122)	ns
Require child 5-11 to complete chores before play, (1) no, (2) sometimes, (3) yes	2.58 (251)	2.59 (208)	2.64 (85)	2.41 (122)	ns
Child 5-11 receives an allowance, percentage yes	47.5 (327)	51.8 (255)	50.4 (98)	53.5 (157)	ns
Allowance for child 5-11 pays for regular chores, percentage yes	60.0 (156)	63.8 (131)	64.5 (48)	50.4 (83)	ns

NOTE: Two cells for stepfamilies were omitted because of small Ns ($N = 12$).

Maternal Control

Beyond setting rules, which we discussed in the first section of this chapter, mothers may exert their control more directly and emphatically by reminding children to do chores, requiring that chores be completed before play, requiring homework to be completed before play, and paying an allowance for children doing regular or extra chores. Among families with children ages 5-11, there are no statistically significant differences across family types regarding these aspects of maternal control. In general, mothers remind children to do chores quite regularly, they usually require chores to be completed before play, about half pay an allowance

Table 5.7 Continued

Item Being Compared	First-Married	Divorced	Stepfamily	Continuously Single	Significance[a]
In addition to allowance, pay child 5-11 for extra chores, percentage yes	38.0 (327)	39.8 (255)	42.6 (98)	39.8 (157)	ns
Require adolescent to complete homework before play, (1) no, (2) sometimes, (3) yes	2.29 (267)	2.07 (260)	2.03 (113)	2.24 (56)	ab
Remind adolescent to do chores, (1) rarely to (4) all the time	2.40 (277)	2.54 (268)	2.63 (115)	2.30 (52)	b
Require adolescent to complete chores before play, (1) no, (2) sometimes, (3) yes	2.32 (277)	2.28 (269)	2.27 (115)	2.33 (51)	ns
Adolescent receives an allowance, percentage yes	51.5 (313)	44.3 (303)	55.6 (129)	38.3 (65)	df
Adolescent allowance pays for regular chores, percentage yes	53.6 (154)	49.2 (138)	52.3 (68)	52.9 (32)	ns
In addition to allowance, pay adolescent for extra chores, percentage yes	34.7 (313)	32.0 (303)	45.5 (129)	30.7 (65)	bd

NOTE: The number of cases varies widely and is shown in parentheses for each cell.
a. The letters indicate which means are significantly different at the $p < .05$ level: a = first-married compared to divorced; b = first-married compared to stepfamily; c = first-married compared to continuously single; d = divorced compared to stepfamily; e = divorced compared to continuously single; f = stepfamily compared to continuously single.

to their school-age children, and about two in five pay their children additional money for extra chores.

Among parents of adolescents there is some variation in maternal control by family type. First-married mothers are most likely to require 12- to 18-year-old children to complete homework before they are allowed to play, but they are followed closely by continuously single mothers. Mothers in stepfamilies are most likely to remind adolescents to do chores, consistent with our findings in Chapter 4 showing greater domestic responsibilities for children in stepfamilies. Parents in stepfamilies are most likely to pay an allowance to their teenage children, with single parents least likely to pay teenagers an allowance. We should remind the reader that these analyses control for our covariates, including family income, so these differences cannot be attributed to the greater financial resources of two-parent families.

Mother-Adolescent Disagreement

To assess the nature and frequency of mother-adolescent disagreement, mothers were asked how often they have disagreements with their child in each of the following areas: how the adolescent dresses, her or his girlfriend/boyfriend, other friends, how late they stay out at night, helping around the house, their sexual behavior, drinking, smoking or drug use, money, school, and getting along with other family members (Table 5.8). Our findings show that mothers in first-married families report the fewest disagreements with their adolescent children. In particular, adolescents in first-married families have fewer disagreements with their mothers concerning friends (including girlfriends and boyfriends), curfew, money, school, and getting along with other family members. The most frequent area of disagreement is how much adolescents should help around the house, whereas sexual behavior and drinking, smoking, and drug use are areas of least frequent disagreement. It is likely that parents and adolescents rarely disagree on these issues because they rarely discuss them. Parent-adolescent conflict tends to involve minor, mundane issues and to be viewed by parents as less severe than it is viewed by adolescents (Montemayor, 1986; Smetana, 1989).

Because some studies suggest that adolescent boys, compared to girls, may be more difficult to control and have more behavior problems, especially in families headed by single mothers (Guidubaldi & Perry, 1985; Hetherington, Cox, & Cox, 1982), we examined the total levels of mother-son and mother-daughter disagreement. The results for all family types combined indicate that mothers report significantly more frequent disagreements with sons than with daughters (sons' mean is 1.83; daughters' mean is 1.73). This overall difference is not large and stems mostly from divorced families, where the daughters' mean is 1.78 com-

Table 5.8 Mother-Adolescent Disagreement

Item	First-Married	Divorced	Stepfamily	Continuously Single	Significance[a]
Combined[b]	1.63	1.85	1.82	1.81	ab
Dress code	2.05	1.89	1.95	1.85	ns
Girlfriend/boyfriend	1.26	1.39	1.37	1.58	c
Friends	1.45	1.74	1.63	2.13	acef
Nighttime curfew	1.45	1.82	1.63	1.89	ac
Helping around the house	2.75	2.92	3.00	2.56	ns
Sexual behavior	1.07	1.13	1.15	1.18	ns
Drinking, smoking, or drug use	1.10	1.22	1.21	1.22	ns
Money	1.63	1.90	1.85	1.71	a
School	1.71	2.17	2.06	1.91	ab
Getting along with other family members	1.89	2.36	2.31	2.08	ab

NOTE: There are 311 to 313 first-married mothers, 300 to 303 divorced mothers, 128 to 129 stepfamily mothers, and 63 to 64 continuously single mothers.
a. The letters indicate which means are significantly different at the $p < .05$ level: a = first-married compared to divorced; b = first-married compared to stepfamily; c = first-married compared to continuously single; d = divorced compared to stepfamily; e = divorced compared to continuously single; f = stepfamily compared to continuously single.
b. All items were scored from 1 for *never happens* to 6 for *happens almost every day*. The combined score is the mean for the 10 individual items.

pared to 1.95 for sons. This corroborates the view that, at least in families where single mothers are residential parents, divorce may be more difficult for boys.

Maternal Role Strain

Previous studies suggest that the responsibilities of parenthood, like other aspects of family labor, fall primarily on mothers (Barnett & Baruch, 1987; LaRossa, 1988; Nock & Kingston, 1988). When mothers in different family types were asked if they wish they could be free from the responsibilities of parenthood, mothers in all four family types tended to disagree with the statement (Table 5.9). Mothers in first-married families expressed the strongest

Table 5.9 Mothers' Parental Role Strain

Item	First-Married	Divorced	Stepfamily	Continuously Single	Significance[a]
Wish could be free from responsibility of parenthood, (1) strongly agree to (5) strongly disagree	4.09	3.89	3.88	3.70	abce
Child care is (1) very unfair to mother to (5) very unfair to husband	2.78	na	2.81	na	ns
Things you do as a mother are					
(1) interesting to (7) boring	2.11	2.27	2.38	2.19	ab
(1) appreciated to (7) unappreciated	2.40	2.71	2.86	2.64	abc
(1) manageable to (7) overwhelming	3.06	3.12	3.13	3.17	ns
(1) simple to (7) complicated	3.54	3.78	3.67	3.97	ac
(1) sociable to (7) lonely	2.37	2.83	2.79	2.61	abce
(1) well done to (7) poorly done	2.13	2.16	2.32	2.11	b
Marital versus postmarital parental role strain					
Parental role is now (1) much worse to (5) much better	na	3.86	na	na	na
Care of children is now (1) much worse to (5) much better	na	3.86	na	na	na
Now married, but if separated, role would be (1) much worse to (5) much better	2.18	na	2.52	na	b

NOTE: The first two items have 1,021 to 1,038 first-married, 648 divorced (first item), 261 to 269 stepfamilies, and 376 continuously single mothers (first item). The items regarding things you do as a mother have 986 to 995 first-married, 610 to 621 divorced, 254 to 260 stepfamilies, and 360 to 363 continuously single mothers. Two items were asked of divorced mothers about their parental role ($n = 458$) and the care of their child ($n = 456$). The last item was asked of 1,002 first-married and 252 stepfamily mothers.
a. The letters indicate which means are significantly different at the $p < .05$ level: a = first-married compared to divorced; b = first-married compared to stepfamily; c = first-married compared to continuously single; d = divorced compared to stepfamily; e = divorced compared to continuously single; f = stepfamily compared to continuously single.

opposition to this view, whereas mothers in continuously single-parent families expressed somewhat less opposition.

Recall that in Chapter 4 mothers reported a general perception of equity in the division of household labor even though mothers do the vast portion of this work. We find the same pattern in mothers' reports of child care: mothers spend much more time on child care than fathers, yet mothers (in married families) typically respond that child care arrangements in their marriage are "fair" to both wife and husband. The scale for this question ranges from 1 (mother disadvantaged) to 5 (father disadvantaged), and a score of 3 signifies perfect equity. The average responses are 2.78 and 2.81 for first-married and stepfamily mothers, respectively. As discussed earlier, it is likely that women are making within-gender rather than between-gender comparisons in assessing fairness. Within-gender comparisons are more likely to engender a sense of fairness (L. Thompson, 1991), but they are also less likely to stimulate women and men to an awareness and understanding of the segregation of family labor by gender.

Mothers also report generally low levels of maternal role strain, with some small differences across family types. Mothers in first-married families are most likely to describe the things they do as mothers as interesting, appreciated, simple, and sociable. Mothers in stepfamilies describe the things they do as somewhat less interesting, less appreciated, lonelier, and not as well done. Mothers in continuously single-parent families describe their mothering activities as most complicated.

Two other questions were asked only of divorced mothers: Compared to the year before you separated, how is your life now as a parent, and how does the care of your children compare to the year before you separated? The average response of divorced mothers was that both being a parent and caring for their children is now "somewhat better" than before they separated. Contrary to the popular view of divorced adults as leading shattered lives, these data show that divorced mothers perceive some postmarital relief and satisfaction in their parenting roles. We explore this further in Chapter 6.

Verbal Aggression and Physical Violence

An important but still understudied area of family relations is verbal aggression and physical violence that parents direct toward their children. Our data show moderate levels of verbal aggression (Table 5.10) with mothers in first-married families, compared to their single-parent counterparts, reporting significantly less yelling at children age 4 and younger. First-married and remarried mothers also yell less often at older children and adolescents. The average responses are between 2 and 3 on a 4-point scale, suggesting that most mothers yell at their children *seldom* or *sometimes.* Across family types, mothers report slightly less yelling at younger children than at school-age or adolescent children.

Mothers were also asked a series of questions about spanking. Across family types more than half the mothers report spanking or slapping their children under age 5 in the past week. This does not vary significantly by family type. Regarding the *number* of times a child under age 5 was spanked in the previous week, mothers in stepfamilies report the highest frequency, nearly three times per week. This is significantly higher than mothers in any other family type. Mothers in the other family types report spanking their young children between once and twice per week.

A much lower but still substantial percentage of mothers spank their children ages 5-11. Mothers in first-married families are less likely than continuously single mothers to spank their school-age children. One fourth of first-married mothers, compared to more than one third of continuously single mothers, spank their school-age children. Mothers in all family types report they spank or slap their older children and adolescents less often than they spank younger children. Mothers in stepfamilies spank or slap their school-age children less often than other mothers, but across family types the average responses indicate that mothers spank or slap children in this age range once every 2 weeks.

We have reviewed several dimensions of mothers' relationships with their children. Our findings suggest that for children of all ages and for all four family structures, mothers are very supportive. They express this support by frequently praising and hugging their children and by occasionally allowing them to help

Table 5.10 Verbal Aggression and Physical Violence

Item	First-Married	Divorced	Stepfamily	Continuously Single	Significance[a]
Yells at child 0-4 (1) never to (4) very often	2.33 (326)	2.68 (65)	na	2.73 (133)	ac
Yells at child 5-18 (1) never to (4) very often	2.68 (718)	2.82 (591)	2.73 (247)	2.91 (260)	acf
Spank or slap child 0-4 in past week, percentage yes	56.3 (320)	63.2 (101)	62.0 (40)	62.6 (157)	ns
Number of times spanked child 0-4 last week (ranged from 0 to 20)	1.62 (328)	1.69 (101)	2.76 (40)	1.51 (157)	bdf
Spank child 5-11 in past week, percentage yes	24.8 (328)	27.2 (255)	28.9 (99)	35.5 (157)	c
Number of times spanked child 5-11 last week (ranged from 0 to 20)	.49 (328)	.51 (590)	.42 (246)	.51 (157)	ns
Spank or slap child 5-18 (1) never to (4) very often	1.99 (713)	2.08 (255)	1.83 (246)	2.07 (256)	bdf

NOTE: The number of cases is in parentheses. The cell with "na" is not reported because there were only 12 cases.
a. The letters indicate which means are significantly different at the $p < .05$ level: a = first-married compared to divorced; b = first-married compared to stepfamily; c = first-married compared to continuously single; d = divorced compared to stepfamily; e = divorced compared to continuously single; f = stepfamily compared to continuously single.

set rules. Similarly, mothers' control of school-age children and adolescents is very similar across family types. In some areas, married mothers exhibit somewhat greater control over their adolescents than single mothers do, but the differences, where they exist, are small. Mothers' perceptions of relationships with their adolescents suggest that disagreements occur infrequently, with mothers in first-married families reporting the lowest level of disagreement.

Across diverse family structures, mothers report little strain in their parenting role. Reflecting their different life situations, mothers in first-married families portray their role in a somewhat more favorable light than other mothers, whereas continuously single mothers describe their activities as most complicated. Regardless of children's age, mothers in first-married families are less likely than their counterparts in other family types to yell at their children. Curiously, mothers in stepfamilies report the highest frequency of spanking children under age 5 (an average of three times per week), yet they are least likely to spank or slap their school-age children. In general, spanking is less common as children grow older, and yelling at children increases.

Fathers' Relationships With Children

For the two family types in which fathers reside in the household, we have the fathers' reports of their interaction with children. Whereas all the fathers in first marriages are talking about their own biological children, usually stepfathers are describing relationships with stepchildren.

On several dimensions of father-child and stepfather-stepchild relationships, fathers in first-married families are more involved and have more positive relationships than fathers in stepfamilies (Table 5.11). Fathers in first-married families have more enjoyable times with children, fewer arguments, more private talks, eat meals together more regularly, and spend more time together in a range of leisure, play, work, and homework activities. On less direct measures of parental involvement, such as fathers' participation in community, religious, youth sports, or PTA activities, there are no differences between fathers in first-married and stepfamilies.

We can also compare levels of mothers' involvement, discussed earlier, with levels of fathers' involvement. Whereas mothers in all family types report they have enjoyable times with their children almost daily (Table 5.5), the data for fathers show enjoyable times with children occurring an average of twice per week (and less often in stepfamilies). Mothers and fathers both report that they argue or have difficulties with their children an average of two to three times per week.

Comparing mothers' involvement with children in various activities (summarized in Table 5.6) with that of fathers, fathers

Table 5.11 Fathers' Relationships With Children:
First-Married and Stepfamilies

Item	First-Married	Stepfamily	Significance[a]
Enjoyable times with child 0-18 last month, (0) never to (5) almost every day	4.06	3.49	*
Arguments or difficult times with child 0-18 last month, (0) never to (5) almost every day	1.75	2.08	*
Number of days had breakfast with child 3-18 last week	2.77	1.96	*
Number of days had dinner with child 3-18 last week	5.45	4.80	*
Leisure activities away from home with child 3-18, (1) never to (6) almost every day	3.35	2.95	*
Work on project or play at home with child 3-18, (1) never to (6) almost every day	4.13	3.56	*
Private talks with child 3-18, (1) never to (6) almost every day	3.49	2.99	*
Help child 3-18 with reading or homework, (1) never to (6) almost every day	3.40	3.06	*
Hours per week with school organization or activities, child 5-18	.81	1.09	ns
Hours per week with religious youth group, child 5-18	.88	.64	ns
Hours per week in community youth group, child 5-18	.26	.61	ns
Hours per week in youth sports program, child 5-18	1.47	1.23	ns

NOTE: An asterisk means the difference is significant at the $p \leq .05$ level. The first eight items had from 771 to 947 first-married and from 194 to 207 stepfamily mothers. The last four items had from 491 to 508 first-married and from 187 to 191 stepfamily mothers.

in two-parent families eat breakfast and dinner with children an average of one day per week less often than mothers. On other activities in which parents and children directly interact with each other, fathers in first-married and stepfamilies spend less time in leisure activities with children, less time working on a project or playing with children, have fewer private talks with children, and help them with homework less often. Whereas the typical responses of mothers in first-married and stepfamilies indicate they have private talks with children and help children with homework a couple of times per week, the data for fathers indicate these types of interaction occur less than once per week. On measures of less direct parental involvement, fathers average slightly lower amounts of time each week in school, religious, and community youth activities. One area where fathers devote more time than mothers is youth sports programs.

Overall, the clear pattern is significantly lower levels of father-child than mother-child interaction. Although mothers are aware that fathers provide much less child care, they typically respond that the division of child care responsibilities is reasonably fair.

Relations With Nonresidential Parents

For mothers in divorced and stepfamilies, a salient feature of family life is relations with their former spouse and the nonresidential parent of their child(ren). In more than 90% of stepfamilies, and an even higher percentage of divorced families, the children's nonresidential father is still living (Table 5.12). But there are many structural barriers to children's involvement with their nonresidential parents. Although distances vary considerably, the average distance between children in these families and their nonresidential fathers is more than 400 miles. For more than one third of children in divorced families, and more than one half of children in stepfamilies, their nonresidential father is remarried. In nearly one fourth of divorced families, and more than one third of stepfamilies, the children's nonresidential father has had a child since the marriage with their mother ended.

Table 5.12   Children's Relations With Nonresidential Parents:
Divorced and Stepfamilies

Item	Divorced	Stepfamily	Significance[a]
Nonresident parent living, percentage yes	97.50	91.10	*
Nonresident parent lives how many miles away?	401.0	431.0	ns
Nonresident parent married, percentage yes	37.00	54.40	*
Nonresident parent has child since your marriage ended, percentage yes	24.40	35.40	*
Phone/letter (1) not at all to (6) several times a week	3.42	2.71	*
Visited (1) not at all to (6) several times a week	3.44	2.47	*
Leisure activities (1) not at all to (6) several times a week	2.79	2.53	ns
Religious activities (1) not at all to (6) several times a week	1.41	1.32	ns
Talking/project/play (1) not at all to (6) several times a week	2.87	2.39	*
School or other organized activity (1) not at all to (6) several times a week	1.58	1.27	*
Influence decisions about education, religion, health care, (1) none to (3) a great deal	1.67	1.47	*

NOTE: An asterisk means the difference is significant at the .05 level. The first six items had from 545 to 623 divorced and from 165 to 216 stepfamily mothers. All other items had from 404 to 491 divorced and 114 to 157 stepfamily mothers.

Comparing children's relationships with nonresidential parents in divorced and stepfamilies, children in divorced families have much more frequent contact with nonresidential fathers. Children in divorced families receive more frequent phone calls, letters, and visits from nonresidential fathers than children in stepfamilies. The average responses suggest, however, that in both types of families contact with fathers typically occurs on a less than monthly basis.

A limitation of group averages is that they conceal cases where some fathers have completely abandoned their own biological children, whereas others routinely write letters to their children and/or talk with them on the telephone. One fourth of children in divorced families, and nearly one third of children in stepfamilies, never talk with their nonresidential fathers. Only one in seven talk with or receive letters from their fathers every week.

Another measure of nonresidential fathers' involvement is the frequency of direct interaction or visitation with their children. Figure 5.3 illustrates that one fifth of children in divorced families, and nearly 30% of children in stepfamilies, never see their nonresidential fathers. Roughly one third of children in divorced families (32%) and stepfamilies (37.1%) see their fathers between once and several times a year. For other children, however, contact is much more frequent. One fifth of children in divorced families (20.8%) and stepfamilies (23.4%) see their fathers one to three times per month. Roughly one in seven children in divorced families (13.8%) see their fathers weekly, compared to roughly half this percentage (6.6%) in stepfamilies. Another group comprising one in seven children in divorced families sees their fathers several times a week, compared to only 3.6% of children in stepfamilies. To be sure, these levels of father-child contact are substantially lower than contact experienced by residential parents, and nonresidential fathers are strikingly uninvolved when their children live in stepfather families.

Comparing the two groups of nonresidential fathers, some specific activities in which fathers of children living in divorced families are more involved include talking with children, playing with them or working on a project together, and school activities. They also exercise more influence in major decisions regarding the children's education, religion, and health care. Children in divorced families average 3 weeks per year staying with their nonresidential father, compared to a little more than 1 week per year for children in stepfamilies.

On other aspects of relationships with nonresidential parents, there are no differences between divorced families and stepfamilies. They are equally likely to have a legal agreement concerning child support, alimony, custody, visitation, and where the child

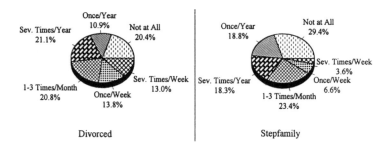

Figure 5.3. How Often Nonresidential Father Visited Child During Last 12 Months

lives. Similarly, there are no significant differences in the use of joint custody, child support payments received or missed, or the number of weeks the child stayed with the nonresidential parent during the prior year.

Other Relatives and Household Members

There are very small percentages of families, in any family type, which have other adult relatives or nonrelatives living in the household. There are adult nonrelatives (typically cohabiting partners) living in the home in 2.7% of divorced families and 2.4% of continuously single-parent families. In 5.5% of continuously single-parent families there are other adult relatives living in the household, most often the children's maternal grandmother. It is extremely rare for other adult relatives or nonrelatives to be living in the households of two-parent families.

SUMMARY AND CONCLUSIONS

We have found that parenting values held by mothers do not vary by family type. Mothers of children of all ages and in all family types attribute considerable importance to children learning and following culturally valued guidelines for behavior. Further, the rules and expectations that mothers establish are similar across diverse family forms. Mothers are opposed to leaving 5 to 11-year-old children alone at home, particularly if parents are going to be away at night or for extended periods of time. In general, mothers allow adolescents to be alone at home, except if parents are going to be away overnight. Mothers in first-married, remarried, divorced, and continuously single-parent families always want to know where their teenage children are. Adolescents in these families average between two and three dates per month, and between 20% and 25% of adolescents have a steady boyfriend or girlfriend. Family values, rules, and expectations for children simply cannot be distinguished based on family structure.

Parent-child interaction patterns, on the other hand, show some differences across family types. Mothers in first-married families report a significantly higher frequency of enjoyable times with their children. The differences are small though, revealing that mothers in all family types have enjoyable times with their children almost daily. Compared to mothers in stepfamilies, first-married mothers also report their spouses have more enjoyable times with the children. Thus, at least according to the perceptions of biological mothers, the frequency of enjoyable interaction with children is greater for biological fathers than for stepfathers. These findings may reflect some role ambiguities in stepfamilies and the hidden agendas confronting stepfathers specifically. There are no differences across family types, however, in the frequency of mothers' or spouses' difficult times with children.

Examining parental involvement in various school-related, religious, community, and youth sports activities, the total level of involvement is significantly higher among first-married mothers. Much of the difference is due to mothers in first-married families spending twice as much time as continuously single mothers in school-related activities. Among mothers of children younger than age 5, there are no differences by family type on most aspects of maternal interaction with children. For mothers of children ages 5-18, the frequency of mothers' leisure activities with children and the frequency with which they help children with reading or homework do not vary across family types.

There are a few, mostly small, differences across family types in maternal support of children. But the clear and consistent pattern, corroborating previous research (Amato, 1987), is high maternal support of children of all ages across all family types. Likewise, maternal control of children ages 5-11 is similar across family types. Among mothers of adolescents, first-married mothers are most likely to require their children to complete homework before they are allowed to play. Mothers in stepfamilies are most likely to remind adolescents to do chores. Mothers in first-married families report the fewest disagreements with their adolescent children, but in all family types mothers report that disagreements occur only periodically.

The picture that emerges is that mother-child relations in first-married families are somewhat more pleasant, more enjoyable, and less stressful. Women in these families describe the things they do as mothers as interesting, appreciated, simple, and sociable. Mothers in stepfamilies describe the things they do as less interesting, less appreciated, lonelier, and not as well done. Continuously single women describe their mothering activities as most complicated. As stressful as single parenting is for many women (M. S. Thompson & Ensminger, 1989), however, it is often better than predivorce marital and family circumstances. The average response of divorced mothers is that both being a parent and caring for their children are now "somewhat better" than before they separated.

The less stressful nature of family interaction in first-married families may also be related to the lower incidence of harsh parenting in these families. Compared to mothers in other family structures, first-married mothers report significantly less yelling at children, regardless of children's age. They also are less likely than remarried mothers to spank their children ages 0-4. Mothers in stepfamilies report the highest frequency of spanking young children, nearly three times per week. Mothers in first-married families also are least likely to spank their school-age children. Possible implications of harsh parenting for children's well-being will be explored in Chapter 7.

On several dimensions of father-child relationships, fathers in first-married families are more involved and have more positive relationships than fathers in stepfamilies. Whereas mothers in all family types report they have enjoyable times with their children almost daily, the data for fathers show enjoyable times with children occurring an average of twice per week (and less often than this in stepfamilies). The clear pattern is significantly lower levels of father-child than mother-child interaction—eating meals together, leisure, playing, private talks, and doing homework. Most fathers engage in the latter two activities less than once per week. These findings substantiate the notion of the technically present but functionally absent father (LaRossa, 1988), highlighting a common pattern of paternal neglect in *two*-parent families. In a cultural climate where two-parent families continue to be cherished, these findings demonstrate that the father's mere presence in the household offers very little in the way of meeting the children's (or mother's) socioemotional needs. Residential status is not to be trivialized, particularly insofar as it is correlated with provision of economic resources, but it offers no guarantee of fathers' participation, involvement, communication, nurturance, or emotional support in the parenting role.

Comparing children's relationships with nonresidential fathers in divorced and stepfamilies, children in divorced families have much more frequent contact with nonresidential fathers. But, in both family types it is less than monthly. Further, despite legal agreements to pay child support, less than one fourth of mothers in divorced families and a smaller percentage of mothers in stepfamilies receive any financial support at all from the children's nonresidential father. These findings suggest a pattern that may be termed the technically absent and minimally functional father, that is, a pattern whereby fathers neglect and, in many cases abandon, their own biological children. Children's relationships (or lack thereof) with nonresidential fathers also highlight an often overlooked distinction between families and households, with nonresidential parents included in families but excluded from households. Although they do not reside in the same household as their children from prior relationships, most of these fathers have opportunities to maintain ties with their children. For most, however, the ties are very loose, and for others, they are broken. Many nonresidential fathers appear to step aside as stepfathers move in. We found, for example, that children in divorced families average 3 weeks per year staying with their nonresidential father, compared to a little more than 1 week per year for children in stepfamilies. Other studies corroborate our findings that paternal involvement following divorce is infrequent (Furstenberg et al., 1987) and that fathers' contact typically diminishes over time (Maccoby & Mnookin, 1992). Seltzer and Bianchi (1988) suggest that we are witnessing a pattern of *serial parenthood*, whereby "noncustodial parents discard ties to their biological children with divorce, and the ties are replaced through remarriage" (p. 674). It is widely speculated that reduced involvement with nonresidential fathers is damaging to children's well-being, and we will explore these relationships and their consequences for children in Chapter 7.

NOTE

1. The lack of stepfamilies with children under age 5 is partially because, in defining our sample, we chose to study only stepfamilies in which mothers had a child by a former marriage. Many of our stepfamily mothers had a child from a prior marriage who was 5 or older at the time of the interview. The set of questions we examine here was answered by mothers who had a child under 5, but none older than age 5.

Family Structure and Mothers' Well-Being

Personal well-being has many dimensions, and mothers may have different and sometimes conflicting feelings about their lives. Personal happiness, self-esteem, depression, and physical health are some dimensions of mothers' well-being we examine in this chapter. The first question we address is how these dimensions of well-being compare across family types. Are divorced mothers depressed compared to mothers in other family types? Is the well-being of remarried mothers better or worse than that of divorced mothers? How do married mothers compare to those who are continuously single?

The theories we outlined in Chapter 2 suggest different answers to these questions. The structural-functionalist perspective emphasizes that role differentiation within the family is vital. According to this view, mothers in single-parent families should experience greater role strain and lower well-being. A social exchange perspective suggests that the quality of marital (or nonmarital) interaction is more important than marital status in explaining adult well-being. From this perspective, we would expect mothers' well-being to be higher in situations where they rate their family relationships more favorably and where their current situations compare favorably to their comparison level for alternatives. A feminist perspective directs attention to the highly variable, gendered, and contentious nature of marital and family dynamics. Traditional marriages, as opposed to egalitarian or feminist marriages, have fewer benefits for women than for men. Some women, however, may fare better than others. Women living in more equitable arrangements and in families where male partners are more involved, supportive, nurturant, and affectionate should exhibit higher well-being.

A second question guiding our analysis is whether differences in mothers' well-being across family types are attributable to other factors that are associated with family structure and background variables. In other words, do differences across family types disappear when we control for variables such as household size, age of youngest child, marriage length, or years since divorce? What happens when we control for background and family resource variables such as household income and mother's education? Or is there a systematic effect of family type that goes beyond these background resources?

Finally, we address a third question: How important are family process variables to mothers' well-being? Although many studies suggest that mothers are profoundly influenced by relationships with their children and spouses, relatively few studies have examined how mothers are influenced by continuing relationships with former spouses. For divorced or remarried mothers, an important aspect of relationships with former spouses is the co-parental relationship. We saw in Chapter 5 that many nonresidential fathers have limited involvement with their children from previous marriages, and some former spouses have very conflicted relationships with each other, whereas others have very little contact and few disagreements. In this chapter we examine how mothers' well-being is influenced by relationships with members of their immediate and divorce-extended families. Another question is how important family relationships are compared with other variables such as family structure and family resources. To examine this, we will compare the importance of resources (such as education and income) to family process variables (such as family conflict, marital instability, and parent-child relations) for mothers in our four family types.

MEASURING MOTHERS' WELL-BEING

The National Survey of Families and Households (NSFH) offers several indicators of mothers' well-being. Psychological well-being is measured in three ways. First, global well-being is assessed by a single question. Mothers were asked to give an overall evaluation of themselves and their lives on a 7-point scale ranging from *very unhappy* to *very happy*.[1] Second, a 12-item scale was used to measure depression. It asked how many days in the last week the mother felt or behaved in ways reflecting depression. The topics included: feeling bothered by things that usually don't bother you, not feeling like eating, feeling that you could not shake off the blues, having trouble keeping your mind on what you were doing, feeling depressed, feeling that everything you did was an effort, feeling fearful, sleeping restlessly, talking less than usual, feeling lonely, feeling sad, and feeling you could not get going. All of us feel some of these ways on occasion, but people who experience many of these feelings several days a week are considered depressed.

A mother's self-esteem is also an important component of her well-being. We measured self-esteem using three standard items from widely used self-esteem scales (e.g., Hughes & Demo, 1989; Rosenberg, 1979). The questions asked if she felt satisfied with herself, if she could do things as well as other people, and if she felt she was a person of worth. The responses were coded from 1 for *strongly disagree* to 5 for *strongly agree*. The higher the average on this scale, the higher the mother's self-esteem.

Health is a critical aspect of well-being. The mother's health was measured using a single, global item: Compared with other people your age, how would you describe your health? The choices ranged from 1 if she felt her health was *very poor* to 5 if she felt her health was *excellent*. Research has shown that this single item is a strong indicator of a person's health. Idler and Kasl (1991) show that such self-evaluation of health status is a strong measure of health and that it predicts mortality above and beyond the prediction based on health problems, physical disability, biological, or lifestyle risk factors.

MOTHERS' WELL-BEING ACROSS FAMILY TYPES

Family structure affects mothers' well-being. Table 6.1 presents the averages on our four measures of well-being (depression, global well-being, self-esteem, and health) for each family type. Panel A presents the averages without adjusting for differences in the control variables we have used throughout the book. The findings suggest that depression varies significantly across family types, and that it is common for a typical mother to experience some depression in any given week. For the 12 items we used to measure depression, the average score was 1.14 for first-married mothers. What does this mean? If each feeling were equally likely (e.g., if you were as likely to feel lonely as you were to have trouble sleeping or to feel sad), the average mother would experience each of the 12 feelings more than once a week. In practice, any individual mother may experience some feelings two or three times a week and others not at all. This means they experience several types of depressive feelings slightly more than once a week. This finding does not suggest a high level of depression, but we should not underestimate it either.

First-married mothers report significantly fewer depressive feelings than stepfamily mothers. Larger differences occur, however, between married and single mothers. Divorced and continuously single mothers are substantially more depressed than married mothers, regardless of whether the married mothers are in their first marriage or a remarriage. Thus, marital status is a more important factor than whether the married mothers are in their first marriage or not, or whether single parents are divorced or continuously single. Figure 6.1 illustrates that marital status is a key variable. Among married mothers, those who are remarried report more depression than first-married mothers, but the difference is small. Among single mothers, the divorced and continuously single are not significantly different from each other in their level of depression. But single mothers tend to be much more depressed than married mothers.

As shown in Panel B of Table 6.1, the results are similar when we adjust for differences across family types in income, education,

Table 6.1 Mothers' Well-Being by Family Type

Panel A: Without Adjusting for Control Variables

Measure of Well-Being	First-Married	Divorced	Stepfamily	Continuously Single	Significance[a]
Self-esteem, average of 3 items, (1) strongly disagree to (5) strongly agree	4.15 (1,026)	4.10 (639)	4.11 (269)	3.98 (371)	cef
Depression, average days/ week for 12 items	1.14 (1,073)	1.71 (663)	1.38 (275)	1.88 (406)	abcdf
Global well-being, (1) very unhappy to (7) very happy	5.60 (948)	4.99 (601)	5.42 (245)	5.11 (355)	abcdf
Health, (1) very poor to (5) excellent	4.16 (1,045)	3.95 (632)	3.97 (269)	3.88 (376)	abc

Panel B: Adjusting for Control Variables

Measure of Well-Being	First-Married	Divorced	Stepfamily	Continuously Single	Significance[a]
Self-esteem, average of 3 items, (1) strongly disagree to (5) strongly agree	4.14 (997)	4.08 (638)	4.10 (267)	4.02 (371)	c
Depression, average days/ week for 12 items	1.20 (1,044)	1.73 (662)	1.41 (273)	1.69 (406)	abcdf
Global well-being, (1) very unhappy to (7) very happy	5.61 (923)	4.98 (600)	5.46 (243)	5.06 (355)	acdf
Health, (1) very poor to (5) excellent	4.10 (1,017)	3.99 (632)	3.95 (269)	3.99 (376)	ab

NOTE: Control variables include whether the mother was in the oversampled group, household income, mother's education, mother's race, mother's age, the number of hours per week the mother is employed, household size, age of youngest child, and whether there is a cohabiting partner (relevant only for divorced and continuously single mothers). The numbers in parentheses show the number of respondents upon which each mean is based.
a. The letters indicate which means are significantly different at the $p < .05$ level: a = first-married compared to divorced; b = first-married compared to stepfamily; c = first-married compared to continuously single; d = divorced compared to stepfamily; e = divorced compared to continuously single; f = stepfamily compared to continuously single.

race, age, hours per week the mother is employed, household size, age of youngest child, and whether there is a cohabiting partner (relevant only for divorced and continuously single mothers). Even when we adjust for these background variables, there is still

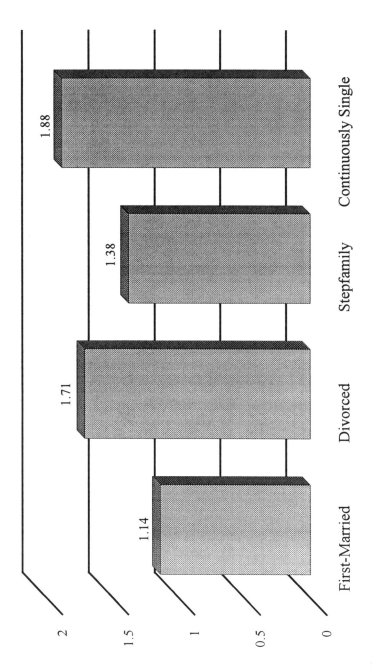

Figure 6.1. Mothers' Depression by Family Type, Without Adjusting for Control Variables

149

a significant difference between married and single mothers. Married mothers report lower levels of depression than single mothers, consistent with previous studies (Gove et al., 1983; Mirowsky & Ross, 1989).

Mothers' global well-being exhibits a slightly different pattern. Without control variables (see Table 6.1, Panel A), first-married mothers are significantly happier than stepfamily mothers, but the difference is small. When control variables are taken into account (Table 6.1, Panel B), there is no significant difference. Divorced and continuously single mothers are not significantly different from each other, but both groups demonstrate significantly lower well-being than married mothers. Again, marital status seems to be the key. It is less important whether the mother is in a first marriage or a stepfamily. Similarly, when the mother is single, it is less important whether she is divorced or continuously single.

Self-esteem does not vary much by family type. Mothers in their first marriage, remarried mothers in stepfamilies, and divorced mothers have average self-esteem levels between 4.10 and 4.15 (on a 5-point scale). Continuously single mothers have significantly lower self-esteem than the other groups, but the difference is fairly small. When control variables are included (Table 6.1, Panel B) the differences are even smaller and the only significant difference is that continuously single mothers have lower self-esteem than first-married mothers.

The differences in the general health of a mother depend on whether she is in her first marriage or not. Mothers in their first marriage report significantly better health than mothers in the other family types. It should be noted that the differences are small, although statistically significant. Mothers in all family types report an average score of about 4, signifying *very good* health on the 5-point scale. Although most previous studies have not distinguished family types as finely as we have here, reviews of the literature conclude that "marriage has large, significant, consistent, positive effects on physical health by increasing social support" (Ross, Mirowsky, & Goldsteen, 1991, p. 346).

These comparisons of mothers in different family structures illustrate an interesting and consistent pattern: marriage is good for the well-being of mothers. In general, mothers in their first marriage have the highest well-being, stepfamily mothers fare nearly as well, and divorced and continuously single mothers have the lowest well-being. Some may contend that these results occur because the higher well-being of married and remarried mothers stems from other factors, such as their greater economic resources compared to single mothers. However, even when these factors are controlled (Table 6.1, Panel B), the same pattern persists.

It is important to bear in mind some limitations of comparing mothers' well-being across diverse family types. First, it is possible that some of the differences in mothers' well-being are due to self-selection into particular family types. For example, mothers with lower well-being may be more likely to divorce or may have lower marriageability. The cross-sectional nature of our data prevent us from examining these possibilities. Similarly, although divorced and remarried mothers may exhibit some adjustment problems in comparison to first-married mothers, the well-being of divorced and remarried mothers may still be higher than that of first-married mothers who are unhappy with their marriages. In a later section of this chapter we will examine the importance of marital adjustment and other family process variables in explaining mothers' well-being.

FACTORS INFLUENCING WELL-BEING

Whereas many family scholars have focused on the effects of divorce or single-parent status on mothers' well-being, we have stressed the fact that there may be more proximate causes. Here we outline some relevant factors and briefly explain why they are important to include as control variables.

Resources and Other Background Variables

Although the background variables we have examined do not explain differences in the well-being of mothers living in different types of families, these variables may still be important. They may explain variation in well-being *within* each family type. For example, among continuously single mothers, those who fare worse on measures of social and psychological well-being may have fewer resources than those who do not. Socioeconomic resources such as education and income are essential for single mothers to support themselves and their children. For divorced women, loss of income is an important predictor of postdivorce adjustment (Gongla & Thompson 1987; Kitson, 1992; Raschke 1987). Unlike their former husbands, whose financial situations typically improve following divorce (Burkhauser & Duncan, 1989; Duncan & Hoffman, 1985; Weitzman, 1985), divorced women generally find the economic consequences of divorce to be severe and long-lasting. Depending on their predivorce family income, women experience declines in family income averaging 23% to 71% in the year following divorce (Weiss, 1984; Weitzman, 1985). For many women, including many heading mother-only families, the economic result of divorce is poverty. Morgan (1989) found that more than one fourth of divorced women fall into poverty during the 5 years following the end of their marriage. On average, by the fifth year postdivorce, women's family income is still only 71% of predivorce income (Duncan & Hoffman, 1985).

Economic decline may force single mothers to reduce material consumption and move their families to poorer neighborhoods. They may face discrimination in locating housing (Raschke, 1987). Poorer neighborhoods are associated with inferior schools and higher rates of crime and delinquency, factors that could influence children's and mothers' well-being.

Mothers' age also may be a relevant factor. We know from our discussion of mothers' background characteristics (in Chapter 3) that continuously single mothers tend to be younger and that remarried mothers tend to be older. Thus we need to control for age to have confidence that differences in mothers' well-being across family types are not due to mothers in one type being younger or older than those in another type. Many studies report increasing competence, self-esteem, and subjective well-being through early and middle adulthood (Clausen, 1991; Demo, 1992b; Herzog, Rodgers, & Woodworth, 1982). For those who divorce, however, age may have different effects. Hetherington, Cox, and Cox (1978) found that 1 year after a divorce, older mothers feel less competent, feel that they failed as spouses and parents, and doubt their abilities to adjust. Kurdek (1981) discovered that older women often experience a more difficult adjustment to divorce both emotionally and financially.

Race is another background variable that may influence mothers' well-being. Several studies find that, controlling for relevant variables, blacks have higher self-esteem than whites, although other studies find no consistent differences (Cross, 1985; Rosenberg, 1989). Compared to whites, blacks report lower levels of happiness, life satisfaction, and other measures of psychological well-being and report worse physical health (Campbell, 1981; Herzog et al., 1982; Thomas & Hughes, 1986; Veroff, Donovan, & Kulka, 1981).

The hours a mother is employed may also influence her well-being. Steady, full-time employment can have a positive effect by increasing income and extending social networks. In addition, mothers may derive meaning, satisfaction, confidence, and self-esteem from employment. Alternatively, full-time and overtime employment schedules restrict the hours available for personal leisure and for the completion of family labor. This can create stress. Booth, Johnson, White, and Edwards (1984) found that women who work longer hours outside the home (especially those working overtime) spend less time with their spouses, do less housework, have more frequent disagreements with their spouses, and have less happy and less stable marriages.

Having a large family and having young children in the home changes family and marital dynamics and creates additional family responsibilities. The number of young children in a family may be an important source of stress for mothers. This may be especially likely in single-parent households or in families where the mother is employed. Many studies suggest that mothers with preschool children are particularly vulnerable to low marital adjustment, personal happiness, and life satisfaction (Abbott & Brody, 1985; Campbell et al., 1976; Glenn & McLanahan, 1982; Hoffman & Manis, 1978). For these reasons, family researchers have argued that in addition to examining age of parents and, for married respondents, length of marriage, it is important to include a separate variable to measure the presence and number of young children (McLanahan & Adams, 1987; Menaghan, 1982; Spanier & Lewis, 1980). We thus control for household size and the age of the youngest child. For single mothers, we also control for the presence of a cohabiting partner, a potentially valuable resource and an additional influence on mothers' well-being.

For married mothers we include the length of the current marriage and for divorced mothers we include the length of time since the divorce. Although it is difficult to disentangle effects associated with age, parenthood, and duration of marriage, there is considerable evidence that marital quality declines during the transition to parenthood and that the decline persists through the childrearing years (for summaries, see Ade-Ridder & Brubaker, 1983; Glenn, 1990). Further, compared to men, women tend to be more involved in parenting and family activities. As a result, mothers make more adjustments through the life course in response to changing family needs and responsibilities (Glenn, 1990; Rollins & Galligan, 1978; Spanier, Lewis, & Cole, 1975). Similarly, research has shown that the initially adverse effects of divorce are often mitigated by time. The longer the mother has been single after a divorce, the less damaging the stress of the divorce on her well-being. Including marital and divorce duration as control variables takes into account that mothers' well-being may be influenced by factors associated with the stage or length of the marriage, remarriage, or separation.

In sum, the resource and background variables we include as predictors of mothers' well-being are household income, mother's education, mother's age, race, the hours per week the mother is employed, household size, age of the youngest child, presence of a cohabiting partner (for single mothers), length of the current marriage (for married mothers), and length of time since divorce (for divorced mothers).

Family Process Variables

Some family process variables that are potentially important apply to all mothers, whatever the family type. The child's well-being, difficulties interacting with the child, and enjoyable times with the child may be important factors in predicting which mothers have high well-being, regardless of the type of family.

The importance of other family process variables may vary depending on marital status. Married mothers, whether in their first marriage or a stepfamily, are influenced by marital dynamics. These involve marital happiness, conflict, violence, stability, equity, and the mother's perception of how marriage compares to being divorced. But first-married families can be distinguished from the other three family types we study in that stepfamilies, divorced families, and continuously single-parent families involve relations with the children's nonresidential father. In these families, the mother's well-being is likely to be influenced by her interaction and conflict with the children's father, her satisfaction with his child support, and her feelings about his interaction with and influence on the child(ren). It is worth noting that mothers in stepfather families are simultaneously influenced by relations with a current husband/stepfather. Further, for first-married and remarried mothers, there may be a sense that their marriage compares favorably or unfavorably to what their lives would be like if they were divorced, with this evaluation affecting their general well-being. For divorced mothers, an important influence may be how they compare their current life situation to that in their previous marriage.

In Chapter 2 we presented some theoretical reasons for expecting family processes to influence mothers' well-being. Although some would argue that family resources are more important than family relationships, we feel that family process variables are at least as important, and in some ways more important, as predictors of mothers' well-being. In making this point we are not saying that poverty and lack of education are unimportant. Instead, we are saying that for a given level of resources (e.g., considering families with the same income), family process variables have an important influence on the mother's well-being. In some cases, different theories lead to different predictions concerning mothers' well-being.

Two elements of family dynamics that should directly lower the mother's sense of well-being are frequent or intense marital conflict and marital violence (Coontz, 1992; Dobash & Dobash,

1979). Instability of the marriage, referring to thoughts and feelings about the marriage being in trouble, or about the possibility of divorce, is a constant source of stress and should adversely influence well-being. Equity in the marital relationship is associated with lower depression (Mirowsky, 1985), but exchange and equity theories suggest different evaluation processes and lead to different predictions. Equity theory suggests that partners evaluate their marriage, including their division of labor (their own contributions and their partners' contributions), and what each partner gets out of the relationship (their outcomes), and are happiest when arrangements are fair to both (Michaels, Edwards, & Acock, 1984). Exchange theory, on the other hand, emphasizes that individuals are motivated to maximize their benefits and minimize their costs, so that mothers should be happiest when they do less of the housework and child care, and husbands do more.

Exchange theory also posits that we must consider the rewards of a particular relationship by comparing them to the rewards of alternative relationships (Michaels, Acock, & Edwards, 1986; Thibaut & Kelley, 1959). The well-being of a mother who is married needs to be considered in the context of what she thinks it would be if she were divorced. Despite the absolute well-being or misery she experiences, exchange theory predicts that she will stay in the marriage as long as she feels she is better off than she would be if she were divorced. Because most researchers focus on mothers in just one marital status, they may exaggerate the negative effects on well-being associated with divorce. For example, a divorced mother may have significant well-being problems, but these problems may be less severe than before she was divorced.

In sum, the family processes that are relevant for mothers' well-being are widely variable across family types. For married mothers, we examine marital happiness, marital conflict, marital violence, marital stability, and marital equity. Mothers of children with a nonresidential father may also be influenced by their own interaction and conflict with their former spouse, the father's interaction with and influence on the child, and satisfaction or dissatisfaction with the father's child support. For single mothers, we examine whether they have a cohabiting partner, and for both married and divorced mothers, we include a comparison level variable. For all mothers, we examine the child's well-being, difficulties interacting with the child, and enjoyable experiences with the child.

CORRELATES OF MOTHERS' WELL-BEING

Before examining the correlations between mothers' well-being and the background and family process variables, it is important to consider how background characteristics and family processes are similar and different across the four types of families. In Chapter 3 we saw that many background/resource variables, such as income and education, differ sharply across family types. For example, family income is much lower in single-parent families, especially those that have been continuously headed by a single mother. Other differences also are important to keep in mind. The average age of the youngest child in continuously single-parent families (4 years) is less than half that of the youngest child in divorced families (8.86 years). This is another illustration of the importance of distinguishing between different types of single-parent families. Continuously single mothers also are much more likely to have a cohabiting partner at the time of the survey (27.5% for continuously single mothers, compared to 15.3% for divorced mothers).

We can also think of certain family processes as varying across family types, whereas other family processes are similar across family types. In Chapter 4 we saw that marital happiness is quite similar (and tends to be high) in first marriages and remarriages. Regarding parent-child relationships, we observed in Chapter 5 that childrearing values are very similar across family types, but that both mothers and fathers in first-married families tend to be more involved—and tend to have more enjoyable relationships with their children—than parents in other family types. Relationships that mothers have with their children's nonresidential fathers are important for three of our family types. Mothers in stepfamilies report the lowest levels of interaction and conflict with their children's nonresidential fathers, and they report the lowest level of nonresidential father's interaction with, and influence on, the child(ren). In some ways the lower contact may be seen as good for mothers in stepfather families. Clearly, this reduced conflict is associated with a reduced role (i.e., diminished interaction and influence) of the nonresidential fathers.

We can approach the influence of the background and family process variables in two ways. First, we can examine the correlation each of them has with each measure of well-being. Those factors that are significantly correlated with health, self-esteem, depression, and global well-being are of special interest. Second, we can identify the independent effect of each of the variables, while controlling for all the other variables.

In previous chapters we focused on the effects of family structure without dealing extensively with other relevant variables. In this chapter, we expand our coverage to include the effects of selected additional variables. A researcher who is interested in developing a complete model to explain a particular aspect of well-being surely would include other factors that go beyond the scope of our book. For example, characteristics of women's employment, job conditions, and relationships with their aging parents may be important factors influencing women's well-being (Mancini & Blieszner, 1989; Menaghan & Parcel, 1990; Spitze, 1988). Our purpose, however, is to identify the effects of family structure, related background characteristics, and selected family process variables. The importance of these family processes is that they offer an alternative explanation of mothers' well-being. Rather than the type of family structure determining well-being, the nature of marital and family interaction may be the more proximate cause.

The bivariate correlations of each of the measures of mothers' well-being (self-esteem, depression, global well-being, and health) with the background and family process variables are shown in Appendix B, Table B.1. There are too many correlations to report them all in the text. We have four outcome variables for mothers (self-esteem, depression, global well-being, and health), four family types, and up to 22 predictors (including background, resource, and family process variables). Although we will discuss the patterns of the correlations in the text, the interested reader will want to examine the actual values in Appendix B.

Some of the features of the correlations are illustrated in Figure 6.2. This figure involves a single outcome, mothers' global well-

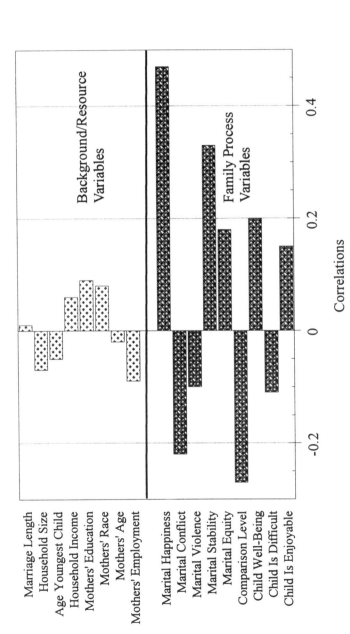

Figure 6.2. Background/Resource Versus Family Process Variables as Predictors of Mothers' Global Well-Being (first-married)

being, and a single family type, first-married mothers. However, it illustrates nicely the pattern of the results for other outcomes and other family types. Correlations can range from a negative one (−1.0) to a positive one (1.0). We expect some of the correlations to be positive and others to be negative. For example, we expect household income to be positively correlated with mothers' global well-being. In contrast, we expect marital conflict to be negatively correlated with her well-being. The figure includes a vertical line representing a correlation of zero—meaning the variables are unrelated. The bars that extend to the left of this vertical line indicate variables that are associated with lower global well-being. The bars that extend to the right of this vertical line indicate variables associated with higher global well-being. The size of each bar reflects the strength of the relationship.

The data illustrated in Figure 6.2 and presented fully in Table B.1 of Appendix B, demonstrate the predominant effect of family process variables compared to background and resource variables. For the background and resource variables, most of the bars are small, indicating weak relationships with mothers' well-being. In contrast, most of the bars for family process variables are larger, graphically illustrating that family processes are far more strongly correlated with mothers' well-being.

We will focus on the statistically significant results in Appendix B Table B.1, but it is also important to note correlations that are not significant. A broadly representative sample such as the NSFH can show that some earlier findings, based on limited samples, may be misleading.

First-Married Mothers

The results are clear and consistent for mothers in first-married families. Most of the correlations for family process variables are significant and all of them are in the expected direction. For example, the comparison level variable, involving a perception that marriage is worse than life would be if divorced, is associated with lower self-esteem, greater depression, lower global well-being, and worse health. A more equitable division of labor between the wife and husband leads to slightly higher self-esteem, global well-being, and health. Marital happiness is significantly related to each measure of well-being and is especially important as a predictor of global well-being.

In contrast, marital conflict significantly decreases self-esteem, global well-being, and health, and it increases depression. The child's well-being, reflecting the quality of interaction between the mother and child, increases her self-esteem, well-being, and health, whereas parent-child conflict is associated with lower self-esteem and well-being and with greater depression. The clear and consistent pattern is that, compared to the influence of background and resource variables, the family and child process variables are more important. However, the most important background variables are mothers' education and household income, signifying the importance of socioeconomic resources to mothers' well-being.

One of the items used to measure the comparison level of marriage is whether the mother believes her parental role would be better or worse if she were divorced. Most mothers in their first marriage (60.9%) are likely to think their parental role would be worse or much worse if they were divorced. Interestingly, about one third (32.7%) feel it would be the same, and small percentages feel it would be better (4.5%) or much better (1.9%). For about two in five first-married mothers then, marriage is not necessarily providing the most desirable context in which to parent.

Mothers in Stepfamilies

A similar pattern emerges for remarried mothers. Judging that the remarriage is worse than life would be if divorced is strongly associated with depression and lower global well-being for mothers in stepfamilies. It is worth noting that because they have been divorced at some point in their lives, remarried women are not merely speculating about what life would be like if they were divorced. They are likely to have realistic perceptions and vivid memories of what it is like to be a divorced, single parent. Compared to first-married mothers, those in stepfather families are more ambivalent in their feelings about what parenting would be like if they were divorced. More than two fifths (42.7%) feel their parental role would be worse or much worse, but nearly half (48.0%) report it would be the same. A small percentage (9.1%) of mothers in stepfamilies think their parental role would be better if they were divorced.

For mothers in stepfamilies, greater equity in the division of household labor increases self-esteem and global well-being, while reducing depression. Marital conflict is associated with greater depression, lower well-being, and worse health. The child's well-being is associated with increased global well-being and better health, along with reduced depression, whereas parent-child conflict (difficulties) is significantly associated with depression and lower self-esteem.

As is the case for first-married mothers, the social background and resource variables have few significant effects on the well-being of mothers in stepfather families. Higher household income and mothers' education are associated with better health, education tends to reduce depression, and longer marriages are related to lower self-esteem and lower global well-being. Most of these effects are weak to moderate in magnitude. It is clear that in stepfamilies, the mother's well-being is more strongly influenced by family processes than by resources.

Divorced Mothers

For divorced mothers, the comparison level of her life as a divorced person with what it had been when she was married is associated with all aspects of well-being. Consistent with our expectations, judgments that their lives now are better than before they divorced are related to lower depression and higher self-esteem, global well-being, and general health. Mother-child difficulties reduce self-esteem and increase depression.

Children's well-being is significantly correlated with all measures of mothers' well-being for divorced mothers. In fact, the correlations between children's well-being and mothers' well-being are stronger among divorced mothers than they are among first-married or stepfamily mothers. This is important because it suggests that the child's outcomes are more central to the well-being of divorced mothers than to that of married mothers. This is a startling counterpoint to the popular view of some social commentators who question the divorced mother's interest in her child's outcomes.

Divorced mothers' relations with their former spouses and their children's relations with nonresidential fathers have a very limited influence on mothers' well-being. Conflict between mothers and nonresidential fathers and dissatisfaction with child support paid by fathers tend to increase mothers' depression. Dissatisfaction with child support also is negatively related to mothers' health. The other variables involving nonresidential fathers have no significant influences on mothers' well-being. We also note that the presence of a cohabiting partner is associated with slightly higher levels of depession among divorced mothers. Considering the resource and other background variables, household income and mothers' education are significantly related to divorced mothers' self-esteem and health. Income also is related to global well-being, and education is associated with lower depression. The length of time since divorce has one small, but significant effect, negatively influencing mothers' health.

The most interesting resource variable is the hours the mother is employed. For married mothers and continuously single mothers, the hours the mother is employed has few consequences. In the case of divorced mothers, by contrast, it is a very important variable. The more hours the divorced mother is employed, the higher her self-esteem, the lower her depression, the greater her global well-being, and the better her health. It is especially important to compare these findings to the case of continuously single mothers. In Chapter 3 we saw that one clear difference between divorced and continuously single mothers is the much higher level of employment among divorced mothers. The bivariate correlations suggest that this has great benefits for divorced mothers' well-being, whereas for continuously single mothers, the hours of employment are not significantly related to well-being.

Continuously Single Mothers

In most other respects, the pattern for continuously single mothers is similar to that of divorced mothers. Continuously single mothers who judge their children's well-being to be good also judge their own well-being, self-esteem, and health to be higher. This sheds further doubt on speculation that children's well-being is not central or important to continuously single mothers. Parent-child conflict (difficulties) is correlated with greater depression. Having enjoyable times with the child is related to both higher self-esteem and global well-being. Cohabiting is also associated with higher global well-being.

The role of the nonresidential father appears to be more important for the well-being of continuously single mothers than it is for either divorced or stepfamily mothers. Dissatisfaction with child support increases depression and reduces global well-being. The more the nonresidential father interacts with the child, the lower the mother's depression and the better her reported health. Similarly, the greater the influence the nonresidential father has on the child, the lower the mother's depression, the better her global well-being, and the better her health. Previous research on nonresidential fathers is limited and typically examines divorced families. Our findings suggest that an important avenue for further research is continuously single-mother families, the involvement and influence of nonresidential fathers in these families, and the consequences for mothers' (and children's) well-being.

Family background and resources have few significant effects on the well-being of continuously single mothers. This does not mean these variables are unimportant. Rather, it means that for the aspects of family resources and mothers' well-being that we have examined, few significant effects have been observed. Mothers' education improves self-esteem and health, and older mothers report worse health. Other variables such as household income, age of youngest child, race, and mothers' hours of employment have no significant effects on mothers' reported level of well-being. It is very likely that the dearth of previous research on continuously single mothers has greatly handicapped our ability to model and explain the well-being of this group of mothers.

MODELS OF MOTHERS' WELL-BEING

The first section of this chapter demonstrated that family type has a significant effect on mothers' self-esteem, depression, global well-being, and health. Most of these differences persisted when relevant background variables were controlled. The second section showed that several family background, resource, and family process variables are correlated with mothers' well-being. In this section we will evaluate models that test the independent effects of each variable. One limitation of the correlations (presented in Appendix B, Table B.1) is that they do not control for any of the background variables or family process variables we have discussed. Controlling for other variables greatly increases the complexity of the analysis, but it is necessary to assess the independent effects of the variables.

Because there are so many predictors, we eliminated several of them before doing analyses involving multiple regression. First, we eliminated any variable that did not have a significant correlation ($p < .05$) with the particular well-being variable. For example, Table B.1 in Appendix B shows that household size has a correlation of $-.02$ with the health of mothers in stepfamilies. This correlation is not significant and therefore this variable was not included in the model for that family type. Second, we eliminated variables that had a large amount of missing data. Entering them in the multiple regression would result in too small a sample to obtain reliable estimates of the other independent effects. An example of this is the nonresidential father's interaction with the child in continuously single-parent families. The missing data for these questions may signify that many nonresidential fathers have especially limited roles in this family type. The only other variable that was eliminated because of missing data is the comparison level of divorce for divorced mothers. Third, we eliminated any variable that was not significant in the multiple regression at the .10 level. We then reestimated the model. In some cases we had to reestimate the model again if there was still a variable that was not significant at the .10 level. The .10 level was used because there is limited prior research involving many of these relationships, and we wanted to include any variable that was marginally significant.

Because equity theory specifies a quadratic relationship between equity and well-being, we included a quadratic term (equity^2) along with equity. Equity theory predicts that the coefficient for the linear term, equity, should have a positive sign. That is, as the relationship becomes more fair to the mother, her well-being should be higher. However, because relationships that are unfair to one's partner can also be stressful, a high level of unfairness to the husband should also cause stress. This should appear as a negative coefficient for equity^2. We included both the linear and the quadratic forms of equity only when both had a significant correlation ($p < .05$), and when both were significant in the regression model at the .10 level or better.

Tables 6.2 to 6.5 present the final results for predicting self-esteem, depression, global well-being, and health, respectively. All variables that are significant at the .10 level are included in the models. The coefficients reported in the table are standardized beta weights. These can range from a negative one (–1.0) to a positive one (1.0). A negative sign signifies a negative relationship and a positive sign signifies a positive relationship. For example, in Table 6.2, for first-married mothers, education increases her self-esteem. In other words, the more education she has, the higher, on average, we expect her self-esteem to be. At the bottom of the tables we report the R^2 and sample size (N). We present two separate R^2 statistics for each family type. First, we present the R^2 for the model that contains only the background/resource variables. Below that, we present the R^2 for the model that includes all the independent variables. The pair of R^2s at the bottom of each column tells us how much of the variance can be explained by the background/resource variables alone, and by the background/ resouce variables in combination with the family process variables.

Table 6.2 Predicting Mothers' Self-Esteem

Predictors	First-Married	Divorced	Stepfamily	Continuously Single
Background variables				
Sample		.10*		
Marriage length			−.12*	
Household income		.09*		
Education	.14***	.17***		.13**
Family process variables				
Marital happiness	.14***			
Marital conflict	−.07*			
Marital stability	.11**		.19**	
Marital equity	−.44*			
Marital equity^2	.38†			
Comparison level, marriage	−.08*			
Child well-being	.06†	.19***		
Child difficulties	−.06*	.14***	−.14*	.16**
R^2 background variables only (N)	.02*** (1,026)	.05*** (639)	.03** (264)	.02** (384)
R^2 with all relevant variables (N)	.12*** (905)	.12*** (633)	.07*** (246)	.05*** (384)

NOTE: The coefficients are standardized beta weights. The inclusion of independent variables was based on the following criteria. First, all variables with significant correlations with self-esteem were included in a regression. Second, those background and family process variables that were significant at the .10 level or better were kept and the model was reestimated. Variables that did not meet the criteria for any family type were dropped from the table.
†$p < .10$; *$p < .05$; **$p < .01$; ***$p < .001$.

Mothers' Self-Esteem

Combining background and family process variables explains a modest portion of the variance in self-esteem. The explained variance ranges from 5% for continuously single mothers to 12% for divorced mothers. Collectively, family process variables account for more variance in mothers' self-esteem than do the set of background variables.

For first-married mothers, factors associated with higher self-esteem include education, marital happiness, marital conflict, marital stability, equity and its square term, comparison level of marriage, the child's well-being, and difficulties with the child. With the exception of the equity variables, all of the effects are in the expected direction. That is, marital happiness, stability, and child's well-being are associated with higher self-esteem, whereas marital conflict, judging marriage as worse than divorce, and difficulties interacting with the child are related to lower self-esteem.

Equity includes both a linear and a quadratic (square) term. The signs for these were in the opposite direction to what was predicted. It should be noted that the square term was significant at the .05 level. A separate regression model including just the linear equity term has the same R^2, and the coefficient for equity is not significant at the .10 level.

Compared to mothers in their first marriage, fewer family process variables are significantly related to the self-esteem of mothers in other family types. Child-related variables, however, are important across family types. The strongest predictor of the self-esteem of divorced mothers is how well their children are doing, and difficulties interacting with their children are related to lower self-esteem. Child-related variables are more closely tied to the self-esteem of divorced mothers, compared to first-married mothers. We also find that in stepfamilies and continuously single-parent families, difficulties with the child are important predictors of mothers' self-esteem.

Two background variables are positively related to divorced mothers' self-esteem: mothers' education and household income. Education also has a significant effect on the self-esteem of mothers in their first marriage and those who are continuously single.

Mothers' Depression

Table 6.3 shows the results for predicting mothers' levels of depression. There is enormous range in the amount of the variance we can explain across family types. With all the variables included, we explain just 3% of the variance in depression for continuously single mothers, but 24% for mothers in stepfamilies. Within each family type, the variance explained by resource and

Table 6.3 Predicting Mothers' Depression

Predictors	First-Married	Divorced	Stepfamily	Continuously Single
Background variables				
Education	−.16***		−.17**	
Race—(1) white (0) nonwhite	−.08**			
Mother's hours employed		.14***		
Cohabiting		−.09*		
Family process variables				
Marital happiness	−.09**		−.26***	
Marital conflict	.23***			
Marital stability			.14*	
Marital equity			−.73*	
Marital equity^2			.69*	
Comparison level, marriage	.17**			
Child well-being		−.18***		
Child difficulties	.09**		.17**	.18***
Conflict with nonresident father		.10*		
R^2 background variables only (N)	.03*** (1,072)	.03*** (663)	.02* (275)	
R^2 with all relevant variables (N)	.14*** (951)	.08*** (586)	.24*** (248)	.03* (402)

NOTE: The coefficients are standardized beta weights. The inclusion of independent variables was based on the following criteria. First, all variables with significant correlations with depression were included in a regression. Second, those background and family process variables that were significant at the .10 level or better were kept and the model was reestimated. Variables that did not meet the criteria for any family type were dropped from the table. The number of cases is in parentheses.
*$p < .05$; **$p < .01$; ***$p < .001$.

background variables is quite small compared to the variance explained by the family process and child variables. This reaffirms our finding based on analyzing the correlations.

Marital happiness is significantly and negatively associated with depression for both first-married and stepfamily mothers, although it is relatively more important for the latter group. Having difficulties with children is also significant for both family types. Marital conflict and a judgment that the current marriage is worse than divorce would be are significant predictors of depression for first-married mothers. Both education and race are significant background variables. The greater the mother's education, the lower her level of depression. Also, whites have slightly lower levels of depression than nonwhites.

For mothers in stepfamilies, marital stability and marital equity are associated with a reduced likelihood of depression. Both the linear and the quadratic terms for equity are important. This means that as the division of labor moves from being unfair toward being fair, the mother's depression lessens. But when the division of labor moves farther toward being unfair to her husband (a rather uncommon occurrence), the depression increases. Education is the only background variable that is a significant predictor of depression for mothers in stepfather families.

Divorced mothers' depression is greater among those who cohabit, although the effect is weak. Cohabiting has no significant effect on the level of depression for continuously single mothers. For divorced mothers, but not for continuously single mothers, the more hours they are employed, the less depressed they are. We saw in Chapter 3 that divorced mothers are employed significantly more hours than their continuously single or first-married counterparts. Here we find that this employment reduces depression for divorced mothers. Higher child well-being also is related to less depressive feelings among divorced mothers, but conflict with the children's nonresidential father is associated with greater depression. For continuously single mothers, the only variable that is significantly related to depression is having difficulties with their children.

Mothers' Global Well-Being

Table 6.4 shows substantial differences in how well our background and family process variables explain mothers' global well-being across the four types of families. This ranges from just 4% for continuously single mothers to 31% for stepfamily mothers. As with self-esteem and depression, the family process and child-related variables are far more important than the background and resource variables.

Table 6.4 Predicting Mothers' Global Well-Being

Predictors	First-Married	Divorced	Stepfamily	Continuously Single
Background variables				
Marriage length			.10†	
Mother's hours employed		.13**		
Cohabiting				.10*
Family process variables				
Marital happiness	.34***		.45***	
Marital stability	.11**			
Marital equity	.50*		.12*	
Marital equity^2	−.47*			
Comparison level, marriage	−.08*			
Child well-being	.10***	.22***	.12*	.17*
Child enjoyable times	.08**			
R^2 background variables only (N)		.01** (601)	.03* (241)	.01* (355)
R^2 with all relevant variables (N)	.27*** (943)	.06*** (600)	.31*** (228)	.04*** (355)

NOTE: The coefficients are standardized beta weights. The inclusion of independent variables was based on the following criteria. First, all variables with significant correlations with global well-being were included in a regression. Second, those background and family process variables that were significant at the .10 level or better were kept and the model was reestimated. Variables that did not meet the criteria for any family type were dropped from the table. No background variables remained significant when the family process variables were included for first-married families. Without the family process variables, only education among the background variables had a significant effect ($p < .01$). Education explained just under 1% of the variance in mothers' global well-being. The number of cases is in parentheses.
†$p < .10$; *$p < .05$; **$p < .01$; ***$p < .001$.

One variable, the well-being of the child, is a consistently significant predictor across all four types of families. It is worth noting that the magnitude of the effect of this variable is greater in single-parent families, whether they are divorced or continuously single, than for married families. The multivariate nature of this analysis strengthens our earlier finding that children's well-being may be more central to the well-being of single mothers than it is to that of married mothers.

Several other variables are significantly related to first-married mothers' well-being. Marital happiness, stability, equity, and enjoyable times with the child also increase the global well-being of mothers in their first marriage. First-married mothers who compare their current marriages unfavorably to what their lives would be like if they were divorced experience a reduced sense of well-being. Consistent with equity theory, both the linear and quadratic terms for equity are significant. That is, as the marital relationship moves from unfair to the mother toward an equitable relationship, her global well-being improves. Further, the quadratic term suggests that when mothers perceive marital relationships as unfair to their husbands, mothers' global well-being is lower.

Among remarried mothers, two variables reflecting marital processes are significantly related to well-being: an equitable division of household labor and marital happiness. For these mothers, marital happiness is the dominant influence on their global well-being. Among single mothers, the well-being of the child is the only family process variable with a significant effect.

Of the myriad background variables we examined, none related to the overall well-being of first-married mothers. Marriage length is weakly related to mothers' well-being in stepfamilies. Having a cohabiting partner has a weak, but significant, positive effect on the well-being of continuously single mothers. Perhaps the most interesting effect of a background variable, consistent with our earlier findings, is that divorced mothers' well-being is enhanced by being employed more hours.

Mothers' Health

Unlike the aspects of psychological well-being examined above, mothers' health is related more strongly to the background and resource variables than to family processes (see Table 6.5). Across all four family types, at least one of the two key socioeconomic variables (household income and mothers' education) is significantly related to mothers' health. In addition, for divorced mothers, two other background/resource variables are related to health: weekly hours of employment and time since divorce. The longer the time since the divorce, the worse the mothers' health, al-

Table 6.5 Predicting Mothers' Health

Predictors	First-Married	Divorced	Stepfamily	Continuously Single
Background variables				
Household income	.09**		.24***	
Education	.18***	.13**		.20***
Mother's age				−.10*
Mother's hours employed			.21***	
Months since divorce		−.07†		
Family process variables				
Marital violence	−.08*			−.16**
Marital equity	.42*			
Marital equity^2	−.37*			
Child well-being	.09**	.13**		.08*
Dissatisfaction with child support		−.07†		
R^2 background variables only (N)	.06*** (1,045)	.08*** (625)	.05*** (269)	.06*** (376)
R^2 with all relevant variables (N)	.08*** (961)	.11*** (566)	.08*** (250)	.07*** (376)

NOTE: The coefficients are standardized beta weights. The inclusion of independent variables was based on the following criteria. First, all variables with significant correlations with health were included in a regression. Second, those background and family process variables that were significant at the .10 level or better were kept and the model was reestimated. Variables that did not meet the criteria for any family type were dropped from the table. The number of cases is in parentheses.
†$p < .10$; *$p < .05$; **$p < .01$; ***$p < .001$.

though this is a weak effect. For continuously single mothers, age is negatively associated with health.

Regarding family process variables, marital violence is associated with worse health among first-married and remarried mothers, whereas marital equity and children's well-being are associated with better health for first-married mothers. Divorced mothers' overall health is enhanced by children's well-being, and adversely affected by dissatisfaction with child support. Of the variables we studied, the only family process or child-related variable important to continuously single mothers is the child's well-being.

SUMMARY AND CONCLUSIONS

In this chapter we identified several dimensions of mothers' well-being and examined differences across family types. The first stage of our analysis involved simple comparisons across family types without controls for relevant variables. We found that single mothers have lower well-being and tend to be much more depressed than married mothers. Continuously single mothers have significantly lower self-esteem than mothers in other family types, and first-married mothers report significantly better health than other mothers. Overall, these findings suggest that marriage, and especially a first marriage, is advantageous to mothers' well-being. Mothers in their first marriage enjoy the highest well-being, stepfamily mothers fare nearly as well, and divorced and continuously single mothers have the lowest well-being.

Because family structure is related to many other characteristics of families, we also examined mothers' well-being across family types, controlling for a series of social background and resource variables. We found that significant differences in aspects of well-being persist across family types. The most pronounced differences are on measures of depression and global well-being, where married mothers exhibit higher well-being than single mothers. Divorced and continuously single mothers are generally happy and satisfied with their lives, but they are not as happy as married mothers. Compared to mothers in other family types, first-married mothers also enjoy slightly higher self-esteem and somewhat better overall health.

These findings refute the idea that differences in mothers' well-being across family types are entirely due to socioeconomic, racial, age, or employment differences associated with family type. It bears repeating that, in general, mothers in all family types report fairly high levels of well-being and that differences across family types are small. Still, married mothers tend to be advantaged. One explanation for this is that marriage provides social support, social integration, and an opportunity for role differentiation. From a structural-functional perspective, married mothers experience higher well-being because they can divide family labor with spouses and thus experience less role strain.

However, as we found in Chapter 4, mothers' household labor is substantial across family types, and the absence of a husband does not significantly increase the time mothers spend on most tasks. If household labor is as demanding for married mothers as it is for single mothers (largely because of the additional work created by the husband's presence), why do single mothers have lower well-being?

Consistent with other studies, our findings suggest that the answer lies in a variety of other family and marital processes. Single mothers and married mothers experience parenthood differently. Long-term single parenting, usually performed by employed women, is a chronic stressor (Thompson & Ensminger, 1989). Compared to their married counterparts, most single mothers have no relief from the responsibilities and burdens of parenting. Marriage typically provides social support, particularly emotional support, so that spouses have someone to talk to, someone to listen, someone who cares about them as individuals and who cares about their problems (Ross et al., 1991). Married mothers also receive instrumental support from their husbands. If she has conflicting or competing demands, she can often rely on her husband to "help out." While the wife/mother cares for one child, for example, the husband/father may help another child with homework. In other situations, the husband/father may chauffeur a child, play with children, or be there when his wife needs someone to listen. By contrast, single mothers often are on their own. Research shows that emotional support reduces depression, anxiety, and other psychological problems and that both social support and psychological well-being enhance physical health (Ross et al., 1991).

All marriages are not alike, however, and all are not equally happy, stable, or equitable. Consistent with social exchange theory, our findings show that mothers' well-being is higher when they rate their marriages as better than their alternatives and when they describe their family relationships favorably. For both groups of married mothers, aspects of marital process are tied to personal well-being. First-married mothers' self-esteem and global well-being are bolstered by marital happiness, marital stability, and by a judgment that the current marriage is better than an alternative relationship or arrangement. Similarly, marital conflict is associated with reduced self-esteem and greater depression. Remarried mothers also benefit psychologically from marital happiness, stability, and equity. These findings corroborate previous studies suggesting that the quality of marital relationships is critical to mothers' well-being (Coontz, 1992; Gove et al., 1983).

Parent-child relations also are central to mothers' self-esteem and overall well-being (Demo, Small, & Savin-Williams, 1987). Of the many dimensions of marital and family relationships we examined, the child's well-being is clearly the strongest and most consistent predictor of mothers' well-being. Substantiating previous studies (Greenberger & O'Neil, 1990), we also found that difficulties in relationships with their children adversely affect mothers' well-being. As feminist family researchers emphasize, the substantial variability in marital and family relationships dictates that marriage is not always or uniformly beneficial to mothers' well-being. Instead, marriage, parenthood, and family life have the potential to enhance or diminish mothers' well-being, with women in more nurturing and equitable family environments benefiting more than other women.

Interestingly, we have been able to identify many more aspects of family relationships that are important for married mothers than for single mothers. Our selection of variables was guided by dominant theories in family studies and resulted in many significant findings. Yet many variables deemed important in previous research reflect marital processes, and these variables are not relevant for understanding the well-being of single mothers. In particular, we could identify very few family relationships that influence the well-being of continuously single mothers. In part, this occurred because previous research has neglected these families or failed to distinguish between different types of single-parent families. As a result, we know less about these families and their well-being than we do about other family types. But another reason is that we had a relatively small subsample of continuously single mothers, and our analysis was further restricted when pertinent information was not available for some of these families. Still, we found that the well-being of single mothers, like their married counterparts, depends on their children's well-being and on their relationships with their children. Further, divorced mothers' depression is associated with conflict with their children's nonresidential father. An important direction for further research, however, is for family researchers to focus on various types of single-parent (including male-headed) families. Considerable work is needed to correct for this imbalance in family research. Specifically, we need to develop a fuller understanding of the diversity and complexity of cohabiting relationships, co-parenting arrangements, relations with noncohabiting partners, relations with extended kin, and the influences of these relationships on single parents' well-being.

We also examined how dimensions of mothers' well-being are influenced by aspects of their social background. Across all family types, and for all three dimensions of psychologial well-being we examined, family relationships proved to be much more powerful than resource variables in explaining mothers' well-being. This should not be taken to mean that mothers' background characteristics and resources are unimportant. On the contrary, certain aspects of their social structural location and resources exert moderate effects on their well-being. Compared with variables measuring the quality of proximate family experiences, however, background variables are less important in explaining variation in mothers' psychological well-being.

Controlling for other variables, household income is related to only one aspect of mothers' psychological well-being, positively influencing divorced mothers' self-esteem. It is also related to the physical health of first-married and remarried mothers. With other factors considered, race is generally unrelated to aspects of mothers' well-being. This finding is consistent with research on other national samples showing that, when relevant social structural variables are controlled, African Americans and whites have comparable levels of self-esteem, personal efficacy, and psychological well-being (Hughes & Demo, 1992a, 1992b). Compared to other background and resource variables, mothers' education is a more powerful resource, bolstering self-esteem, reducing feelings of depression, and consistently improving evaluations of general health. Marital duration has few significant effects. For divorced mothers in particular, the most consistent predictor of well-being is hours of paid employment, which positively influences all four aspects of their self-reported health and well-being. Thus, although the income of divorced women generally plunges in the years following divorce, many of these women work longer hours in paid employment to provide for themselves and their families, simultaneously enriching their own psychological and physical well-being. For many of these divorced mothers, employment represents more than necessary financial resources; it provides meaning, satisfaction, a sense of personal control, and well-being. In the next chapter we examine the correlates of children's well-being across family types, retaining our focus on background, resource, and family process variables.

NOTE

1. A description of variables we examine in this chapter appears in Appendix A. Specific questions, coding, and the sample sizes for each variable are presented. Where appropriate, we present factor loadings, interitem correlations, and reliability coefficients.

SEVEN

Family Structure and Children's Well-Being

What are the implications of different family structures for children's well-being? In this chapter we examine several aspects of children's social and psychological well-being—including dimensions of socioemotional adjustment, global well-being, and academic performance—in an attempt to disentangle the intricate web of family arrangements and relationships that bear on children. To do this, we examine whether children fare better in one or more of the family structures we have studied throughout the book. Where there are differences, we seek to find out if the differences are due to the type of family the child lives in, the socioeconomic resources of the family, or what we have described as family process variables.

In the first part of the chapter we address the question of how dimensions of well-being compare across family types. Are children in single-parent families more likely to be upset, irritable, or unhappy compared to children in families where mothers are married? Do children whose mothers have been continuously single differ in well-being from those whose mother is divorced? Compared to the adjustment and well-being of children in families headed by divorced mothers, are children advantaged or disadvantaged when their mothers remarry and form stepfamilies?

The theoretical perspectives we outlined in Chapter 2 suggest different answers to these questions. The traditional approach to well-being emphasizes family composition and posits that two parental role models are essential for the normal development and well-being of children. Accordingly, children reared in households where the two biological parents are not present (specifically, children in divorced families, stepfamilies, and continuously single-parent families) would be expected to exhibit lower levels of well-being than children in first-married family units. The economic deprivation perspective, in contrast, suggests that because family income is much higher in two-parent households than in one-parent households, children in two-parent families (first-married and stepfamilies) should experience higher levels of well-being than children in single-parent (continuously single and divorced) families. A third perspective, the family conflict hypothesis, predicts that regardless of family structure, children exposed to high levels of interparental conflict and parent-child conflict experience lower levels of well-being than children in families with less conflict. Finally, the life stress perspective predicts that because more life stress is generally experienced by children in divorced and remarried families, these children should experience lower levels of well-being than those in first-married or continuously single-parent families. Thus, although individual theories can be distinguished in terms of their emphases and central explanatory variables, most theory and research to date suggest that children in first-married family units are advantaged in terms of social and psychological well-being and that children of divorce and children in single-parent families are disadvantaged.

A second question guiding our analysis is whether differences in children's well-being across family types are attributable to children's age and gender. Age is an especially important control variable because children's adjustment problems vary by age, and different family structures tend to have children of different ages. For example, continuously single-parent families are much less likely than stepfamilies to have children ages 12-18. On the other hand, continuously single-parent families are much more likely than stepfamilies to have children under age 5. We also control for gender because there are potential differences between boys and girls in their relationships with parents, their adjustment, and their academic performance.

Finally, we address a third question: How important are family resource variables compared to family process variables? Although many studies suggest that children are profoundly influenced by relationships with their mothers and fathers, as well as by the relationship between the mother and father, relatively few studies have examined how children are influenced by continuing relationships between parents who do not reside together, many of whom were formerly married. Further, it is not clear how important family relationships are compared with other variables such as family structure and family resources. To examine this, we will compare the importance of resources, such as education and income, to family process variables, such as family conflict, marital instability, and parent-child relations, for children and adolescents in our four family types.

MEASURING CHILDREN'S WELL-BEING

Personal well-being has many dimensions, and children may have a variety of different and sometimes conflicting feelings about their lives. The National Survey of Families and Households (NSFH) asked mothers to describe their children on several aspects of well-being. It is important to note that these are the mothers' evaluations and not those of children themselves, their teachers, or their peers. Information from multiple informants would be ideal, but the NSFH did not collect data from children or from nonfamily members. However, there is ample evidence that most mothers are very involved in childrearing, they tend to be closely attached to their children, and are good sources of information about their children (LaRossa, 1988; Rossi, 1984; L. Thompson & Walker, 1989).

Although measured by a single question, the variable we use to measure children's global well-being has substantial face validity. Mothers were asked, "All things considered, how is your child's life going?" The response options ranged from 1 for *not very well* to 4 for *very well*. This question was asked about a particular, randomly selected child.

We use three separate sets of questions to measure children's socioemotional adjustment. The questions were based on whether the focal child was age 0-4, 5-11, or 12-18. For the group ages 0-4, nine questions were used involving the mothers' ratings of how true it was that the particular child was willing to try new things, was fussy or irritable, kept busy, lost her or his temper easily, was happy, was fearful or anxious, bullied others, did what was asked, and got along well with others. Items were recoded so that higher scores for each item indicated better adjustment. We computed adjustment for children 0-4 as the mean response for mothers who answered at least eight of the nine items.

This set of items has strong face validity for assessing the well-being of young children, but children in this age range also exhibit considerable variability on these behaviors from day to day, or even from one moment to the next. A child who is fussy and irritable one day may be cheerful the next, and a child who acts like a bully one morning may get along very well with other children that afternoon. This inconsistency was reflected in a low reliability for the measure (see Appendix A).

For children ages 5-11 and 12-18, we used 10-item scales to measure adjustment. The questions were the same as the items used for younger children, with the addition of a 10th item concerning whether the child did her/his responsibilities. The reliability of these scales was somewhat better, but still not as high as we would like. It is difficult to know the cause of the low reliability on scales with 10 items. We do not have objective data on the children, nor even the children's own reports of their well-being. Unfortunately, these data were not collected in the NSFH survey. Relying exclusively on mothers' evaluations may reduce the reliability. We argued above that for the youngest age group (0-4), a low reliability may be inherent in their day-to-day inconsistency. A similar argument may also apply to adolescents, who seem to have the world in control one day but feel completely out of control the next. Ultimately, the lack of high reliability may reflect the inherent complexity of the well-being concept.

Another important child outcome is academic performance. Mothers whose focal child was 5-11 were asked how the child was doing in school. Response options ranged from 1 for *near the bottom of the class* to 5 for *one of the best students in the class.* Mothers whose focal child was 12-18 were asked the grades the adolescent earned. Their responses were coded into a 9-point scale ranging from 1 for mostly Fs to 9 for mostly As.

CHILDREN'S WELL-BEING
ACROSS FAMILY TYPES

Our findings suggest that family structure has a modest effect on children's well-being. Table 7.1 presents the averages on each of our child outcome variables: global well-being; adjustment of children 0-4, 5-11, and 12-18; and academic performance of children 5-11 and 12-18. Panel A presents the averages without adjusting for differences in the control variables we have used throughout the book.

Children whose parents are both in their first marriage have the highest average score on every child outcome variable, although many differences are small and do not reach statistical significance. There are more differences across family types on children's global well-being than there are on other outcomes, and these values are illustrated in Figure 7.1. For the global measure of well-being, children with first-married parents score significantly higher than children in any other family type.

The sharpest contrast is between children with first-married parents and those whose parents are divorced. Panel A of Table 7.1 shows that children with first-married parents have significantly higher global well-being, adjustment (5-18), and academic performance (5-18). Although these differences are statistically significant, it is easy to exaggerate their importance. A statistically significant difference means that we are confident the mean scores are distinguishable. It does not mean we are confident that the difference is large. For example, the average socioemotional adjustment score of 5 to 11-year-olds in first-married families is 2.58, compared to 2.50 for children from divorced families. Although this is significant, it is still remarkable that they are this close on a scale that ranges from 1 to 3.

Throughout the book we have distinguished between divorced and continuously single mothers. In particular, we have illustrated

Table 7.1   Children's Well-Being by Family Type

Panel A: Without Adjusting for Children's Age or Gender

Measure of Well-Being	First-Married	Divorced	Stepfamily	Continuously Single	Significance[a]
Global well-being, (1) not very well to (4) very well	3.72 (1,084)	3.45 (676)	3.49 (276)	3.65 (418)	abcef
Adjustment of child 0-4, higher on 3-point scale means better adjustment	2.49 (318)	2.44 (101)	2.48 (40)	2.44 (157)	ns
Adjustment of child 5-11, higher on 3-point scale means better adjustment	2.58 (330)	2.50 (255)	2.55 (98)	2.53 (156)	a
Academic performance of child 5-11, (1) for one of worst to (5) for one of best in class	4.04 (304)	3.83 (241)	3.91 (95)	3.74 (152)	ac
Adjustment of child 12-18, higher on 3-point scale means better adjustment	2.61 (314)	2.50 (302)	2.47 (131)	2.53 (64)	ab
Grades in school, 12-18, (1) for mostly Fs to (9) for mostly As	6.98 (300)	6.42 (291)	6.74 (125)	6.55 (60)	a

Panel B: Adjusting for Children's Age and Gender

Measure of Well-Being	First-Married	Divorced	Stepfamily	Continuously Single	Significance[a]
Global well-being, (1) not very well to (4) very well	3.70 (1,067)	3.50 (670)	3.54 (274)	3.60 (410)	abce
Adjustment of child 0-4, higher on 3-point scale means better adjustment	2.49 (314)	2.43 (100)	2.47 (39)	2.44 (153)	ns
Adjustment of child 5-11, higher on 3-point scale means better adjustment	2.57 (325)	2.51 (251)	2.56 (98)	2.52 (153)	a
Academic performance of child 5-11, (1) for one of worst to (5) for one of best in class	4.03 (299)	3.85 (237)	3.92 (95)	3.72 (149)	ac
Adjustment of child 12-18, higher on 3-point scale means better adjustment	2.60 (310)	2.50 (301)	2.47 (130)	2.54 (63)	ab
Grades in school, 12-18, (1) for mostly Fs to (9) for mostly As	6.99 (296)	6.40 (290)	6.69 (124)	6.59 (59)	a

Table 7.1 Continued

Panel C: Adjusting for Children's Age, Gender, Sample, Household Income, Mother's Education, Race, Mother's Age, Hours per Week Mother Is Employed, Number of Children, and, for Single Mothers, Whether She Is Cohabiting

Measure of Well-Being	First-Married	Divorced	Continuously Stepfamily	Single	Significance[a]
Global well-being, (1) not very well to (4) very well	3.70 (1,065)	3.49 (670)	3.57 (272)	3.58 (410)	abcde
Adjustment of child, 0-4, higher on 3-point scale means better adjustment	2.49 (314)	2.42 (100)	2.49 (39)	2.45 (153)	a
Adjustment of child 5-11, higher on 3-point scale means better adjustment	2.58 (323)	2.50 (251)	2.57 (98)	2.52 (153)	ad
Academic performance of child, 5-11, (1) for one of worst to (5) for one of best in class	3.98 (297)	3.86 (237)	3.92 (95)	3.81 (149)	ns
Adjustment of child 12-18, higher on 3-point scale means better adjustment	2.61 (310)	2.50 (301)	2.48 (128)	2.52 (63)	ab
Grades in school, 12-18, (1) for mostly Fs to (9) for mostly As	6.97 (296)	6.42 (290)	6.68 (123)	6.63 (59)	a

The number of cases is in parentheses.
a. The letters indicate which means are significantly different at the $p < .05$ level: a = first-married compared to divorced; b = first-married compared to stepfamily; c = first-married compared to continuously single; d = divorced compared to stepfamily; e = divorced compared to continuously single; f = stepfamily compared to continuously single.

that the socioeconomic resources available to divorced mothers, although scarce in comparison to those of married mothers, are generally much greater than those of the continuously single mothers. Based on an economic deprivation argument, then, one would expect that children in continuously single-parent families would have the lowest well-being of children in the four family types. Yet we find that children in continuously single-parent families are not significantly different from children in other family types on any measures of well-being, with the exception that they score *higher* than children in divorced families on global well-being (Panel A in Table 7.1).

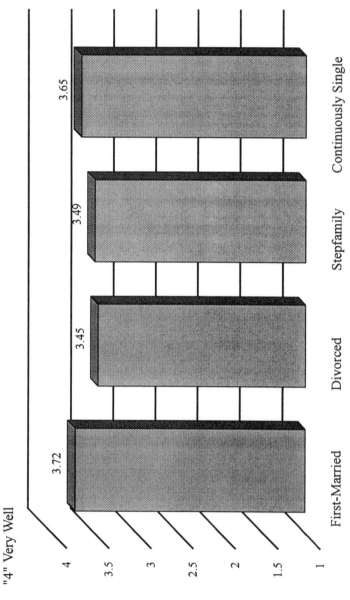

Figure 7.1. Children's Global Well-Being by Family Type, Without Adjusting for Control Variables

Other arguments characterize children in stepfamilies as disadvantaged due to a variety of factors including the absence of a biological parent, the stresses accompanying parental divorce and remarriage, and the ambiguities of stepfamily relationships. Our findings provide limited support for these long-standing arguments. Children in stepfamilies are described as remarkably similar in well-being to children in other family types. Based on mothers' reports, the stepfamily children appear to be intermediate between children in first-married families, who have the highest reported adjustment, and those in divorced families, who have somewhat lower well-being. It bears repeating, however, that most of the differences across family types are quite small.

When we control for children's age and gender (as shown in Panel B of Table 7.1), the results correspond closely to those without controls. Adjusting for children's age and gender, children in first-married families have the highest scores on all variables. On average, children in continuously single-parent and divorced families have similar adjustment levels, although children in the latter group have lower scores on the global well-being variable. In general, children in stepfamilies are intermediate in well-being and socioemotional adjustment, falling between children in first-married and divorced families.

We also examined children's well-being across family types, with controls for a series of variables we have used throughout the book (Panel C of Table 7.1). Adjusting for children's age, gender, race, whether they were in the oversampled group, household income, mothers' education, mothers' age, hours per week mothers are employed, number of children, and for single mothers, whether they were cohabiting at the time of the interview, the pattern of findings is very similar to the pattern without control variables. Including the series of control variables, children in stepfamilies score significantly higher than their counterparts in divorced families on two measures—global well-being and socioemotional adjustment of children ages 5-11. The adjustment of preschoolers in first-married families is significantly higher than that of children in divorced families when covariates are considered, but differences across family types disappear in the academic performance of children ages 5-11.

FACTORS INFLUENCING WELL-BEING

Although many family scholars have focused on the effects of divorce or single-parent status on children's well-being, we have stressed that there are more proximate causes. In Chapter 6, we outlined these causes as they relate to mothers' well-being. Many of the same factors are also relevant in explaining children's well-being. Here we briefly describe some potentially important variables in explaining children's well-being.[1]

Resources and Other Background Variables

Family resources are often acknowledged as having an enormous effect on the well-being of children. Parents who have high education and income can invest these resources in their children. Such parents can provide a neighborhood where there is little crime, where there are excellent schools, and where their children are surrounded by other children who have professional aspirations. Economically oppressed single mothers who have limited education must reduce material consumption and move their families to poorer neighborhoods. Poorer neighborhoods are associated with inferior schools and higher rates of crime and delinquency, factors that could exert stronger and more direct influences than family type on children's well-being. Families with limited resources also may face obstacles such as minimal levels of nutrition and health care. Household size is an important consideration when resources must be divided among family members. As the parents' resources are spread over a larger family, each child receives less attention, emotional support, and economic support (Blake, 1989).

For children in divorced families, the length of time since the divorce is important because the stresses and adversities are greatest during and immediately following parental separation and divorce (Cashion, 1984; Kinard & Reinherz, 1984, 1986). Thus any adverse effects may be mitigated by time. With time the mother and children adjust to their new roles and relationships and may benefit from a social support system comprising new neighbors, friends, co-workers, and extended kin (Milardo, 1987; Savage, Adair, & Friedman, 1978; Stacey, 1991).

For single-parent families, we include whether the mother has a cohabiting partner. The presence of a cohabiting partner may influence family relationships and well-being in several ways. On the one hand, an extra adult may provide supervision, support, and control of children (Dornbusch et al., 1985), reducing stress on the single mother. On the other hand, it may introduce ambiguous or at least changing roles and relationships. Some single parents have other adults in the household who are not cohabiting partners. Whether relatives or nonrelatives, we consider their presence to be another family resource variable.

We saw in Chapter 6 that the number of hours per week that mothers are employed is an important influence on mothers' well-being, especially for divorced mothers. Beyond providing necessary financial resources for themselves and their families, employment enriches mothers' lives, provides a sense of personal control, and expands role models for children. Because maternal employment may influence family relationships and children's well-being in different ways in one family structure than in another, it is necessary that we include hours of paid employment as a control variable.

Other variables we must control to identify the effects of family structure include children's age, race, and gender, and whether the family was in an oversampled group.

Family Process Variables

For children living in families with married parents, several dimensions of marital and family relationships may influence child outcomes. Marital conflict, marital stability, and mothers' marital happiness shape the context in which children live. Studies suggest that levels of marital and family conflict are more important than type of family structure for understanding children's adjustment, self-esteem, and other measures of psychological well-being (Berg & Kelly, 1979; Demo & Acock, 1988; Emery, 1982; Raschke & Raschke, 1979). Marital unhappiness and conflict may confuse, bother, irritate, and distract children, especially younger children (Grych & Fincham, 1990).

Also important for children's development and well-being are relationships they have with their fathers. As often happens with other family relationships, father-child relationships are widely variable (Barnett & Baruch, 1987). Frequent interaction with a residential father may be an advantage if these relationships are positive, supportive, and nurturant (Barber & Thomas, 1986; Rollins & Thomas, 1979), but if the interaction is strained, sporadic, or highly conflicted, child well-being may be compromised (Cooper, Holman, & Braithwaite, 1983; Demo et al., 1987). In the analyses that follow, we consider the influence of fathers' enjoyable times with children, difficult times with children, the amount of time fathers spend in child care, and their involvement in a variety of youth-related activities.

The child's relationship with the mother may be even more important. Mothers, compared to fathers, typically spend more time with their children and invest themselves more directly in caring for their children (LaRossa & LaRossa, 1981; Montemayor, 1986; L. Thompson & Walker, 1989). If mother-child interaction is routine, enjoyable, and supportive, maternal involvement is likely to exert positive effects on children. Mothers also play an important role in monitoring and controlling children's actions, defining limits, and enforcing rules. Where mother-child relationships become difficult, where there is frequent or intense conflict, or where mothers rely on verbal or physical aggression to control their children, we would expect negative effects on child outcomes.

We anticipate that mothers who share culturally approved values about child outcomes (for example, considering it important that children do well in school and get along with peers) will have an advantage in providing an optimal socialization experience for their children. Similarly, we expect that both mother-child relationships and children's well-being will benefit when mothers' well-being is higher.

For children living in stepfather families, there are additional family relationships that may influence children's well-being. Unfortunately, we know much less about children's continuing relationships with nonresidential parents than we do about their relationships with residential stepparents (M. Coleman & Ganong, 1990). Consistent with the patterns we observed in Chapter 5, however, studies suggest reduced contact between children and nonresidential parents following remarriage (Furstenberg & Nord, 1985; Seltzer & Bianchi, 1988). The consequences for children of diminished parental involvement are unclear, but the available evidence suggests their well-being is unaffected (Clingempeel & Segal, 1986; Furstenberg & Nord, 1985). Here we consider nonresidential fathers' involvement with, and influence on, the child; mothers' conflict with nonresidential fathers concerning the child; and mothers' satisfaction with the amount of child support paid by fathers.

When we examine children living in single-parent families, we again consider the variables involving mothers' and children's relationships with nonresidential fathers. Unfortunately, in families headed by continuously single mothers, there often is insufficient information about nonresidential fathers. It is possible that this high level of missing data is due to nonresidential fathers being so uninvolved in these families that mothers chose not to answer questions about their former partners. Whatever the reason, our findings concerning the influence of nonresidential fathers on the well-being of children in continuously single-parent families need to be interpreted very cautiously.

CORRELATES OF CHILDREN'S WELL-BEING

Background Variables

The correlations between the background variables and each measure of children's well-being (global well-being, socioemotional adjustment, and academic performance) are presented in Appendix B, Table B.2. There are four panels (A through D) representing the correlations for first-married families, divorced families, stepfamilies, and continuously single-parent families, respectively. The table also reports in parentheses the number of cases on which each correlation is based. The global well-being variable has a large sample for all family types, but the sample sizes vary widely for other variables. We have relatively few divorced families with children ages 0-4, and we have even fewer stepfamilies with a child aged 0-4. Because continuously single mothers tend to be younger, we have very few continuously single-parent families with children ages 12-18.

A researcher who is interested in developing a complete model to explain a particular aspect of well-being surely would include other factors that go beyond the scope of our book. For example, characteristics of children's schools, neighborhoods (Bronfenbrenner, 1989; Brooks-Gunn, Duncan, Klebanov, & Sealand, 1993), peer relationships (Hartup, 1983), and activities in church and other youth organizations are important factors influencing children's well-being. Our purpose, however, is to identify the effects of family structure, related background characteristics, and selected family process variables. The importance of these family processes is that they offer an alternative explanation of children's well-being. Rather than family structure determining children's well-being, the nature of marital and family interaction may be the more proximate cause.

The bivariate correlations show that most of the background and resource variables have weak correlations with children's outcomes. For children living in first-married families (Panel A) and those living in families headed by divorced mothers (Panel B), household income is significantly correlated with only one variable—academic performance of children ages 5-11. Among children living in stepfamilies, household income is not significantly associated with any measure of well-being (Panel C). For continuously single mothers (Panel D), income is only significantly related to one variable—the socioemotional adjustment of adolescents.

In contrast to income, mothers' education is related to several aspects of children's well-being. The educational attainment of first-married mothers is significantly correlated with children's global well-being and with the socioemotional adjustment of children ages 5-11. In three of our family types, mothers' educational attainment is significantly related to children's academic performance. Continuously single mothers' education is significantly correlated with children's global well-being and with the socioemotional adjustment of children ages 0-4 and 5-11.

The number of hours per week that mothers spend in paid labor is not significantly correlated with any children's outcome variable for children living in first-married or stepfamilies. For children living in single-mother families, however, the number of hours mothers are employed each week is significantly related to both socioemotional adjustment and academic performance of 5 to 11-year-olds (in divorced families) and to the socioemotional adjustment of 12 to 18-year-olds (in continuously single-parent families).

We expected that household size would be negatively related to child outcomes because family resources would need to be spread over more people. The zero-order correlations show that, for first-married families, household size is negatively correlated with the global well-being of children. Greater size is associated with worse adjustment of 5 to 11-year-old children in families headed by divorced mothers. For stepfamilies, household size has no significant effects on children's well-being. In continuously single-mother families, larger household size is associated with lower global well-being of children of all ages, worse socioemotional adjustment of adolescents, and lower grades in school among adolescents.

An important finding regarding background variables is that race, measured as white or nonwhite, has few significant relationships to child outcome variables. In first-married families, race is significantly related to adjustment of children ages 5-11. Notably, children with white mothers have more adjustment problems. In families headed by divorced mothers, children with white mothers have lower global well-being. In continuously single-mother families, race has no significant effects.

We controlled for children's gender and age because of research indicating that boys and younger children have more adjustment problems. In contrast to other background variables, children's gender and age are consistently important. Based on zero-order correlations alone, and regardless of family type, boys tend to have lower global well-being and more adjustment problems. Older children also fare worse than younger children.

Length of marriage is negatively associated with global well-being of children living in first-married families. Marital duration is highly confounded with mothers' age, and the latter variable has an even stronger effect than marital duration does on children's well-being. Interestingly, length of marriage is positively associated with the adjustment of young children. Thus being married longer may provide some advantages for rearing very young children. In stepfamilies, however, there is no significant effect of length of marriage.

We expected that length of time since divorce would be significant in that the initial effects of divorce on children may be mitigated by time as mothers and children adjust to their new family roles. Our data, however, show no effects for length of time since divorce. We note that our cross-sectional data are limited in assessing this hypothesis, but it appears that for children whose parents have divorced, those whose parents have been divorced for several years have no advantage or disadvantage in terms of well-being or adjustment.

We suggested that the presence of a cohabiting partner may be a resource for single mothers or may add ambiguity to family and parent-child relationships. We find that for divorced mothers, having a cohabiting partner is associated with worse school performance among children ages 5-11 and 12-18. The academic performance of adolescents is also worse in families where continuously single mothers have cohabiting partners. These findings suggest that a cohabiting partner's presence may have a disruptive effect on parental involvement in and supervision of children's homework, but multivariate analysis is necessary to examine this and alternative hypotheses.

Family Process Variables

There are four clusters of family process variables, not all of which apply to a particular type of family. The clusters are marital relations, children's relations with residential fathers, children's relations with nonresidential fathers, and children's relations with mothers. The clear and consistent pattern across family types is that children's outcomes are more closely linked to family process variables than to background and resource variables. This pattern is illustrated in Figure 7.2. Although the figure illustrates the

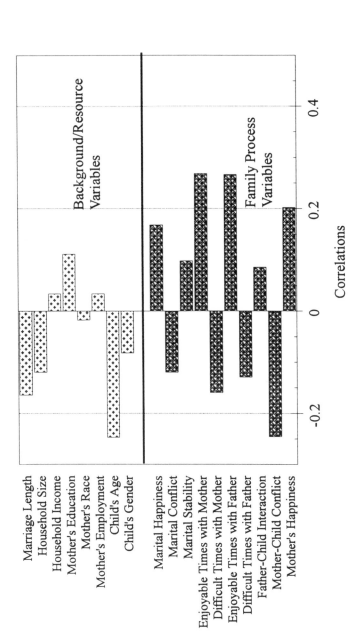

Figure 7.2. Background/Resource Versus Family Process Variables as Predictors of Child's Global Well-Being (first-married)

195

correlations for children in first-married families, the same pattern holds for children in the other three family types.

Marital relations. The bivariate correlations reveal a consistent relationship between parents' marital adjustment and children's well-being. In first-married families, mothers' marital happiness is associated with higher global well-being and better socioemotional adjustment for her children. Marital conflict, on the other hand, is inversely related to the global well-being and adjustment of children of all ages. Marital stability appears to enhance children's global well-being and adjustment and to bolster the academic performance of adolescents. These patterns are consistent across several measures of adjustment and suggest that family processes have a stronger influence than family resources on children's well-being.

In stepfamilies, the influence of marital relations on children's well-being is less pervasive. Children's global well-being is related to parents' marital happiness and to lower levels of marital conflict. Marital conflict in stepfamilies also is associated with diminished socioemotional adjustment of adolescent children. Marital stability is not related to the well-being of children in stepfamilies.

Children's relations with residential fathers. Our findings show that fathers can have a significant influence on their children. Although fathers have much lower levels of interaction with children than do mothers, the amount of time fathers spend with their children and the quality of this time are extremely important correlates of children's well-being. In first-married families, the amount of enjoyable time fathers and children share is related to children's global well-being and socioemotional adjustment, regardless of children's age. Difficult interaction between fathers and children diminishes children's adjustment and well-being and is associated with worse academic performance by adolescents. Other aspects of fathers' involvement, including participation in youth organizations and time spent caring for young children, are unrelated to children's well-being.

The general pattern is similar for stepfather-stepchild interaction.[2] The amount of enjoyable time stepfathers have with children is important, but this variable, compared to biological father-child enjoyable times, is not as consistently correlated with children's well-being. Further, the negative effects of difficult stepfather-stepchild interaction are even more pervasive than in first-married families.

Children's relations with nonresidential fathers. We have stressed that nonresidential fathers need not be absent fathers. Nonresidential fathers may still be involved with children, exercise influence over issues involving their children, provide child support, and cooperate with mothers in parenting. However, some nonresidential fathers choose to be uninvolved, and some are discouraged from involvement by mothers.

Our findings show that positive involvement by nonresidential fathers has some benefits for children, and negative involvement has adverse effects (Appendix B, Table B.2). However, the correlations between nonresidential fathers' involvement and children's well-being are much weaker than the corresponding correlations for children with residential fathers or stepfathers. In families headed by divorced mothers, child-related conflict between mothers and nonresidential fathers is associated with lower global well-being of children and with lower socioemotional adjustment of children five and older. Nonresidential fathers' involvement with children is correlated with two positive outcomes for children, enhancing the academic performance and socioemotional adjustment of children ages 5-11.

In stepfather families, interaction with nonresidential fathers is unrelated to children's well-being. Out of 24 correlations between children's well-being and aspects of nonresidential fathers' relations with their children and former spouses, not one correlation is statistically significant. Consistent with previous studies (Furstenberg & Nord, 1985; Seltzer & Bianchi, 1988), these findings suggest a greatly diminished role for nonresidential fathers, once their children form relationships with stepfathers.

Unfortunately, many questions were not answered pertaining to nonresidential fathers in continuously single-mother families.

Yet despite the fact that statistical significance is harder to achieve with smaller subsamples, mothers' dissatisfaction with child support from nonresidential fathers is significantly associated with lower global well-being of children, lower adjustment for children ages 5 to 11, and lower grades in school for 12 to 18-year-olds. Conflict between mothers and nonresidential fathers also is related to lower academic performance for adolescents. As with children living in divorced families, nonresidential fathers' involvement is positively related to adjustment and school performance of children age 5 and older. The level of influence nonresidential fathers exercise in coparenting also is positively related to children's global well-being.

Children's relations with mothers. Our findings underscore the importance for children's well-being of their relationships with mothers. In most cases, these relationships exert stronger influences than relationships with fathers. Across family types, children's well-being is higher when mothers report higher levels of enjoyable interaction with children, and children's well-being is lower when mothers report interaction with children is more difficult. For all four family types, and most notably in divorced families, mothers' support is consistently associated with positive outcomes for children. Surprisingly, mothers' control, at least as measured here, is uncorrelated with children's well-being.

Mother-child conflict and mothers' aggression toward children are strongly and inversely related to children's adjustment and well-being. Mothers' emphasis on children conforming to culturally prescribed norms is related to children's and adolescents' socioemotional adjustment. For all four family types, children's well-being is higher in families where mothers describe their own global well-being more positively.

Across diverse family structures, the clear pattern is that most variables involving mothers and their interaction with their children are strong and consistent predictors of children's adjustment. The heart of family process, as it pertains to outcomes for children, is the relationship children have with their mothers. The first section of this chapter presented evidence that family structure affects children's well-being. Most of these differences persist when relevant background variables are controlled. The second section illustrated that several family structure, background, and family process variables are correlated with children's well-being. The correlations suggest that family processes are more central than background variables to children's well-being and that relationships between mothers and children are especially important. In the next section we will evaluate a model that tests the independent effect of each variable on the measures of children's well-being. One limitation of the bivariate correlations is that they do not control for any of the background variables or family process variables we have discussed. Controlling for other variables greatly increases the complexity of the analysis, but it is necessary to assess the independent effects of the variables.

MODELS OF CHILDREN'S WELL-BEING

Because there are so many predictors, we eliminated several of them before doing the multiple regression analysis. First, we eliminated any variable that did not have a significant correlation with the dimension of well-being that we were examining. This eliminated quite a few variables. Second, we eliminated variables that had a large amount of missing data. Entering them in the multiple regression would result in too small a sample to obtain reliable estimates of the independent effects of the other independent variables. Most of the variables with a lot of missing data involve aspects of nonresidential fathers' involvement in stepfamilies and continuously single-mother families. The missing data may signify that many nonresidential fathers have especially limited roles in these two family structures.

Third, we eliminated any variable that was not significant in the multiple regression at the .10 level, and then reestimated the model. We continued eliminating variables that were not significant at the .10 level until all variables in the equation were significant at the .10 level or better.

We also restricted analysis to outcome variables that had sufficient cases for multiple regression. The regression analysis was conducted only for those measures of well-being that had at least 100 observations. Because relatively few stepfamilies have young children who are biological children of the mother from a prior marriage, we were not able to estimate a model for socioemotional adjustment or academic performance of young children (ages 11 and younger) in stepfamilies. Similarly, because relatively few continuously single-mother families have older children, we could not estimate a model for the socioemotional adjustment or academic performance of adolescents in this family type.

We conducted multiple regression analyses for each of the six measures of children's well-being described above: global well-being, socioemotional adjustment (measured separately for children ages 0-4, 5-11, and 12-18), and academic performance (measured separately for children ages 5-11 and 12-18). The results are summarized in Tables 7.2 through 7.7. The coefficients are standardized beta weights, which allow us to compare the relative importance of the different background, resource, and family process variables as predictors of children's well-being. Beta weights range from −1.0 to +1.0. A positive coefficient means that as values increase on the independent variable, children tend to have better adjustment. Correspondingly, a negative coefficient means that as values increase on the independent variable, children tend to have worse adjustment. For example, we would expect that mothers' education would have a significant positive coefficient—signifying that the higher the mother's education, the better the adjustment of her children. The standardized beta weights are different from the correlations because we are now controlling for every other variable in the model. For example, both household income and mothers' education may have moderate correlations with children's well-being. The beta weight tries to separate out the net effect of each of them, controlling for the other. Each table also includes the R^2. This is an overall measure of how well we can predict the child outcome variable. It tells us how much of the variability (variance) in the child outcome variable can be explained by the set of independent variables.

Factors Associated with Global Well-Being

When relevant background and family process variables are examined simultaneously, there are few background variables that significantly influence children's global well-being (Table 7.2). Only one of these—age of child—has a significant effect across all family types. The older the child, the greater the problems with global well-being, regardless of family type. This is an important finding because this is the only measure of children's well-being for which we have information on children ages 0-18. This effect is strongest in stepfamilies and weakest in continuously single-parent families. Race has a significant independent effect only in divorced families, with children of white mothers having slightly lower global well-being. Importantly, race does not have a significant independent effect in any other type of family. Boys have somewhat lower global well-being in first-married and stepfamilies, but not in single-parent families.

Mothers' education is associated with slightly better global well-being in first-married families and in continuously single-parent families. The effect for continuously single-parent families is somewhat stronger, suggesting that education of mothers who have never married may be the most important resource for strengthening the global well-being of their children.

Table 7.2 presents the R^2 values for background variables and for the combination of background and family process variables. It is clear that family process variables add a substantial explanatory ability above and beyond that of the background variables. For example, the background variables explain 7% of the variance in the global well-being of children in first-married families. When process variables are included, 17% of the variance can be explained. For divorced families, the background variables alone explain just 5% of the variance, compared to 18% when process variables are included.

Enjoyable mother-child and father-child interaction and higher well-being among mothers bolster children's well-being for children living in first-married families. Difficult mother-child interaction is associated with lower child well-being. Enjoy-

Table 7.2　Predicting Global Well-Being of Children Ages 0-18

Predictors	First-Married	Divorced	Stepfamily	Continuously Single
Background variables				
Race, (1) white, (0) nonwhite		−.09*		
Mother's education	.08*			.16**
Gender of child, (1) male, (0) female	.08**		−.14*	
Age of child	−.18***	−.21***	−.32***	−.10†
Family process variables				
Conflict with Nonresident Father		−.11**		
Dissatisfaction with child support from nonresident father				−.14**
Enjoyable time with father	−.14***		.18**	
Enjoyable time with mother	.07†	.11**		.18**
Difficult time with mother	−.19***	−.27***	−.24***	
Mother's global well-being	.11***	.18***	.11†	
R^2 with background variables only (N)	.07*** (1,067)	.05*** (676)	.15*** (274)	.06*** (418)
R^2 with all relevant variables (N)	.17*** (903)	.18*** (532)	.25*** (237)	.11*** (323)

NOTE: The coefficients are standardized beta weights. The inclusion of independent variables was based on the following criteria. First, all variables that correlated significantly with global well-being were included in a regression. Second, those variables, both background and family process variables, that were significant at the .10 level or better were kept, and the model was reestimated. Variables that met these criteria for any family type were included. †$p < .10$; *$p < .05$; **$p < .01$; ***$p < .001$.

able father-child interaction and higher well-being among mothers bolster children's well-being for children living in stepfamilies, whereas difficult times with mothers lowers well-being of children. Difficult mother-child interaction detracts from children's well-being in three of the family types—first-married, divorced, and stepfamilies. Conflict between mothers and nonresidential fathers in divorced families and dissatisfaction with child support among continuously single mothers reduce children's well-being.

Predicting Socioemotional
Adjustment of Children Ages 0-4

For three of our family types, we were able to examine the socioemotional adjustment of children under age 5 (Table 7.3). As explained above, there are too few cases in stepfamilies for meaningful regression analysis. Our findings indicate that background and resource variables are very limited. Mothers' education is associated with better adjustment among children in divorced and continuously single-parent families. Several variables we might expect to be important, such as household income, have no significant independent effect.

Family processes are very important in understanding the socioemotional adjustment of preschoolers in first-married families. The R^2 for background variables is just 2%, compared to 22% when family process variables are included. Enjoyable father-child interaction facilitates children's adjustment, while marital conflict and difficulties in either mother-child or father-child relations undermine children's adjustment. Curiously, there are no significant family process variables for young children in divorced families. In continuously single-mother families, mothers' own well-being is the most important family process variable, whereas difficult times with the child tends to lower the child's well-being.

Although a moderate portion of the variance in adjustment for young children is explained in first-married families, the variables we have used explain only a small portion of the variance in single-parent families. One problem is that our measure of young children's adjustment is one of the least reliable measures in our study (see Appendix A). At this developmental stage, the mothers' ratings may reflect day-to-day variability in how their child is doing rather than a stable pattern of adjustment. With our data, it is not possible to determine if the adjustment of young children is largely unrelated to family processes or if the problem is one of unreliable measurement.

Table 7.3   Predicting Socioemotional Adjustment of Children
Ages 0-4

Predictors	First-Married	Divorced	Continuously Single
Background variables			
Sample	–.18***		
Mother's education		.19†	.23**
Age of child		.19†	
Family process variables			
Marital conflict	–.19***		
Enjoyable time with father	.20***		
Difficult time with father	–.19***		
Difficult time with mother	–.14†		–.14†
Mother's global well-being			.19*
R^2 with background	.02**	.08*	.04*
variables only (N)	(318)	(101)	(157)
R^2 with all relevant	.22***	.08*	.12**
variables (N)	(294)	(101)	(130)

NOTE: The coefficients are standardized beta weights. The inclusion of independent variables was based on the following criteria. First, all variables that correlated significantly with socioemotional adjustment (ages 0-4) were included in a regression. Second, those variables, both background and family process variables, that were significant at the .10 level or better were kept, and the model was reestimated. Variables that met these criteria for any family type were included.
†$p < .10$; *$p < .05$; **$p < .01$; ***$p < .001$.

Predicting Socioemotional
Adjustment of Children Ages 5-11

The socioemotional adjustment of children in middle and late childhood is only modestly affected by background and resource variables (Table 7.4). Boys tend to have more adjustment problems than girls, but this effect is significant only in first-married families and continuously single-parent families. The single resource variable that is significant for children's adjustment is mothers' education, and this relationship holds only in the case of continuously single-mother families. You will recall that we obtained this same result in examining the adjustment of children ages 0-4. Together, these results suggest that mothers' education

Table 7.4   Predicting Socioemotional Adjustment of Children
Ages 5-11

Predictors	First-Married	Divorced	Continuously Single
Background variables			
Mother's education			.23***
Gender of child, (1) male, (0) female	−.12*		−.16*
Family process variables			
Conflict with nonresident father		−.13*	
Marital conflict	−.16**		
Enjoyable time with mother	.30***		.34***
Difficult time with mother	−.32***	−.44***	−.40***
Mother's support of child		.19***	
Mother's interaction with child		.15**	
Mother's aggression against child		−.14**	
R^2 with background variables only (N)	.01* (325)	.08*** (237)	.08** (153)
R^2 with all relevant variables (N)	.27*** (303)	.38*** (219)	.35*** (153)

NOTE: The coefficients are standardized beta weights. The inclusion of independent variables was based on the following criteria. First, all variables that correlated significantly with socioemotional adjustment (ages 5-11) were included in a regression. Second, those variables, both background and family process variables, that were significant at the .10 level or better were kept, and the model was reestimated. Variables that met these criteria for any family type were included.
†$p < .10$; *$p < .05$; **$p < .01$; ***$p < .001$.

may be a very efficacious way of helping children in families where the mother has never married. Other factors, such has having other adults in the household, household size, hours per week the mother is employed, race, and even household income, have no independent effect on the children's socioemotional adjustment.

Again, family process variables have far greater explanatory power than background variables. Table 7.4 shows that background variables explain from 1% to 8% of the variance in socioemotional adjustment of children between 5 and 11. When family process variables are included, we explain from 27% to 38% of the variance in socioemotional adjustment.

For children with first-married mothers, three family process variables have significant influences on adjustment: enjoyable mother-child interaction strengthens adjustment, whereas marital conflict and difficulties in mother-child relations hamper children's adjustment. Interestingly, no measures of father-child relationships exert significant effects when other variables are controlled.

The socioemotional adjustment of children with divorced mothers is significantly related to five dimensions of family interaction. Our findings demonstrate that children's adjustment is hampered by conflict between mothers and nonresidential fathers and by difficulties in mother-child dynamics, the latter variable exerting a strong negative effect. Mothers' aggressive behavior toward children further detracts from children's socioemotional adjustment. In general, higher levels of mothers' interaction with children improves children's adjustment. The quality of the interaction also is important, however, as divorced mothers who provide more emotional support for their children report their children are better adjusted.

For children with continuously single mothers, the key factor is the quality of time the mother spends with the child. If their interactions are enjoyable, the children are better adjusted. If their interactions are difficult, the children's adjustment is worse.

Predicting Academic
Performance of Children Ages 5-11

Unlike the other aspects of children's well-being we have examined, the academic performance of children in elementary schools is more strongly influenced by background and resource variables than by family process variables for children from first-married or divorced families (Table 7.5). Academic performance represents a dimension of children's behavior that is very different from their general well-being, happiness, or socioemotional functioning. Although these aspects of well-being are correlated with one another, some children are quite happy despite

Table 7.5 Predicting Academic Performance of Children Ages 5-11

Predictors	First-Married	Divorced	Continuously Single
Background variables			
Household Income	.12*		
Mother's education		.13*	.26***
Gender of child, (1) male, (0) female	−.23***	−.16**	−.24**
Age of child	−.14*		
Family process variables			
Difficult time with mother		−.19**	−.24**
Mother's support of child			.26***
R^2 with background variables only (N)	.11*** (299)	.08*** (237)	.07*** (149)
R^2 with all relevant variables (N)	.11*** (299)	.12*** (236)	.21*** (141)

NOTE: The coefficients are standardized beta weights. The inclusion of independent variables was based on the following criteria. First, all variables that correlated significantly with academic performance (ages 5-11) were included in a regression. Second, those variables, both background and family process variables, that were significant at the .10 level or better were kept, and the model was reestimated. Variables that met these criteria for any family type were included.
*$p < .05$; **$p < .01$; ***$p < .001$.

doing poorly in school, whereas others are not happy despite doing very well in their schoolwork.

Background variables account for 11% of the variance in school performance among children in first-married families, and family process variables add nothing to this. Our data show four significant background/resource variables in first-married families: girls and younger students do better, and children's academic performance is facilitated by higher family income and mothers' education. It is noteworthy that, consistent with other aspects of well-being we examined, education has a significant influence over and above the influence of family income.

Earlier we explained that we did not include all possible family process variables. It is likely that there are several family process variables that would explain substantial variance in school performance. For example, we did not include time spent helping the child with homework, time spent in school, or participation in school-related activities. Each of these may have positive effects on school achievement (Astone & McLanahan, 1991; Cochran & Dean, 1991; Maeroff, 1992). When other variables are controlled, however, the more general family processes we have examined are not significantly related to children's school performance.

In divorced families, as in first-married families, girls perform better in school than boys do. Another indication that mothers' education is an important resource is that this variable is a strong predictor of academic perfomance among children in divorced families. One family process variable is significant: Mothers who have difficulty interacting with their children have children who perform worse in school.

A similar pattern exists in continuously single-parent families, with girls outperforming boys in schoolwork. In terms of family processes, mothers who have difficulty interacting with their children have children who perform worse in school, whereas more supportive mother-child relationships are related to children doing better in school.

Predicting Socioemotional
Adjustment of Adolescents, Ages 12-18

Adolescence is widely regarded as a period of enormous change, maturation, and development. Early in this life stage, adolescents experience cognitive changes, notably the development of formal operational thought, as well as physical and physiological changes that stir new ways of thinking about oneself (Demo, 1992b). Adolescents tend to be very introspective and self-conscious, thinking and worrying about their appearance, their popularity, and others' attitudes toward and expectations of them (Damon & Hart, 1982; Rosenberg, 1979). Their social world also changes, evidenced by heightened peer involvement, emancipation from parents, and increasing interest in dating and sexual activity. In these and other ways, adolescence is a crucial and difficult stage for socioemotional adjustment.

Theories of adolescent development typically emphasize extra-familial influences, especially peer group affiliation and friendship relations, and suggest a reduced role for families, as evidenced by adolescents' increasing independence and distancing from parents (Bell, 1981; Douvan & Adelson, 1966; Youniss & Smollar, 1985). Peers, mass media, and other social institutions are posited to supplant the family in shaping adolescents' attitudes and behavior. Evidence for this position would be reflected in family process variables being relatively unimportant influences, and background and family resource variables being very important influences on adolescent adjustment.

The background and resource variables should be prominent because they shape the opportunities children have. For example, higher parental education and family income often provide opportunities for children to attend the best schools and increase exposure to other adolescents who have high educational and occupational goals. By contrast, low income, education, and minority status restrict educational opportunities and increase the exposure to peers who have low educational and occupational aspirations.

Our findings, summarized in Table 7.6, refute the view that family relations are unimportant to adolescents. No social background or family resource variable has a significant influence on the socioemotional adjustment of adolescents in any family type, but several family process variables are important in each family type. Whereas background variables explain none of the variance in adolescent socioemotional adjustment, family process variables explain from 37% to 54% of the variance.

For first-married families, marital conflict has a highly surprising independent effect on adolescent adjustment in that it appears that marital conflict increases the adjustment of adolescents. This nonintuitive finding needs to be interpreted cautiously. There is considerable colinearity between marital conflict, mother-adolescent disagreement, and mothers' aggression toward adolescents. In fact, compared to its correlation with adolescents' adjustment, marital conflict is much more strongly correlated with mother-adolescent disagreement and with mothers' aggression toward adolescents. Because all three of these variables

Table 7.6   Predicting Socioemotional Adjustment of Adolescents, Ages 12-18

Predictors	First-Married	Divorced	Stepfamily
Background variables			
None are significant			
Family process variables			
Marital conflict	.14*		
Difficult time with father			−.29***
Enjoyable time with mother	.18***	.14**	
Difficult time with mother		−.28***	
Mother-adolescent interaction		.14**	
Mothers' support of adolescent			.30***
Mother-adolescent disagreement	−.44***	−.39***	−.46***
Mothers' childrearing values			.20**
Mothers' aggression toward adolescents	−.18**		
Mothers' global well-being	.21***		
R^2 with background variables only (N)	.00	.00	.00
R^2 with all relevant variables (N)	.37*** (234)	.43*** (280)	.54*** (120)

NOTE: The coefficients are standardized beta weights. The inclusion of independent variables was based on the following criteria. First, all variables that correlated significantly with socioemotional adjustment (ages 12-18) were included in a regression. Second, those variables, both background and family process variables, that were significant at the .10 level or better were kept, and the model was reestimated. Variables that met these criteria for any family type were included.
*$p < .05$; **$p < .01$; ***$p < .001$.

involve conflict, we estimated a separate equation that included marital conflict but did not include the two mother-adolescent variables (mother-adolescent disagreement and mothers' aggression toward adolescents). In this regression, marital conflict has a significant negative effect on adolescent socioemotional adjustment. The key finding is that the net effect of conflict is negative. Mother-adolescent disagreement and mothers' aggression toward adolescents are both significant predictors of socioemotional problems for adolescents.

In first-married families, mothers' reports of frequent, enjoyable interaction with their children are significantly associated with better socioemotional adjustment of their adolescent children. Similarly, mothers whose own global well-being is higher have better adjusted children. Importantly, the variables involving first-married fathers have no significant influence on the adjustment of adolescents.

For divorced families, the important family process variables are the quality of interaction between the mothers and adolescents—more frequent and enjoyable interaction increasing adolescents' adjustment and difficult relations detracting from it. Further, as in both first-married families and stepfamilies, mother-adolescent disagreement is the strongest predictor of adjustment problems.

In stepfamilies, another family process adversely affecting adolescent adjustment is difficulties in stepfather-adolescent interaction. Family processes bolstering adolescent adjustment include highly supportive mother-adolescent relationships and mothers holding higher expectations for their adolescent children to conform to culturally valued norms.

Adolescence may be a life stage punctuated by parent-adolescent disagreement (Collins, 1990; Montemayor, 1986) and by increasing peer and extrafamilial involvement, but our findings document the pivotal role that relationships with parents play in shaping the socioemotional adjustment of adolescents. None of the social background and family resource variables we examined exert significant independent effects on adolescent well-being. Our measures of family process, on the other hand, explain from more than one third to more than one half of the variance in adolescent socioemotional adjustment. As important as other contexts are for adolescent development, these results reaffirm the pervasive influence of family relations.

Predicting Academic Performance
in Adolescents, Ages 12-18

Consistent with our findings regarding the academic performance of children ages 5-11, we find that academic performance of

Table 7.7   Predicting Academic Performance in Adolescents, Ages
12-18, Measured by Grades in School

Predictors	First-Married	Divorced	Stepfamily
Background variables			
Mother's cohabiting		−.15**	
Mother's education	.21***	.12*	.17*
Gender of adolescent, (1) male, (0) female	−.15**	−.16**	−.19*
Age of adolescent	−.16**		
Family process variables			
Enjoyable time with father			.17*
Mothers' control of adolescent		.14*	
Mother-adolescent disagreement	−.28***	−.34***	−.31***
Mothers' aggression toward adolescents	−.10†		
R^2 with background variables only (N)	.06*** (296)	.07*** (290)	.08** (124)
R^2 with all relevant variables (N)	.17*** (280)	.20*** (280)	.22*** (122)

NOTE: The coefficients are standardized beta weights. The inclusion of independent variables was based on the following criteria. First, all variables that correlated significantly with academic performance (ages 12-18) were included in a regression. Second, those variables, both background and family process variables, that were significant at the .10 level or better were kept, and the model was reestimated. Variables that met these criteria for any family type were included.
†$p < .10$; *$p < .05$; **$p < .01$; ***$p < .001$.

adolescents is influenced by their age, gender, and mothers' education (see Table 7.7). Mothers' education is associated with better grades for students in first-married families, divorced families, and stepfamilies alike. Girls have higher grades than boys, regardless of family type. Older children have worse grades in first-married families, but this effect is not significant in divorced or stepfamilies.

In divorced families, mothers' having a cohabiting partner is associated with lower grades for adolescents. This is the only outcome variable for children of any age that is influenced by the presence of a cohabiting partner. Clearly, the presence of a cohabiting partner in the household changes roles and expectations for all family members. It may be that mothers in these households spend less time monitoring adolescents' homework and study habits and that cohabiting partners are disinclined to get involved.

Although some background variables are significant predictors of adolescent school performance, the process variables appear to be more important. Background variables explain from 6% to 8% of the variance in school performance. When process variables are included, the models explain between 17% and 22% of the variance. Still, in comparison to adolescents' socioemotional adjustment, school performance is much less sensitive to family process variables.

For all three family types in this analysis, mother-adolescent disagreement exerts the strongest influence, negatively affecting school performance. In first-married families, mothers' aggression toward adolescents also has a significant adverse effect on adolescents' grades in school. In divorced families, mothers' control of adolescents exerts a significant beneficial effect on adolescents' academic performance. An additional influence on adolescents' academic performance in stepfamilies is enjoyable stepfather-adolescent interaction, which boosts adolescents' grades. The set of social background, resource, and family process variables collectively explains a moderate amount of the variance in school grades.

SUMMARY AND CONCLUSIONS

Examining a nationally representative sample of children and adolescents living in four diverse family structures, we find few statistically significant differences across family types on measures of socioemotional adjustment and well-being. For each of six measures of children's and adolescents' well-being, there is the possibility that six statistically significant differences would be obtained by comparing across four family types. Thus 36 statistically significant differences are possible across family types. Controlling for relevant social background variables, we find that one measure (academic performance of children ages 5-11) produces no significant differences, two measures each yield one significant difference, two measures each yield two significant differences, and one measure (global well-being) generates five significant differences (shown in Panel C of Table 7.1). That is, 25 out of 36 comparisons across family types show differences that fail to achieve statistical significance. In other words, the differences in children's and adolescents' adjustment *within* family types are greater than the differences *between* family types.

One comparison yields consistent differences: children and adolescents in first-married families score higher than their counterparts in divorced families on five of the six measures of adjustment and well-being. Although the differences tend to be small, they exist on several important aspects of children's well-being, and they persist when many relevant variables are controlled. It bears repeating that on most measures, the only group of children that can be statistically distinguished from children in divorced families is children in first-married families. On average, children in divorced families are very similar in adjustment to their counterparts in stepfamilies and continuously single-parent families.

The findings described here underscore the pivotal role of family processes in shaping children's socioemotional adjustment and well-being. Children and adolescents who are happier, get along well with others, and are less anxious and fearful are those who have enjoyable relationships with their mothers and fathers, have relatively low levels of conflict with their parents, and whose mothers enjoy a stronger sense of well-being. Collectively, family process variables account for between one third and one half of the variance in children's and adolescents' well-being.

The strongest and most consistent predictors of adjustment problems for children and adolescents are variables measuring mother-child disagreement and mothers' aggression directed toward their adolescent children. The magnitude and consistency of these effects across several dimensions of children's well-being provide strong support for the family conflict hypothesis. We also need to recognize that these relationships are likely to be reciprocal. Although we have stressed that family relationships—and parental behaviors in particular—influence children's and adolescents' adjustment, the statistical associations we have observed also reflect the common experience in which children's behavior problems irritate and anger parents, who respond with parental reprimands, sanctions, and/or aggression. In some families this may become a vicious cycle in which parents verbally (and sometimes physically) abuse their children, thus harming children's adjustment, and as the adjustment worsens, this causes the parents to be even more aggressive against the children. Although the cross-sectional nature of our data prevents us from estimating the magnitude of such reciprocal effects, there is ample evidence that family relationships are highly interdependent, that child-related concerns are stressors for parents, and that children's behavior and well-being influence both mothers' and fathers' behavior and well-being (Demo et al., 1987; Greenberger & O'Neil, 1990; Kidwell, Fischer, Dunham, & Baranowski, 1983).

High levels of conflict between parents and children clearly are disadvantageous for children and deleterious to their well-being. But we also need to recognize that much, perhaps most, of the conflict between generations is minor (Collins, 1990; Montemayor, 1986) and that some conflict is important and necessary. Disagreements between parents and adolescents, for example, are important in that they bring issues out into the open, prompt relationships to be renegotiated, and facilitate adolescent adjustment and individuation (Holmbeck & O'Donnell, 1991). It may be that the relationship between parent-child conflict and children's well-being is curvilinear, with moderate levels associated with optimal adjustment.

We have observed that few social background or family resource variables are significantly associated with children's or adolescents' well-being *within* family types. This is not to say that factors such as race, mothers' education, and household income are unimportant to children's well-being. We illustrated in Chapter 3 that there is substantial variability *across* family types on these domains. For example, compared to mothers in other family structures, continuously single mothers tend to be younger, are more likely to be black, and tend to be poor. But the analyses described here show that family process variables are much more important than background or resource variables in accounting for variation in children's and adolescents' well-being within family types. Children's age and gender are important, however, with older children and boys having more adjustment problems, at least according to mothers' reports. It is worth reiterating that we are relying on mothers' perceptions of children's well-being. Mothers may see more problems as children get older, children may cause more problems or more significant problems for mothers as they get older, deflating mothers' accounts of children's well-being. Consistent with previous research, girls are also described as having far fewer adjustment problems than boys have (Guidubaldi & Perry, 1985; Hetherington et al., 1982). We also note that mothers' education is strongly related to the well-being of children in continuously single-mother families. This effect is independent of income and indicates that education is a valuable resource that provides knowledge, meaning, and skills for single mothers and their families.

Unlike most measures of children's and adolescents' socioemotional adjustment and well-being, their academic performance is more strongly influenced by social background and family resource variables than by family processes. Children and adolescents from higher income families and with more highly educated mothers perform better in school and earn higher grades. Girls also outperform boys. In Chapter 8 we discuss the broader implications of family resources and family processes for children's well-being, and the importance of socioeconomic resources, in particular, for family stability and well-being.

NOTES

1. Parts of Chapter 7 are derived from work by F. Carson Mencken and Alan C. Acock (1989).

2. Our subsample of stepfamilies is defined by the presence of at least one child who was born before the current marriage. For these children, the residential father is a stepfather. In some of these families, however, there may be children who were born during the current marriage, for whom the residential father is the biological father.

EIGHT

Beyond Family Structure

At the beginning of this book we reflected on American marriage and family life—how families have been reshaped by high rates of teenage and nonmarital childbearing, sharp increases in the divorce rate, postponed marriage and childbearing, smaller families, single-parent families, stepfamilies, and dual-earner marriages. We sought to examine how these developments have influenced marital, postmarital, and parent-child relationships. Were family members better served by the traditional family? Are today's diverse arrangements meeting family members' needs just as well, or even better? How important is *family structure* in shaping family relationships? Does family structure have an important influence on the social and psychological well-being of family members? How important are *family processes*? Could family processes be as important or even more important than family structure?

In searching for answers we analyzed extensive data collected from a nationally representative sample of American families and households. We concentrated on a subsample of 2,457 families, all of which included children and their biological mothers living in the same household. We examined many aspects of relationships between wives and husbands, between former spouses and coparents, and between parents and children. One of our objectives was to describe common characteristics of family relationships in first-married, remarried, divorced, and continuously single-parent families. Another objective was to trace the consequences of these diverse family experiences for the well-being of mothers and their children.

Several important patterns and consistent themes emerged. One long-standing pattern we observed is the tremendous amount of household labor performed by women. Many other studies have documented the lopsided division of labor in two-parent families, with women typically performing three fourths of all housework (Berk, 1985; Huber & Spitze, 1983). Few studies have explored how single-parent families divide domestic responsibilities (Voydanoff, 1987). Further, many studies have relied on small convenience samples of white, middle-class families (Spitze, 1988). Our findings suggest that across a broad spectrum of American families—across single-parent, two-parent, first-married, and remarried families; across families of diverse socioeconomic and racial backgrounds; and across families in which women are employed as well as those in which they are not employed—women do two to three times as much housework as their husbands or cohabiting partners. Increasing family diversity has not changed the division of domestic labor.

Other family processes are firmly established and resistant to change, despite profound changes in the composition and structure of American families. Although they are often physically present in the household, husbands, male partners, fathers, and stepfathers tend not to be significantly involved in family life. This theme is evident across many dimensions of family labor and caregiving. As fathers, many men in two-parent families are functionally absent (LaRossa, 1988). Compared to fathers, mothers in two-parent households are deeply and routinely involved in their children's lives. In both first-married and stepfamilies, fathers spend less time than mothers in leisure activities with children and working on a project or playing with children, have fewer private talks with children, help them with homework less often, eat meals with them less regularly, and spend less time caring for them. Stated simply, parenting, like housework, is gendered family labor. Other studies document numerous additional familial responsibilities shouldered by women, including emotion work, kinkeeping, and caregiving for aging parents, parents-in-law, and ill spouses (Abel & Nelson, 1990; Boyd & Treas, 1989). In general, "everyday and ultimate responsibility for marriage, housework, and parenthood usually remains with women; and responsibility for breadwinning usually remains with men" (Thompson & Walker, 1989, p. 864). Collectively, these findings provide compelling evidence that popular descriptions of changes in gender, marital, and family roles have been overstated. Although images abound in the popular culture and literature portraying "liberated" men who are fully involved in their families, the evidence indicates this is not typical in American families. Furthermore, a focus on role change obscures more complex dynamics. For example, although further research is necessary to substantiate our conclusion, it appears that many men *are* doing more housework than men did in the 1960s. However, more important patterns are often overlooked—that while some men are doing substantially more housework than their predecessors a generation ago, most men are doing only slightly more; that most women are doing more housework than their predecessors and substantially more than their husbands or male partners; and that a focus on how men have changed masks persisting aspects of gender inequality.

There are also some noteworthy similarities and differences in parent-child and couple relations across family types. Mothers of children of all ages and in all family types attribute considerable importance to children learning and conforming to culturally valued guidelines for behavior. This is significant because popular commentators, politicians, and some social scientists blame many societal problems on single mothers, claiming that they represent a decline in family values, rules, and expectations (Whitehead, 1993). The evidence suggests that any problems associated with single-parent families cannot be attributed to "poor" childrearing values, lack of rules, or low expectations for children. Instead, disadvantages for parents and children in single-parent families typically stem from sustained economic hardship (Lempers et al., 1989; McLoyd, 1990).

Parent-child interaction processes are distinguishable across family structures, revealing some strengths of first-married families and revealing both strengths and concerns involving stepfamilies. Although previous studies suggest unique stresses and less emotional closeness associated with stepparent-stepchild relationships (Ganong & Coleman, 1987; White & Booth, 1985), less is known about parent-child relationships following remarriage (Coleman & Ganong, 1990). The extensive information collected in the National Survey of Families and Households (NSFH) enables us to compare many relationships across family types. Mothers in their first marriage report the highest levels of enjoyable interaction with their children and describe relations with their children as more pleasant and less stressful. Mother-child, father-child, and stepfather-stepchild relations in stepfamilies are described in less favorable terms. Mothers in stepfamilies describe the things they do as less interesting and not as well done and themselves as less appreciated and lonelier. They also report more verbal and physical aggression directed toward children. Compared to first-married, biological fathers, stepfathers have less frequent enjoyable interaction with their stepchildren. Children in stepfather families interact less frequently with their nonresidential fathers than children in divorced families. Collectively, these findings suggest that children in stepfather families are disadvantaged in that they spend less time with a variety of parents and stepparents, and the time they spend together is less enjoyable. However, it is important to keep in mind that most of these differences across family types are small. Further, and consistent with previous research (Amato, 1987), we find high levels of maternal support for children of all ages in all four family structures.

Comparing numerous aspects of marital relationships in first marriages and remarriages, our findings call into question the view of remarriage as an incomplete institution (Cherlin, 1978). For intergenerational relations, and at the level of stepfamily life, remarriages with stepchildren seem less satisfactory and more stressful for children. But at the couple level, remarriages with stepchildren have many strengths in comparison to first marriages, including more frequent marital interaction and sexual intercourse and less arguing. Previous studies found remarriages to be very similar to first marriages in marital satisfaction, quality, interaction, tensions, and conflict (Vemer et al., 1989; White & Booth, 1985), although remarriages with stepchildren were identified as having lower marital quality (White & Booth, 1985). Yet all of the remarriages we studied included stepchildren, and mothers described the marriages in very favorable terms, as happy and stable marriages, and as superior to first marriages in some respects. Mothers are the biological parents in our sample, however, and stepfathers may describe things differently. We were not able to examine this possibility, but White and Booth (1985) report that in remarriages with stepchildren, stepparents judge marital quality to be lower than biological parents do.

FAMILY STRUCTURE, FAMILY PROCESSES, AND MOTHERS' WELL-BEING

There are several differences in mothers' well-being across family types, with single mothers generally having lower well-being and feeling more depressed than married mothers. Being married, especially for mothers in their first marriage, appears to enhance mothers' well-being. It is important to note that this pattern may not hold for other groups of women, such as nonparents or parents of adult children. But the evidence suggests that, for many women, the rewards of marriage outweigh the costs, that marriage provides social integration, and that husbands provide a source of social support, including forms of emotional and instrumental support. Husbands and fathers typically limit themselves to "helping out" in family labor and caregiving, and as we saw in Chapter 4, single women and married women perform about the same amount of household labor. But without fathers' contributions to parenting, single mothers take on added responsibilities, burdens, anxieties, and stresses (Thompson & Ensminger, 1989).

The key to mothers' happiness and well-being lies not in family structure, but in family processes. Important correlates of mothers' well-being include the nature and quality of marital relations, mother-child relations, and children's well-being. First-married and remarried mothers benefit psychologically from marital happiness, stability, and equity, and from low levels of marital discord. But perhaps the single most important determinant of mothers' well-being is the sense that their children are doing well. Where there are difficulties in mother-child relationships, mothers' well-being diminishes (Greenberger & O'Neil, 1990). Single mothers, although maligned in the popular culture, depend even more than married mothers on their children's well-being. Problems experienced by children in single-mother families are not due to reduced psychological investment in children any more than they are due to poor values.

Another important dimension of family processes is children's relations with their fathers. Our findings illustrate that, for both children and mothers, the regularity and quality of fathers' involvement are more important than fathers' physical presence. Residential husbands and fathers who are significantly involved in family life, who are supportive and affectionate, contribute in meaningful ways to the well-being of mothers and children. When they are not involved, or when they are negatively involved, mothers' and children's well-being suffer. Many divorced mothers describe their current parenting role as preferable to their preseparation parenting role, presumably because there are fewer disagreements and tensions regarding fathers' involvement in parenting. For both divorced and continuously single mothers, there is substantial variation in the frequency and quality of interaction with their children's nonresidential fathers. When this interaction is constructive, there are clear benefits for both mother and children.

FAMILY STRUCTURE, FAMILY PROCESSES, AND CHILDREN'S WELL-BEING

As with mothers' well-being, family process variables are more influential than family structure in shaping children's well-being. Across six measures of children's and adolescents' well-being, differences within family types are far greater than differences between family types. It is clear that if we are to understand the most important forces influencing children and adolescents, we need to move beyond studies designed to compare children's adjustment across two or more social addresses (Bronfenbrenner & Crouter, 1983) and accept the challenge of identifying more proximate familial and extrafamilial experiences shaping children's lives.

Family process variables are especially important for children's socioemotional adjustment and global well-being, explaining between one third and one half of the variance in these dimensions of children's well-being. Characteristics of family relations that enhance children's socioemotional adjustment and well-being include enjoyable mother-child and father-child interaction, low levels of parent-child conflict, and higher maternal well-being. Aggression directed toward children is strongly associated with lower well-being among children of all ages. By contrast, with family process variables controlled, background characteristics and family resources explain only a small amount of the variance in children's outcomes.

Although we have documented few differences in children's well-being across a broad variety of family structures, there is one important exception to this pattern: children and adolescents living in postdivorce, mother-headed families consistently exhibit lower well-being than their counterparts living in first-married families. Generally, the differences are small, consistent with findings obtained in other studies. Amato and Keith (1991) reviewed 92 studies comparing the well-being of children living in divorced single-parent families with that of children in continuously intact two-parent families, and found a median effect size of .14 of a standard deviation.

Still, it is important that we identify the family arrangements and processes that are detrimental to children who experience parental divorce. Several aspects of children's relationships with residential mothers and nonresidential fathers are significantly and consistently associated with children's well-being in these families. Particularly troubling for children are frequent disagreements with parents, difficulties interacting with them, persistent conflict with both mothers and nonresidential fathers, and parental aggression. Indeed, the typical life course of children whose parents divorce is marked by multiple forms of family conflict. Many children suffer lingering effects from sustained predivorce marital discord (Emery, 1982; Grych & Fincham, 1990; Porter & O'Leary, 1980) and a concomitant deterioration in parent-child relationships (Hess & Camara, 1979; O'Leary & Emery 1984). One mechanism through which marital conflict weakens parent-child bonds is inconsistent parenting practices (Emery, 1982). Other consequences of marital conflict include interspousal aggression and parent-child aggression (Jouriles, Barling, & O'Leary, 1987). Thus, for many children in divorced families, lower postdivorce well-being stems, in part, from lower predivorce well-being. Marital conflict and interspousal aggression also reduce mothers' well-being, inhibiting mothers' parenting and their abilities to satisfy their children's needs. Compounding these problems are a series of processes associated with persisting postdivorce inter-parental conflict and hostility: children being drawn into conflicts, feeling caught between parents (Buchanan, Maccoby, & Dornbusch, 1991) and pressured to take sides, or trying to remain close with both parents and experiencing loyalty conflicts (Clingempeel & Segal, 1986; Wallerstein & Blakeslee, 1989). Whereas in many families parent-child and parent-adolescent disagreements tend to be minor, the range of conflicts commonly experienced in divorced families may serve to fuel, aggravate, and intensify everyday disagreements arising between parents and children.

Consistent with previous studies (Amato & Keith, 1991), our findings provide strong support for the family conflict hypothesis. We recognize, however, that some types of conflict probably have beneficial effects. There are many situations in which mothers, fathers, and children have different interests, and some conflict is inevitable if they assert themselves. The complete absence of conflict implies that the distinct interests of mothers, fathers, and/or children are being suppressed. We examined many aspects of family conflict, most of which could be considered destructive rather than constructive in nature. Violence and aggression, in particular, have consistently adverse effects. Interparental and parent-child conflict also are inversely related to children's well-being. But we need to recognize that periodic and mild forms of conflict, such as marital disagreements or disagreements between parents and children, may be constructive and adaptive. Further, the cross-sectional nature of our research prevents us

from determining the direction of the effects, and we need to ac-
knowledge that children's socioemotional and behavioral problems
increase the likelihood of parent-child and interparental conflict.

Our study adds considerable support for the importance of
family processes in shaping children's well-being, but we do not
want to overlook the infuence of family resources. Mothers'
education, in particular, facilitates children's well-being across
family types. Further, when mothers' education and household
income are included in the same model, mothers' education is the
dominant variable. This suggests an important aspect of maternal
education that has been neglected in economic studies that gauge
education largely in terms of its effect on income. Mothers' education may improve the quality of family processes—parenting
practices, support, family communication—in ways not tapped
by income alone. Background and resource variables exert their
strongest effects in boosting the academic performance of children, and are less important for explaining the social and emotional adjustment of children.

THEORETICAL IMPLICATIONS

Much of the research done on contemporary families is guided
by standard structural-functionalist assumptions and concepts
(Kingsbury & Scanzoni, 1993). Essential concepts including norms,
roles, and interdependent institutions helped to organize our
study. However, traditional structural-functional thought on the
family has received only limited support. Like modern families,
postmodern families exhibit a substantial degree of role differentiation. But as women have increased involvement with institutions outside the family (principally through employment) they
remain the primary source of family labor. Parsonian structural
functionalists, in particular, emphasized the distinction between
instrumental and expressive leaders. In many postmodern families, however, women enact both roles. Women, who often had
important instrumental roles in modern families, have greatly
increased these activities in postmodern families, whereas any
increase in men's expressive activities is minimal. Many men's

reluctance to become more involved in their families, or even to be committed to their families, has been to the disadvantage of women and children. We have observed throughout this study that there are numerous benefits for women and children when husbands and fathers are actively and positively involved in both instrumental and expressive activities.

Nontraditional family structures (postdivorce families, stepfamilies, and continuously single-mother families) are far less problematic than suggested by traditional structural functionalism. Affective solidarity appears to be much more important than structural functionalism would predict. The concept of nonresidential fathers and stepfathers as potentially active participants in the family was not anticipated by structural functionalists, but regular and meaningful involvement by these nontraditional parents has consistently positive consequences for children.

Social exchange and equity theories posit the importance of maximizing individual rewards and balancing profits in relationships, but the complexity lies in the different ways people define what they value. There seems to be an inherent contradiction between the assumption that individuals are purely rational and the reality that many mothers (including employed mothers) perceive the division of household labor as equitable when they are doing most of the work. It is difficult to ascertain the values that drive particular comparisons, as well as the reasons that a particular group is chosen over others as a comparison group. Greater theoretical precision may be attained if aspects of reference group theory were integrated with social exchange theory. The concept of comparison level seems especially important in how mothers evaluate their own cost/benefit ratio. Rather than comparing their ratio to that of their husband, many women seem to be comparing their ratio to that of other mothers who are similarly disadvantaged. Because other mothers define their comparison level, these mothers may be satisfied with a situation that an objective observer would see as an unjust or inequitable relationship.

Social exchange and equity theories also provide important foundations for the prediction that family processes are more important than family structure for individual well-being. In this respect, the theories are strongly supported. Our study produced consistent evidence that family structure per se has limited and modest effects on mothers' and children's well-being, and we found impressive empirical support for the influence of family process on both mothers' and children's well-being.

In support of both equity theory and feminist theories, we found that balanced relationships strengthen mothers' well-being. However, it is important to distinguish between psychological equity and objective equity. Feminists have argued that women need to be aware of the objective inequity. There is evidence supporting this position. For example, although many women feel their relationships are equitable, the degree to which relationships are perceived as equitable is a significant predictor of mothers' well-being.

Families have always been much more diverse than is suggested by the nostalgia associated with the monolithic nuclear family of the 1950s and early 1960s. Growing diversity in family structure means that most families no longer resemble this idealized family form. Yet many family processes, dynamics, and arrangements characterizing traditional families have changed very little. In particular, women continue to do the vast majority of household labor and family caregiving. Prevailing paradigms that focus on popular concepts such as family change and role change obscure more important realities and complexities of family dynamics.

The work women and men do in families needs to be recognized and valued, not trivialized. Family labor is necessary and important and it is much more than "women's work." Yet boys continue to be taught that housework is not important and, in many households, they are asked to do very little of it (Berk, 1985; Goldscheider & Waite, 1991). Sons are also more resistant than daughters to assume housework responsibilities in families where mothers are employed (Goldscheider & Waite, 1991). To challenge prevailing assumptions, debunk myths, and foster a learning environment in which equality is firmly valued, "educators and practitioners must think, teach, and act in ways that will bring change in their own lives, the lives of those they teach and serve, and in society" (Allen & Baber, 1992, p. 379).

IMPLICATIONS FOR PRACTITIONERS

Family therapists are likely to see many female clients who are quite angry about their marital or cohabiting relationships. Many of these women may be confused and distraught because of the contradictions between the images and messages in the popular culture that portray contemporary relationships as egalitarian and the burdensome, oppressive reality of their own lives. The men with whom these women live may hold egalitarian beliefs and attitudes, and they may feel righteous because they do more housework and child care than their fathers did. The women may feel angry and exhausted because they do all the family labor their mothers did while at the same time managing the responsibilities associated with paid employment. Importantly, the division of housework is associated with women's, but not men's, marital and personal happiness (Thompson & Walker, 1989). For wives, lower marital satisfaction and personal well-being are associated with husbands' unwillingness to share in household labor (Pleck, 1985; Staines & Libby, 1986). Premarriage and marriage counselors need to help couples develop strategies to negotiate housework and housework standards. For example, who decides who does the laundry, who decides how the laundry shall be done, and who decides when it shall be done? Hawkins and Roberts (1992) argue that for interventions of this kind to be effective, they must focus on couples rather than individuals. They suggest several strategies for increasing male involvement and facilitating equity, including strengthening marital communication, encouraging wives to request involvement by their husbands, helping wives to relinquish responsibility for housework, and connecting housework with child care.

LIMITATIONS AND STRENGTHS OF THE STUDY

Because process variables are difficult to measure, they are rarely included in studies based on large, nationally representative samples (Dawson, 1991). The major strength of this study is its ability to evaluate the importance of family process variables. We have been able to compare the independent effects of different family process variables and to compare their effects with the effects of family resources, background variables, and family structure.

Many studies on the effects of family structure have been limited to small or clinical samples. In contrast to a sample of a special population, such as people who see counselors because of adjustment problems, we have a probability sample. For example, our sample includes divorced families that have adjustment problems, families where the problems are serious, and families where there are no adjustment problems. A probability sample allow us to represent the full range of experience within each family type.

The comparative nature of our study also is a major strength. Many studies are limited by samples that focus on one family structure, such as children living in single-parent families, precluding comparisons with other types of families. Other studies involve two family structures, typically comparing single-parent and two-parent families, but they blur important distinctions within single-parent families and within two-parent families. We have been able to compare four prevalent family types. Many other studies have used samples that were too small to make statistically reliable interpretations. Because the NSFH is a large sample, we have been able to make many estimations that would not have been possible with other studies.

Despite these strengths, there are still noteworthy limitations to this study. First, there are limitations imposed by cross-sectional data. When we compare the global well-being of children in divorced families to children in first-married families, we may exaggerate the effects. Changes in marital status are not random events. Mothers who are happy and have happy children are not likely to get divorced. To estimate the effects of divorce on children, the ideal study would compare these children's well-being to what it had been before the divorce. Longitudinal data (which will be available with Wave 2 of the NSFH) will permit much more precise evaluation of the true effects of family structure.

There are other limitations of our study. Although we have made important distinctions between family structures, such as between divorced and continuously single mothers, it would be useful to have even greater differentiation between family types. For example, continuously single mothers are disproportionately poor and black, but a rapidly growing group of continuously single mothers is white. There is an emerging group of white, predominantly professional mothers who choose not to marry. We have tried to address this by using statistical controls; future studies will need to examine more refined family typologies. Some other important avenues for future research include family relationships in different types of stepfamilies (Coleman & Ganong, 1990) and estimation of how parents and children are affected by multiple transitions in family structure through the life course.

An important limitation of our descriptions of American families is that we have relied almost exclusively on mothers' reports of family relationships and family members' well-being. The perspectives of other family members surely would be different and would alter the pattern of findings. This limitation is perhaps most serious in our analysis of children's and adolescents' well-being. Ideally, we would compare mothers' reports with those of fathers, children, and perhaps teachers. The NSFH did not collect information from children or members outside the household, but data were collected from many fathers and stepfathers. As explained in Chapter 3, we elected to examine mothers' reports for all families rather than have mothers' reports for some families and fathers' reports in other families.

CONCLUSIONS

The findings presented in this book call into question a number of common assumptions and popular stereotypes associated with traditional nuclear family ideology. Across numerous aspects of marital relations, parent-child relations, mothers' well-being, and children's well-being, the strikingly consistent pattern is that *the variance within each family type is greater than the variance across family types*. These findings present a challenge to family researchers who continue to be guided by simplistic classifications of family structure and by an assumption that a first-married nuclear family (preferably with the mother unemployed, but at least with the mother principally responsible for childrearing) is the optimal environment for marital happiness and for rearing healthy, adjusted children. The evidence is persuasive that these structural variables alone tell us very little about the everyday interaction patterns and proximate experiences that shape family members' social and psychological well-being.

The findings also refute many popular stereotypes. For example, teachers, politicians, and popular commentators are simply wrong if they assume that single mothers do not value their children's education, do not have high educational expectations for their children, or do not impose family rules. What is needed to support these families is not rhetoric but changes in social policy and the provision of social programs and special services to meet their needs. Policymakers need to recognize differences between single mothers who are divorced and those who are continuously single. Continuously single mothers work fewer hours and have dramatically less income. The average continuously single mother has family income that exceeds the poverty level by roughly $400. This means she has virtually no money to invest in herself or her children. To support continuously single mothers and their children, we need social programs and policies that support women's employment, such as more accessible and more affordable quality child care. Employers need to expand options such as flextime, job sharing, sick leave, and maternal leave, and workers need to be supported and encouraged to take advantage of such programs when companies offer them (Hochschild, 1992).

The goal of this book was not to write an apology for any family type, nor to attack any family type. The goal was to describe the realities and complexities of family interaction across diverse family structures. But a clear message that resonates from the findings is that the future strength of single-parent and two-parent families rests on greater responsibility and more nurturant involvement of residential and nonresidential fathers. Their presence per se can be advantageous or disadvantageous for children as well as for the children's mothers. But in the end, fathers must understand, appreciate, and fulfill their responsibilities whether they are physically present or not.

APPENDIX A

Coding and Items
Used in Analysis

Who should read this appendix? The National Survey of Families and Households (NSFH) data are in the public domain. For the benefit of interested scholars who may want to replicate or extend our analyses, we provide details on the specific items we used and how we coded them. Where scales were used, we also include information on reliability. Rather than detract from the continuity of the text, we provide this technical information in this appendix. Most readers will be able to understand the entire text without reading this appendix, though many readers may want to refer to the appendix at various points for specific information.

The NSFH includes more than 4,200 actual or computed variables for each household. Although we use a large number of variables, our data include only a subset of the variables listed in the codebook. The following is a listing of the specific questions, organized by chapters. We provide the exact wording of each question used in the analysis for each chapter, along with other pertinent information for each item. We report the item name as shown in the National Survey of Families and Households Codebook. The codebook labels all items answered by the respondent in the main interview with an *M*, followed by the question number (e.g., M205 would be main interview, question 205). Items answered by the respondent in a self-administered questionnaire start with an *E*, followed by the number of the questionnaire schedule, and finally by the item number (e.g., E705 refers to a self-administered/enumerated questionnaire Number 7, Item 5). Some items involve the response of the spouse/partner to a self-administered questionnaire. A few items were worded differently if a person was cohabiting: the word *partner* was substituted for any reference to a spouse. These items start with an *S*, followed by the item number. Items with other starting letters represent variables computed by the NSFH staff.

There are several general conventions we used to recode the items. Some items refer to a particular child who is randomly selected from a list of eligible children. This may be a child under 5, a child living with the mother who has a nonresident father, and so on. Where a particular child is the reference for an item we have put *(child)* or *(he/she)* in the item. In the actual interview, the name of the child would be substituted. Questions that involved a dichotomy such as yes or no were typically recoded so that a score of 1 signified yes and a 0 signified no.

Some items were worded in a positive direction and some in a negative direction. We recoded the answers so that a higher score represents more of the variable. For example, when we use a scale to measure depression, a higher score means the person is more depressed. When we use a scale to measure adjustment, a higher score means better adjustment.

CHAPTER 1:
FAMILY STRUCTURE IN CONTEXT

We eliminated many of the respondents because they did not meet our requirements. All respondents with any of the following characteristics were deleted: M2DP01 = 2 indicates the respondent was a male. MFOCAL1 = 96 indicates there was no child aged 0 to 18. M2NUM = 1 indicates it was a one-person household. M2CP01 = 2, 4, or 9 indicates the mother was separated, widowed, or did not indicate her marital status. M95 = 99 means the mother did not indicate how many times she had married.

Defining Family Types

The following variables were used in the definitions of the family types and were applied to the respondents remaining after Step 1 above. Some of the items appear to be redundant. This provided separate checks on the coding scheme. Thus any mothers who gave inconsistent answers (e.g., by saying she was married at one point in the survey and saying she was not married at another point) were eliminated.

Item M2CP01 asked the marital status of the respondent: 1 for married, 2 for separated due to marital problems, 3 divorced, 4 widowed, 5 continuously single. MARCOHAB was computed by the NSFH staff using the following code: 1 married, living with spouse; 2 married, spouse absent; 3 cohabiting—separated; 4 cohabiting—divorced; 5 cohabiting—widowed; 6 cohabiting—continuously single; 7 not cohabiting—separated; 8 not cohabiting—divorced; 9 not cohabiting—widowed; 10 not cohabiting—continuously single. HHTYPE was computed by the NSFH staff using the following code: 1 married couple household, 2 one-parent family, 3 other family household, 4 one-person household, 5 cohabiting couple household, 6 other nonfamily household. M95 asked: "Altogether, how many times have you been married?" (number of times from 0 to 7 coded). S50 asked the spouse/partner: "How many times have you been married?" (1 for once, 2 for twice, 3 for three times, or 4 for four or more times). K2 is a computed variable indicating whether the mother has any biological children under 18 who are not the biological children of her spouse/partner living in the household (1 yes and 0 no). This was used in limiting stepfamilies to those where the mother had a biological child. The final variable used was NUMBER, meaning the number of children a mother had who were not the child of her spouse/partner and were conceived while she was in a prior marriage. We computed this using three variables: M204, the number of children to whom the mother had given birth; M205p01m-M205p012m, the date of birth of each child; and MAREND, the date the previous marriage ended. NUMBER was given a value of 1 if at least one of the mothers' children was born prior to the end of her last marriage or up to 10 months after her last marriage ended. This means that the child was born, or at least conceived, while she was married.

First-married mothers. First-married mother families consisted of families in which the mother answered 1 on M2CP01 (meaning married), answered 1 for MARCOHAB (meaning married, living with spouse), 1 on HHTYPE (meaning married couple household), 1 for M95 (meaning she had been married just once), and for S50, answered either 1 or more than 4 (meaning her husband said this was his first marriage, or we did not have an answer from him on that item). As a further check, we used M2EP02 to M2EP15 to ensure that there was no household member who was a stepchild (4) of the mother.

Divorced mothers. Divorced mother families consisted of families with M2CP01 = 3 (meaning divorced), MARCOHAB = 4 or 8 (meaning divorced, living without a cohabiting partner, or divorced, living with a cohabiting partner), HHTYPE = 2 (meaning it was a one-parent family), NUMBER = 1 (meaning she had a child in her previous marriage or within 10 months after it ended). HHTYPE = 2 was used only for those with a 4 on MARCOHAB.

Stepfamily mothers. Stepfamily mother families consisted of families in which the mother answered 1 for M2CP01 (meaning married), 1 for MARCOHAB (meaning married, living with spouse), 1 on HHTYPE (meaning married couple household), a score of more than 1 on M95 (meaning she had been married more than one time), and a 1 on K2 (meaning she had a biological child in the household who was not a biological child of her spouse).

Continuously single mothers. Continuously single mother families consisted of families with these answers: M2CP01 = 5 (never married), HHTYPE = 2 (meaning single-parent family), MARCO-HAB = 6 or 10 (cohabiting, never married, or not cohabiting never married), M2EP03 to M2EP11 not equal 4 (no stepchildren present), and F1REL not equal 4 (verifying no stepchildren). HHTYPE = 2 was used only for those with a 10 on MARCOHAB.

CHAPTER 3:
RESEARCH DESIGN
AND PROFILE OF AMERICAN FAMILIES

Deleting Cases and Defining Family Types (See Chapter 1)

Weighting. Some parts of Chapter 3 use weighted data to estimate the values for the United States. The weighting was done using the variable labeled WEIGHT. This was used to account for whether the mother was in the main sample or the oversampled group, the selection probability based on the number of adults in the household, differences in response rates for various groups, and a poststratification adjustment to replicate the U.S. population by age, race, and sex based on the Current Population Survey. For this weighting the individual mother is the unit of analysis. Mothers who were oversampled for any reason are weighted less than other mothers.

Mothers' education. EDUCAT is a variable computed by the NSFH staff to measure years of education. It ranges from 0 for *no formal education* to 20 for *doctorate or professional degree.* The scoring attempts to take into account the class standing of a respondent who enrolled in college or professional school but did not receive a degree, and to redefine postgraduate work to identify those who obtained a degree and those who began working on a degree but did not complete it.

Race. M484 asked: "Which of the groups on this card best describes you?" (1 Black; 2 White—not of Hispanic origin; 3 Mexican American, Chicano, or Mexicano; 4 Puerto Rican; 5 Cuban; 6 Other Hispanic; 7 American Indian; 8 Asian; or 9 other). RACE was coded as a 1 if M484 was 2; otherwise, RACE was coded 0. Thus RACE represents white, non-Hispanics versus all others.

Age and gender. The mothers' age was measured by Item M2BP01, age of respondent, in years. Many of the items about children focused on a randomly selected child. MFOCAL1 refers to a randomly selected child under age 19 who is a biological, step, adopted, or foster child of the mother or a child of her cohabiting partner. MFOCAL2 refers to a biological child of the mother under age 19 living in the household with only one biological parent in the household. Items F1AGE and F2AGE measure the age of the child. Items F1SEX and F2SEX identify their sex (1 male and 2 female). Items F1REL and F2REL measure their relationship to the mother (3 biological child, 4 stepchild, 5 adopted child, 6 foster child, 7 child of lover/partner). AYOC is a computed variable, age of the youngest child. The child must be the biological, step, adopted, foster child, or child of lover/partner. LSTA1NUM is the number of children on List A (MFOCAL1) who are age 4 or younger. List A includes all children age 18 and younger on household roster with relationship of biological child, stepchild, adopted child, foster child, or child of lover/partner. LSTA2NUM is the number of children on List A who are 5 to 18.

Household income. IHTOT2 is a variable computed by the NSFH staff. It represents the household's total income, including income of respondent and spouse from interest, dividends, and other investments. IRTOT2 is the amount of this income, in dollars, that the wife provides. IPOVLINE is a computed variable showing the poverty line income for a family of a given size and number of related children. The difference between the income and this figure was used to compute income above the poverty level.

Mothers' hours of employment. A series of items was used to estimate the hours a mother is employed outside the home. M528 asked: "Now let's talk about your full-time and part-time work experience. Are you currently working for pay in any job?" (1 yes, 2 no, 3 currently in armed forces). Mothers who answered no to M528 were assigned no hours of employment. Mothers who answered that they were currently in the armed forces were assigned 40 hours of employment. M535 asked: "How many hours did you work last week?" (coded as hours). M536 asked: "Do you have a job from which you were absent last week?" (1 yes and 2 no) and M537 asked: "Is this the number of hours that you usually work?" (1 yes and 2 no). Those for whom the answer was yes to either M536 or M537 answered M538: "How many hours a week do you usually work?" If there were no answers to M535, M536, or M537, the mother was defined as not employed any hours.

Other household characteristics. N2NUM asked the number of people living full time in the household. ADNONREL asked how many of them were adult nonrelatives. ADREL asked how many of them were adult relatives. E1306 asked if the maternal grandmother was in the household. E1316 asked if the maternal grandfather was in the household. All of these were coded 1 for yes and 2 for no. AYOC asked the age of the youngest child in the household.

Location. METRO is a computed variable: 1 if living in standard metropolitan statistical area, or 2 if living in an area outside a standard metropolitan statistical area. REGION is a computed variable coded 1 for Northeast, 2 for North Central, 3 for South, and 4 for West.

Sample versus oversample group. Blacks, Chicanos, Puerto Ricans, one-parent families, cohabiting couples, and persons who were recently married were among those oversampled. The computed variable SAMPLE (1 if in main sample and 2 if in oversample) was used as a control variable.

CHAPTER 4:
MARITAL, POSTMARITAL,
AND NONMARITAL RELATIONS

Role allocation and domestic division of labor. Spouses who reported spending extremely high amounts of time on particular tasks, amounts equivalent to more than three standard deviations above the mean, were recoded to the value corresponding to three standard deviations. The value of three standard deviations was computed using weighted data. Some respondents had a difficult time estimating the hours they work and estimated impossibly large numbers. Truncating at three standard deviations above the mean eliminates such outliers.

Questions used for household tasks. The NSFH used the following format to determine how household chores were handled: "The questions on this page concern household tasks and who in your household normally spends time doing those tasks. Write in the approximate number of hours per week that you, your spouse/ partner, or others in the household normally spend doing the following things." The variables are shown in Table A.1

Table A.1   NSFH Data on Household Tasks

| | | Variable Names | | |
| | | Spouse/ | Other | Other |
Variable	Mother	Partner	Under 19	Over 19
Preparing meals	E1A1	E1A2	E1A3	E1A4
Washing dishes	E1B1	E1B2	E1B3	E1B4
Cleaning house	E1C1	E1C2	E1C3	E1C4
Outdoor Tasks	E1D1	E1D2	E1D3	E1D4
Shopping	E1E1	E1E2	E1E3	E1E4
Washing, ironing	E1F1	E1F2	E1F3	E1F4
Paying bills	E1G1	E1G2	E1G3	E1G4
Auto maintenance	E1H1	E1H2	E1H3	E1H4
Driving	E1I1	E1I2	E1I3	E1I4

Role strain regarding household chores. Table A.2 shows the semantic differential items used to measure role strain on a scale from 0 to 7. The items involve polar opposites regarding housework. The items were labeled E203A to E203F. Items were coded so a higher score indicated greater strain.

Table A.2   NSFH Data on Role Strain Involving Housework

QUESTION: Circle the number that describes the work you do around the house								
interesting	0	1	2	3	4	5	6	7	boring
appreciated	0	1	2	3	4	5	6	7	unappreciated
overwhelming	0	1	2	3	4	5	6	7	manageable
complicated	0	1	2	3	4	5	6	7	simple
lonely	0	1	2	3	4	5	6	7	sociable
poorly done	0	1	2	3	4	5	6	7	well done

Sexual relations. Item E705 asked: "About how often did you and your husband have sex during the past month?" (number of times).

Quality of relationship and frequency of interaction. Two items were used. Item E701 asked: "Here are a few questions about your current marriage. Taking things all together, how would you describe your marriage?" Responses ranged from 1 for *very unhappy* to 7 for *very happy.* Item E704 asked: "During the past month, about how often did you and your husband spend time alone with each other, talking, or sharing an activity?"

Role strain regarding marital relations. This used the same semantic differential scale shown above for role strain regarding household chores. The question was, "How would you describe the things you do as a wife?" The items were labeled E206A to E206F. They were coded so a higher score indicated greater role strain.

Husband-wife disagreement. This was measured using nine items, seven of which have the same format. The seven are based on answers to the question, "The following is a list of subjects on which couples often have disagreements. How often, if at all, in the last year have you had open disagreements about each of the following?" The answers ranged from 1 for *never* to 6 for *almost every day.* The items and their topics were: E706A—household tasks, E706B—money, E706C—spending time together, E706D—sex, E706E—having another child, E706F—in-laws, and E706G—the children.

The other two items are based on answers to the following questions: (E707B) "There are various ways that married couples deal with serious disagreements. When you have a serious disagreement with your husband, how often do you discuss your disagreements calmly?" The answers ranged from 1 for *never* to 5 for *always.* E707C involved arguing heatedly or shouting at each other.

Marital instability. Five items were used to assess marital instability. Item E715 asked: "During the past year, have you ever thought that your marriage might be in trouble?" (1 for yes or 2 for no). Item E716 was a follow-up question: "Do you feel that way now?" (1 for yes and 2 for no). Item E717 asked: "During the past year, have you and your husband discussed the idea of separating?" (1—"yes, I brought it up the first time," 2—"yes, my husband brought it up the first time," or 3—no). Item E718 asked: "It is always difficult to predict what will happen in a marriage, but realistically, what do you think the chances are that you and your husband will eventually separate or divorce?" (answers ranged from 1 for *very low* to 5 for *very high*).

Spousal violence. Two items were used to assess spousal violence. Item E707D asked mothers: "There are various ways that married couples deal with serious disagreements. When you have a serious disagreement with your husband, how often have you ended up hitting or throwing things at each other?" (answers ranged from 1 for *never* to 5 for *always*). Item E708 asked: "Sometimes arguments between partners become physical. During the last year has this happened in arguments between you and your husband?" (1 for yes or 2 for no).

Divorced and stepfamilies: Postmarital relations of mother and non-resident parent. We used four items:

- M356: "Next, I'd like to ask you some questions about the child and his/her father. Is (child's) father still living?" (1 for yes and 2 for no).
- M358: "About how far away from here does he live?" (actual or estimated miles).
- M366: "How often do you talk about (child) with his/her father?" (1 for *not at all*, 2 for *about once a year*, 3 for *several times a year*, 4 for *one to three times a month*, 5 for *about once a week*, and 6 for *several times a week*).
- E412: "During the past year, how often have you had any contact with your former husband (by phone, mail, visits, etc.)?" (coded the same as M366 above).

Divorced and stepfamilies: Conflict with former spouse. Three sets of questions were used. The first series asked: "How much conflict do you and (child's) father have over each of the following issues?" (1 for *none*, 2 for *some*, and 3 for *a great deal*). The issues included M368A—where the child lives, M368B—how the child is raised, and M368C—how the mother spends money on the child. Three items were used to measure dissatisfaction, M385A to M385C. Answers ranged from 1 for *very satisfied* to 5 for *very dissatisfied*. All mothers who had experienced a marital separation since January 1, 1977, were asked E402: "How would you describe your current relationship with your former husband?" (1 *very unfriendly* to 5 *very friendly*). E402 was reverse coded with a 1 signifying *very friendly* to a 5 signifying *very unfriendly*.

CHAPTER 5: PARENT-CHILD RELATIONS

Childrearing values for children ages 0-4. Mothers were asked: "How important is it to you that your children. . ." (answers ranged from 1 for *not at all important* to 7 for *extremely important*). The items we used were:

E903A—importance of following the rules
E903B—do well in school
E903C—be independent
E903D—be kind and considerate
E903E—control their temper
E903F—importance of always doing what is asked
E903G—carry out responsibilities on their own
E903H—do well in creative activities such as music, art, or drama
E903I—keep busy by themselves
E903J—get along well with other kids
E903K—do well at athletics
E903L—try new things.

All items have a loading of .48 to .72 on the first principal component. The alpha reliability for this scale was .854.

Childrearing values for children ages 5 to 18. Mothers were asked: "How important is it to you that your children. . ." (answers ranged from 1 for *not at all important* to 7 for *extremely important*). The items we used were:

E1005A—always follow family rules
E1005B—do well in school
E1005C—be independent
E1005D—be kind and considerate
E1005E—control their temper
E1005F—always do what you ask
E1005G—carry out responsibilities on their own
E1005H—do well in creative activities such as music, art, or drama
E1005I—keep busy by themselves
E1005J—get along well with other kids
E1005K—do well in athletics
E1005L—try new things.

Loadings of the first principal component ranged from .53 to .69. The alpha reliability for this scale was .856.

Rules for children 0 to 4. M301 asked: "Do you restrict the amount of television that (child) watches?" (1 for *yes*, 2 for *no*, 3 for *don't have a television*; an answer of 3 was recoded to 1 because this restricts television time). M302 asked: "Do you restrict the type of programs that (he/she) watches?" (1 for *yes*, 2 for *no*).

Rules for children 5 to 11. Nine items were asked regarding rules for children between 5 and 11. Five of these asked: "Would (child) be allowed to be at home alone? (coded 1 for *yes*, 2 for *sometimes/it depends*, and 3 for *no*). The items are:

M312A—in the morning before school
M312B—in the afternoon after school, between 3:00 and 6:00 p.m.
M312C—all day, when there is no school
M312D—at night, if you were gone until midnight
M312E—overnight, if you went on a trip.

Item M313 asked: "When (child) is away from home, is (he/she) supposed to let you know where (he/she) is?" (answers ranged from 1 *all of the time* to 4 *hardly ever*). This was recoded so that a higher score signified more supervision. M314 asked: "Do you restrict the amount of television that (he/she) watches?" (1 *yes*, 2 *no, 3 try but not successful).* This was recoded so *try but not successful* was between yes and no. The coding was also reversed so that a score of 1 indicated no restrictions and a score of 3 indicated there were restrictions. M315 asked a similar question concerning restrictions on the type of programs. It was scored the same way. M316 asked: "Does (he/she) have regular chores to do around the house?" (1 for yes, 0 for no).

Rules for children 12 to 18. M335 asked: "When (child) is away from home, is (he/she) supposed to let you know where (he/she) is?" (1 for *all the time* to 4 for *hardly ever*). This was reverse coded so a 1 indicated *hardly ever* and a 4 indicated *all the time.* M336 asked: "Do you restrict the amount of television that (child) watches?" (1 for *yes,* 2 for *no,* and 3 for *try*). Responses of 3 were recoded to between yes and no, and the item was reverse coded so 1 was no restriction and 3 was restriction. M337 asked: "Do you restrict the type of programs that (he/she) watches?" This was recoded as M336 above. M338 asked if the child had regular chores and it was coded using a 1 for yes and a 0 for no. M347 asked if the child was allowed to earn money outside of the family. It was coded so a 1 signified yes and a 0 signified no. The number of times the child dated in the last month was measured by Item M351. Five items asked: "Would (child) be allowed to be at home alone?" (1 for *yes,* 2 *sometimes/it depends,* or 3 for *no*). The items were:

> M334A—in the morning before school
> M334B—in the afternoon after school, between 3:00 and 6:00 p.m.
> M334C—all day, when there is no school
> M334D—at night, if you were gone until midnight
> M334E—overnight, if you went on a trip.

Finally, E1360B asked their agreement to the statement: "It is all right for unmarried 18-year-olds to have sexual relations if they have strong affection for each other" (1 *strongly agree* to 5 *strongly disagree*).

Educational expectations. Item M277 asked: "Even though it may be a long way off, how much education do you think (child 0 to 18) will probably get?" (1 *not finish high school,* 2 *graduate from high* school, 3 *graduate from vocational or trade school,* 4 *graduate from a 2-year junior or community college,* 5 *complete 1 to 3 years of college,* 6 *graduate from a 4-year college or university,* 7 *complete a master's or doctorate degree).* E1359D asked mothers' opinion on the statement: "Parents ought to help their children with college expenses" (1 *strongly agree* to 5 *strongly disagree*).

Overall involvement with children. M284 asked: "During the past 30 days, how often did you have an especially enjoyable time with (child)?" M285 asked: "How often in the past 30 days did you argue or have a lot of difficulty dealing with him/her?" M286 asked: "What about your (husband/partner)? During the past 30 days, how often did he have an especially enjoyable time with (child)?" (scored same as M284). M287 asked: "And how often did he argue or have a lot of difficulty dealing with the child?" All of these questions were recorded on a scale of 1 *never* to 6 *almost daily.*

All mothers were asked: "During the past 12 months, how much time did you and your husband or partner spend in an average week in each of the following organized youth activities as a participant, advisor, coach, or leader (hours per week)?" The items were E1004A1—parent-teacher organizations, E1004B1—religious youth group, E1004C1—community youth groups (e.g., scouts), E1004D1—team sports or youth athletic clubs. Respondents were given their mean response for the four items as long as they answered at least three of them.

Interaction with children 0 to 4. The first two items were asked if there was a child ages 1 to 4. M291 asked: "Does (child) attend a nursery or preschool?" (1 *yes* and 2 *no*). This was recoded so a 1 was yes and a 0 was no. M292 asked: "How many days each week does (he/she) attend (actual number of days)?"

Three items were asked of mothers who had a child age 0 to 4 but no child age 5 to 18 in the household. These mothers were asked: "How often do you spend time with your children..." (1 for *never or rarely* to 6 for *almost every day*). The items were E901A—on an outing away from home (at parks, museums, zoos, etc.), E901B—at home playing together, and E901C—reading to child.

The last three items concern a specific child 0 to 4 without other restrictions. M298A asked: "About how many hours in a typical day do you spend taking care of (child's) physical needs, including feeding, bathing, dressing, and putting (him/her) to bed (number of hours/day)?" M298B asked: "About how many hours in a typical day does your (husband/partner) spend taking care of (child's) physical needs, including feeding, bathing, dressing, and putting (him/her) to bed (number of hours/day)?" M303 asked: "During the past week, about how often did you get a chance to read to (child)?" (1 *not at all* to 4 *almost every day*)?

Mother-child interaction for children ages 5 to 18. Item E1001A asked: "How many days last week did you eat breakfast with at least one of the children?" (0 for *no days* to 7 for *every day*)? Item E1001B asked: "How many days last week did you eat dinner with at least one of the children?" (coded same as E1001A). Four items were asked about other activities using the stem: "How often do you spend time with the children. . ." (responses ranged from 1 for *never or rarely* to 6 for *almost every day*). Item E1002A asked about leisure activities away from home such as picnics, movies, sports; item E1002B asked about time at home working on a project or playing together; item E1002C asked about having private talks; and item E1002D asked about helping with reading or homework.

Maternal support and control. For mothers with children under age 5, but none 5 or older, maternal support was measured by two items. Mothers were asked: "Listed below are several ways that parents behave with their children. Please indicate how often you do each" (1 for *never* to 4 for *very often*). Item E902A asked about praising the child, and item E902C asked about cuddling or hugging the child. Maternal support was measured by three items for mothers with children between 5 and 18. Mothers were asked: "Listed below are several ways that parents behave with their children. Please indicate how often you do each" (1 for *never* to 4 for *very often*). Item E1003A asked about praising the child, E1003B asked about allowing child to help set the rules, and E1003D asked about hugging the child.

Control was measured separately for children 5 to 11 and 12 to 18. Five items concerned children 5 to 11. M317 asked: "How often do you remind (child) to do (his/her) chores?" (1 for *all the time* to 4 for *rarely or never*). M319 asked: "Is (he/she) required to complete (his/her) chores before playing, watching television, or going out?" (1 for yes, 2 for no, and 3 for *sometimes/it depends*). M320 asked: "Does (child) receive an allowance?" (1 for *yes* and 2 for *no*)? Those answering yes were also asked M322: "Does this allowance pay (him/her) for work that (he/she) regularly does around the house?" (1 for *yes* and 2 for *no*). M323 asked: "In addition to this allowance, is (he/she) paid for extra jobs done around the house?" (1 for *yes* and 2 for *no*). The yes/no items were recoded so a 1 signifies *yes* and a 0 signifies *no*.

Six items concerned children 12 to 18. M330 asked: "Is (he/she) required to complete (his/her) homework before playing, watching television, or going out after school?" (1 for *yes*, 2 for *no*, and 3 for *sometimes/it depends*). M339 asked: "How often do you remind (child) to do (his/her) chores?" (1 *all of the time* to 4 *rarely or never*). M341 asked: "Is (he/she) required to complete (his/her) chores before playing, watching television, or going out?" (1 *yes*, 2 *no*, or 3 *sometimes/it depends*). M342 asked: "Does (child) receive an allowance?" (1 *yes*, 2 *no*). Those answering yes were also asked M344. M344 asked: "Does this allowance pay (him/her) for work that (he/she) regularly does around the house?" (1 *yes*, 2 *no*). M345 asked: "In addition to this allowance, is (he/she) paid for extra jobs done around the house?" (1 *yes*, 2 *no*). The yes/no items were recoded so a 1 signifies *yes* and a 0 signifies *no*.

Areas of mother-child disagreement for children ages 12 to 18. Mothers with children ages 12 to 18 were asked how often they disagreed with the child on 10 issues. The stem was: "In the last 12 months, how often have you had open disagreements with (child) about each of the following?" (1 for *never* to 6 for *almost every day*). The items were

M350A—dress code
M350B—girlfriend/boyfriend

M350C—friends
M350D—how late (he/she) stays out at night
M350E—helping around the house
M350F—(his/her) sexual behavior
M350G—(his/her) drinking, smoking, or drug use
M350H—money
M350I—school
M350J—getting along with family members.

Maternal role strain as a parent. Table A.3 shows the semantic differential items used to measure parental role strain on a scale from 0 to 7. The items involve polar opposites regarding the parenting role. The items were labeled E205A to E205F.

Table A.3   NSFH Data on Parental Role Strain

Circle the number that describes the things you do as a parent

interesting	0	1	2	3	4	5	6	7	boring
appreciated	0	1	2	3	4	5	6	7	unappreciated
overwhelming	0	1	2	3	4	5	6	7	manageable
complicated	0	1	2	3	4	5	6	7	simple
lonely	0	1	2	3	4	5	6	7	sociable
poorly done	0	1	2	3	4	5	6	7	well done

Two additional items were used. E703D asked: "How do you feel about the fairness in your relationship in each of the following areas?" (1 *very unfair to me* to 5 *very unfair to him*). E703D focused on child care. E1360N asked: "I often wish I could be free from the responsibility of being a parent" (1 *strongly agree* to 5 *strongly disagree*).

Maternal role strain for marriage compared to postmarriage. Mothers who experienced marital separation after January 1, 1977, were asked: "In each of the following areas, how is your life now, compared to the year before you separated?" (1 *much worse* to 5 *much better*). E413H asked about being a parent and E413I asked about care of their children. Mothers who were currently married were asked: "Even though it may be very unlikely, think for a moment about how various areas of your life might be different if you separated. For each of the following areas, how do you think things would change?" (1 *much worse* to 5 *much better*)? Item E713F concerned being a parent.

Verbal aggression and physical violence. Mothers with a child under 5, and no child over 5, were asked Item E902D: "Please indicate how often you yell at (child)" (1 for *never* to 4 for *very often*). The corresponding question, E1003E, was asked of mothers who had a child 5 to 18.

Three items were used to measure physical violence for mothers of children under 5. Mothers with no children older than 5 were asked E902B: "Please indicate how often you spank or slap (child)" (1 for *never* to 4 for *very often*). Mothers with a child under 5 were asked M296: "Sometimes children behave well and sometimes they don't. Have you had to spank (child) when (he/she) behaved badly in the past week?" (1 for *yes* and 2 for *no*). They were also asked M297: "How many times have you had to spank (child) in the past week?" (number of times recorded). Items M306 and M307 parallel M296 and M297, but are focused on a child 5 to 11. Mothers with a child 5 to 18 were asked E1003C: "Please indicate how often you spank or slap (child)" (1 for *never* to 4 for *very often*).

Spouse's relationship with children (first-married and stepfamilies). Item S98 asked fathers: "During the past 30 days, how often did you have an especially enjoyable time with any of the children?" (0 for *never* to 5 for *almost every day*). S99 asked him: "During the past 30 days, how often did you argue or fight or have a lot of difficulty dealing with any of the children?" (0 for *never* to 5 for *almost every day*). Fathers with a child 3 to 18 were asked S102A: "How may days last week did you eat breakfast with at least one of the children?" and S102B: "How many days last week did you eat dinner with at least one of the children?" These fathers were asked: "How often do you spend time with the children . . . ?" (1 for *never or rarely* to 6 for *almost every day*). Specific items were S103A—

leisure activities away from home (picnics, movies, sports, etc.), S103B—at home working on a project or playing together, S103C—having private talks, and S103D—helping with reading or homework.

Mothers with a child 5 to 18 reported the hours per week their spouse/partner spends on certain activities:

E1004A2—parent-teacher organizations or other school activities,
E1004B2—religious youth group
E1004C2—community youth groups (e.g., scouts)
E1004D2—team sports or youth athletic clubs.

Postmarital relations with nonresident parent: Divorced and stepfamilies. Mothers with a child 0 to 18 whose father is absent were asked a series of items. M356 asked: "Is (child's) father still living?" (1 for *yes* and 2 for *no*). M358 asked: "About how far away from here does he live (actual or estimated miles)?" M359 asked: "Is he currently married?" (1 for *yes* and 2 for *no*). M360 asked: "Has he had any children since those he had with you?" (1 *yes* and 2 *no*). M361 asked: "During the past 12 months, about how often did (child) talk on the telephone or receive a letter from his father?" (1 *not at all* to 6 *several times a week*). M362 asked: "During the past 12 months, how often did (child) see his father?" (1 for *not at all* to 6 for *several times a week*). Four items asked the mother: "How often does (child's) father spend time with (him/her) in each of the following activities?" (1 for *not at all* to 6 for *several times a week*). The activities were M365A—leisure activities such as picnics, movies, sports, or visiting family or friends, M365B—religious activities, M365C—talking, working on a project, or playing together, and M365D—school or other organized activities. M367 asked: "How much influence does (child's) father have in making major decisions about such things as education, religion, and health care?" (1 *none*, 2 *some*, or 3 *a great deal of influence*). M364 asked: "How many weeks did (he/she) stay with (his/her) father during the past 12 months? This does not include short visits, such as weekends" (number of weeks recorded).

Legal agreements with the absent father were measured using several items. M369 asked: "Do you and (child's) father have a legal agreement regarding child support, alimony, custody, or visitation?" (1 for *yes* and 2 for *no*). M370 asked: "Is there a legal agreement about where (child) lives?" (1 for *yes* and 2 for *no*). M276 asked: "Today, many states allow for joint legal custody, which means that regardless of where the child lives, both parents have equal decision-making rights. Does your legal agreement give (child's) father an equal say in making decisions about (him/her)?" (1 for *yes* and 2 for *no*). M377 asked: "Is there a legal agreement that (his/her) father is supposed to pay child support?" (1 *yes* and 2 *no*). M380 asked: "In the past 12 months, how many of the payments have been missed?" (1 for *none* to 6 for *all*). M382 asked: "Does (child's) father pay anything toward (his/her) support?" (1 *yes* and 2 *no*).

Family, kin relations, and their surrogates. The item ADNONREL indicates if there were any adult nonrelatives in the household (1 for *yes* and 2 for *no*). ADULTREL indicates if there were any adult kin in the household (1 for *yes* and 2 for *no*). Item E1306 asked if the maternal grandmother lives in the household (0 if *living in the household* and 1 to 11 for *living in other places*). Item 1316 asks the same information about the maternal grandfather.

CHAPTER 6:
FAMILY STRUCTURE
AND MOTHERS' WELL-BEING

Chapter 6 uses four dependent variables to represent broad issues in the well-being of mothers in different types of families. These variables are self-esteem, depression, global well-being, and health.

Self-esteem. This variable was measured using three items. E1359L stated: "I feel that I'm a person of worth, at least on an equal plane with others" (1 *strongly agree* to 5 *strongly disagree*). Item E1360E stated: "On the whole, I am satisfied with myself" (1 *strongly agree* to 5 *strongly disagree*). Item E1360M stated: "I am able to do things as well as other people" (1 *strongly agree* to 5 *strongly disagree*). Each item was recoded so a higher score corresponded to higher self-esteem. The variable, self-esteem, was computed as the mean response on the three recoded items.

For mothers in each type of family a single factor emerged, and the loadings for the four family types ranged from .73 to .79. The alphas (a measure of reliability) were .64, .66, .61, and .57 for first-married, divorced, stepfamily, and continuously single families, respectively. The scale involves data for 1,026 first-married, 639 divorced, 269 stepfamily, and 384 continuously single mothers.

Depression. A 12-item scale was used to measure depression. This consisted of items E202A to E202L that used the following stem: "Next is a list of the ways you might have felt or behaved during the past week. On how many days during the past week did you . . . ?" (number of days from 0 to 7). The items were:

E202A—feel bothered by things that usually don't bother you

E202B—Not feel like eating; your appetite was poor

E202C—feel that you could not shake off the blues even with help from your family or friends

E202D—have trouble keeping your mind on what you were doing

E202E—feel depressed

E202F—feel that everything you did was an effort

E202G—feel fearful

E202H—sleep restlessly

E202I—talk less than usual

E202J—feel lonely

E202K—feel sad

E202L—feel you could not get going.

We computed the mean of the 12-item scale for all mothers who answered at least 11 of the 12 items.

For each family type a single factor emerged, and loadings ranged from .57 to .84. The alpha reliability coefficients were .92, .94, .92, and .93 for first-married, divorced, stepfamily, and continuously single mothers, respectively. The scale has scores for 1,073 first-married, 666 divorced, 275 stepfamily, and 406 continuously single mothers.

Global well-being. A single item, E201, was used to measure global well-being. It asked the respondent to take things all together and rate how they felt about their well-being. The response options ranged from 1 for *very unhappy* to 7 for *very happy*. There were 948 first-married, 601 divorced, 245 stepfamily, and 355 continuously single mothers answering this question.

Health. The mothers' health was measured using a single item. E207 asked: "Compared with other people your age, how would you describe your health?" (1 *very poor* to 5 *excellent*). There were 1,045 first-married, 632 divorced, 269 stepfamily, and 376 continuously single mothers answering this question.

Measurement of Predictors of Mothers' Well-Being

Our measures of the socioeconomic and other structural variables are described above. Briefly, family type is measured by the TYPEC variable, cohabiting status by the COHAB variable, length of current marriage by the MARLGTH variable (century month of interview—century month of end of last marriage), and time since previous marriage ended by DIVLGTH (century month of interview—century month marriage ended). Household size is measured using M2NUM, age of youngest child is measured by AYOC, household income is measured with IHTOT2, mothers' education with EDUCAT, race with RACE, mothers' age with M2BP01, and mothers' hours of employment by HOURS.

Family process variables involve different clusters of predictors for each type of family. The number of mothers for each independent variable appears in Table A.4. Where scales are used the lowest and highest factor loading on the principal component as well as the alpha reliability coefficient are also presented. Marital happiness is measured by a single item, E701, which asks mothers to take all things together and rate their marriage. Responses range from 1 for *very unhappy* to 7 for *very happy*. Marital conflict is measured by a scale, MARCONF, that uses seven items, E706A to E706G. These items asked the mother to rate different

Table A.4   Variables Used to Predict Mothers' Well-Being: Number of Observations, Factor Loadings, and Alpha Reliability Coefficient

Independent Variable	First-Married	Divorced	Stepfamily	Continuously Single
Socioeconomic and background characteristics				
Cohabiting	na	667	na	418
Length of marriage	1,084	na	272	na
Time since previous marriage ended	na	668	na	na
Household size	1,085	677	277	418
Age of youngest child	1,085	677	277	418
Household income	1,085	677	277	418
Mothers' education	1,085	677	277	418
Race	1,085	677	275	418
Age of mother	1,085	677	277	418
Hours per week mother is employed	1,085	677	277	418
Family processes				
Comparison level of divorce, divorce better	na	473, 60-79, 81	na	na
Mother's interaction with nonresident father	na	607	197	330
Dissatisfaction with nonresident parent's economic support	na	607	194	326
Conflict with nonresident parent over child	na	604, 63-73, 76	196, 57-71, 70	329, 67-74, 79

areas of potential disagreement on a scale from 1 for *never* to 6 for *almost every day.* The areas of potential conflict include household tasks, money, time together, sex, having a(nother) child, in-laws, and children. The score is the mean of the items if they answered at least six of the seven items.

Marital violence was measured using a single item, E708, that was recoded so a 1 indicated that sometimes arguments became physical and 0 indicated that this never happened. Marital stability was also measured with a single item, E718. Mothers reported the chances of an eventual separation or divorce. This

Table A.4 Continued

Independent Variable	First-Married	Divorced	Stepfamily	Continuously Single
Marital happiness	1,035	na	263	na
Marital conflict	1,011, 41-75, 76	na	258, 43-81, 76	na
Marital violence	981	na	252	na
Marital stability	991	na	255	na
Marital equity	1,054, 61-70, 55	na	265, 64-79, 62	na
Comparison level of marriage, marriage worse	1,004, 59-84, 83	na	256, 46-74, 79	na
Parent-child interaction and child well-being				
Child well-being	1,084	676	276	418
Child difficult times	1,074	669	276	414
Child enjoyable times	1,078	675	276	413
Nonresident parent interaction with child	na	406, 58-84, 74	116, 63-81, 71	187, 64-83, 69
Nonresident parent's influence on child	na	435	119	196

NOTE: Numbers appearing in the cells are first, the number of cases; second, the range (from lowest to highest) in factor loadings on the first principal component across all items and all family types; and third, the alpha reliability coefficient. For example, 473, 60-79, 81 means there are 473 cases for the variable, the lowest factor loading of any item in any family type is .60 whereas the highest is .79, and the alpha reliability is .81.

was recoded so a 1 meant chances were very high and a 5 meant chances were very low. The equity of the marital relationship was measured with four items, E703A to E703D. These concerned whether household chores, the mother's work role, the decisions about spending, and child care were unfair to the mother or to the father. The responses ranged from 1 *unfair to wife* to 5 *unfair to husband*. Equity was computed as the mean of those items answered for mothers who answered three or four of the items. Because inequity is directional, a high score means that the relationship was unfair to the husband. As the score moves from 1 to 3 (fair to both) the disadvantage of the mother decreases. As the score moves from 3 to 5 the mother becomes advantaged by inequity.

Because inequity can be to the advantage of either the husband or the wife, we have included two variables: EQUITY, and EQUITYSQ—the square of equity. In predicting well-being, the coefficient for equity should be positive, indicating the less the mother is disadvantaged, the higher her level of well-being. However, the coefficient for EQUITYSQ should be negative, because those mothers who are advantaged by inequity may have lower well-being. In this way, a positive sign for EQUITY raises the mothers' well-being as you move from the mother being disadvantaged toward a balanced relationship. EQUITYSQ has a negative sign and lowers the mothers' well-being as you move toward her husband being disadvantaged.

Married mothers were asked a series of six items, E713A to E713F, in which they compared marriage to what their life would be like if they were divorced. We refer to this scale as comparison level of marriage. A higher score signifies that marriage is worse than divorce would be. The items covered their standard of living, social life, career opportunities, happiness, sex life, and parental role. The response options ranged from 1 (these areas of life would be much worse if they were divorced) to 5 (these areas would be much better if they were divorced). A variable called MARWRSE was computed as the mean of the responses for those answering five or six of the items.

A second set of variables is relevant for divorced mothers, and some of these are relevant to stepfamily mothers or continuously single mothers. The comparison level of divorce is based on a 7-item scale, E413A to E413G. These items asked mothers to rate their situation now compared to the year before they separated from their former husband. The answers ranged from 1 for *much worse now* to 5 for *much better now*.

Mother's interaction with nonresident father was measured by a single item, M366, that assessed the frequency of child-related interaction between the nonresident father and the mother. The frequency of their interaction concerning the focal child ranged from 1 for *not at all* to 6 for *several times a week*. The mother's dissatisfaction with nonresident parent's economic support was measured using M385C. Answers ranged from 1 for *very satisfied* to 4 for *very dissatisfied*. Conflict with nonresident parent, ABSCONF, was measured using M368A to M368F. Respondents were asked: "How much conflict do you and (child's) father have over each of the following issues?": M368A, where child lives; M368B, how (he/she) is raised; M368C, how you spend money on the child; M368D, how he spends money on (child); M638E, his visits with (child); and M368F, his contribution to (child's) support.

A third set of variables examined the child's well-being and interaction between the parents and the child. The child's well-being was measured using M276. This asked the mother to rate how well the focal child's life was going. Responses were recoded so they ranged from a 1, which signified the child's life was *not going well at all* to a 5, indicating the child's life was *going very well*. Nonresident parent interaction with child, ABSINVOL, was measured using four items, M365A to M365D. These items covered leisure, church, interaction, and organizational activities. The response options ranged from 1 for *never* to 6 for *often*. The score was computed as the mean of the items for respondents who answered three or four of the items. The nonresident father's influence on child was measured using one item, M367, for which the response options ranged from 1 for *none* to 3 for *a lot*.

CHAPTER 7:
FAMILY STRUCTURE
AND CHILDREN'S WELL-BEING

Measuring Child Outcome Variables

We identified a number of outcome variables. Because outcomes may vary by child within any given family, we used items that referred to a particular focal child. One of the items concerned a focal child from 0 to 18. The other outcome variables focused on a child in a smaller age group, namely 0 to 4, 5 to 11, or 12 to 18. The items and scales are shown in Table A.5.

Table A.5 Dependent Child Well-Being Variables

Dependent Variable	0-18	0-4	5-11	12-18
ADJUST12—Adjustment scale for focal child 12-18, M325A-M325J coded from (1) to (3) for most adjusted				M325B D En G Hn In Jn
ADJUST11—Adjustment scale for focal child 5-11, M305A-M305J coded from (1) to (3) for most adjusted			M305B D En G Hn In Jn	
ADJUST04—Adjustment scale for focal child 0-4, M295A-M295I Coded from (1) to (3) for most adjusted		M295B D En G Hn In		
Grades for 12-18, (1) Fs to (9) As				M331N
Child gets homework done, (1) rarely to (4) always				M329N
School performance, (1) bottom of class to (5) best in class			M309N	
Child's life going from (1) not well to (4) very well	M276N			

Child well-being, child 0 to 18. A general well-being item was asked about a randomly selected child 0 to 18. M276 asked: "The next questions are about (child). All things considered, is (child's) life going . . . ?" (coded as 1 *very well* to 4 *not very well*). This was recoded so that a higher score reflected higher well-being.

Child adjustment, child 0 to 4, 5 to 11, or 12 to 18. A slightly different measure of a randomly selected child was used depending on whether the child was 0 to 4, 5 to 11, or 12 to 18. ADJUST04 was used to measure the adjustment of a child 0 to 4. Nine questions were asked about a randomly selected child 0 to 4 using the statement: "I am going to read some statements that might describe a child's behavior. Please tell me whether each statement has been often true, sometimes true, or has not been true of (child) during the past three months" (1 for *often true*, 2 for *sometimes true*, and 3 for *not true*). The items were:

M295A—is willing to try new things
M295B—is fussy or irritable
M295C—keeps self busy
M295D—loses temper easily
M295E—is cheerful and happy
M295F—is fearful or anxious
M295G—bullies others
M295H—does what he/she is asked
M295I—gets along well with others.

All items were coded so a higher score reflected better adjustment on the part of the child. A factor analysis had a strong principal component, but indicated that the positive and negative items loaded on separate scales when a varimax rotation was done. The alpha for the 9-item scale was .57. An alpha was also computed for the positive and negative items separately, but it was no higher. ADJUST04 was computed as the mean of items as long as at least eight of the nine items were answered.

ADJUST11 was used to measure the adjustment of a child 5 to 11. Ten questions were asked consisting of those listed above plus whether the child does his/her responsibilities. A factor analysis produced results comparable to those for ADJUST04. The $\alpha = .67$ was somewhat better than for the younger children. ADJUST12 was used to measure the adjustment of a child 12 to 18. It used the same items as for ADJUST11 and with the same results. For a child 12 to 18 the $\alpha = .69$.

Academic Performance. Mothers with a child 5 to 11 were asked M309: "How well does (child) do in school? Is (he/she . . .)?" (recoded as 1 for *near the bottom of the class* to 5 for *one of the best students in (his/her) class.* Mothers with a child 12 to 18 were asked M331: "What sort of grades does (child) get? Would you say it is mostly As, Bs, Cs, Ds, or what?" (recoded as 1 for *mostly Fs* to 9 for *mostly As).*

Measuring Variables That Predict Child Outcome Variables

There are many factors that predict how children will do in different types of families and there are many background and control variables. Table A.6 provides a complete list of the predictors, background, and control variables. Because most of these variables have been used in previous chapters we will not discuss their measurement here. Now, we will focus on how we measured variables that we have not used previously.

Presence of adults other than cohabiting partners. The variable, EXADULT, combines two variables, namely, ADULTREL and ADNOREL. A household with any extra adults is coded as 1 whereas households with no extra adults is coded 0. This variable is used in single-parent households. It is problematic because there are relatively few households in the data set that have any extra adults present.

Because the dependent variable refers to a particular child, we have included the age (F1AGE) and gender (F1SEX) of the child as predictors. The analysis is organized by age groups, 0 to 4, 5 to 11, and 12 to 18, but there is still variation within each group by age. The potential problems a 12-year-old faces are qualitatively different from those faced by a 17-year-old. We control for gender because of possible sex differences in outcome variables. Both F1AGE and F1SEX were constructed by the NSFH staff to indicate the age and sex of the focal child.

An index of mother's support, MOMSUP5, was computed for families with children 5 to 18 using the mean of two items (E1003A and E1003D). These concerned praising the child and hugging the child (responses ranged from 1 for *never* to 4 for *very often*. The items have a correlation of .35. Parallel items were asked for families with children under 5, but there was too little variation for this to be an explanatory variable—97% of mothers reported hugging their young child very often.

Mother-child disagreement, DISAGREE, was measured for focal children ages 12 to 18 using items M350A to M350J. These asked how often the mother and focal child openly disagreed in the last 12 months about a series of issues including how the child dresses, boyfriends/girlfriends, friends, staying out late, helping around the house, sexual behavior, drinking/smoking/drugs, money, school, and getting along with family members. Answers to each item ranged from 1 *never* to 6 *almost every day*. The loadings on the principal component range from .41 to .68. The alpha is .75. DISAGREE was computed as the mean of the items answered as long as the mother responded to at least 9 of 10 items.

Childrearing values for parents of children 0 to 4, VALUE04, was measured using items E903A to E903L. VALUE04 was computed as the mean of these items if the mother responded to at least 10 of the 11 items. The items concerned conforming to socially approved values, such as following the rules, doing well at school, being independent, being kind, controlling one's temper, doing what is asked, carrying out responsibilities, being creative, keeping busy, getting along well with peers, doing well at athletics, and trying new things. Responses ranged from 1 for *not at all important* to 7 for *extremely important*. Loadings on the principal component range from .48 to .72 and alpha is .85. These items were asked only in families with a child 0 to 4 and no child 5 to 18. Hence the number of cases is too small for multivariate analysis. Childrearing values for parents of children 5 to 18, VALUE518, was measured using a parallel set of items, E1005A-E1005I. Loadings on the principal component range from .52 to .68 and alpha is .86.

For families with children 0 to 4 and no older children, the mother's aggression toward the child, AGRESS04, was computed using a two-item index, E902B and E902D. E902B concerned spanking or slapping the child and E902D asked about yelling at the child. Response options ranged from 1 for *never* to 4 for *very often*. The correlation between these items is .55. For families with children 5 to 18, parallel items, E1003C and E1003E, were used to form an index of mother's aggression, AGRESS. The correlation between these items is .32.

For families with children 5 to 18 the interaction between the mother and child, MOMINT5, was measured using E1001A, E1001B, and E1002A-E1002D. The first items asked how many days the mother and child had breakfast and dinner together, with answers ranging from 0 for *none* to 7 for *every day*. The last four items focused on activities including leisure activities, working on a project, pri-

Table A.6   Predictors of Child Outcome Variables

Independent Variable	0-18	0-4	5-11	12-18
Sample SAMPLE	SAMPLE	SAMPLE	SAMPLE	SAMPLE
Cohabiting COHAB	COHAB	COHAB	COHAB	COHAB
Other adults in household ADULTREL + ADNONREL = EXADULT	EXADLT	EXADLT	EXADLT	EXADLT
Time since divorce CMINT-MAREND = DIVLGTH	DIVLGTH	DIVLGTH	DIVLGTH	DIVLGTH
Length of current marriage MARLGTH	MARLGTH	MARLGTH	MARLGTH	MARLGTH
Size of household M2NUM	M2NUM	M2NUM	M2NUM	M2NUM
Household income— IHTOT2	IHTOT2	IHTOT2	IHTOT2	IHTOT2
Mothers' education— EDUCAT	EDUCAT	EDUCAT	EDUCAT	EDUCAT
Mothers' employment HOURS	HOURS	HOURS	HOURS	HOURS
RACE	RACE	RACE	RACE	RACE
Gender of child F1SEX	F1SEX	F1SEX	F1SEX	F1SEX
Age of child F1AGE	F1AGE	F1AGE	F1AGE	F1AGE
Marital happiness E701	E701	E701	E701	E701
Marital conflict MARCONF	MARCONF	MARCONF	MARCONF	MARCONF
Marital stability E718N	E718N	E718N	E718N	E718N
Father-child enjoyable times last 30 days M286	M286	M286	M286	M286
Father-child conflict: difficult times with child M287	M287	M287	M287	M287
Father's interaction/ care with child, 0-4 M298B		M298B		
Father's time in child-related organizations, 5-18 DADACTV			DADACTV	DADACTV
Dissatisfaction with child support M385C	M385C	M385C	M385C	M385C

Table A.6 Predictors of Child Outcome Variables

Independent Variable	0-18	0-4	5-11	12-18
Talk with nonresident father about child M366	M366	M366	M366	M366
Conflict with nonresident father about child ABSCONF	ABSCONF	ABSCONF	ABSCONF	ABSCONF
Nonresident father's interaction with child ABSINVOL	ABSINVOL	ABSINVOL	ABSINVOL	ABSINVOL
Nonresident father's influence on child M367	M367	M367	M367	M367
Mother-child enjoyable times last 30 days M284	M284	M284	M284	M284
Mother-child conflict: difficult times with child M285	M285	M285	M285	M285
Mother's support for child, 5-18	—		E1003A, E1003D	E1003A, E1003D
Mother's control of child, 12-18	—			MOMCD18
Mother-child interaction, 5-18 MOMINT5		E901A - E901C	E1001A, B, E1002AD	E1001A, B, E1002AD
Mother-adolescent disagreements, 12-18 DISAGREE		DISAGREE	DISAGREE	DISAGREE
Mother-child verbal and physical aggression, 0-4 AGRESS04		AGRESS04		
Mother-child verbal and physical aggression, 5-18 AGRESS	AGRESS		AGRESS	AGRESS
Mother's childrearing values, 0-4		VALUE04		
Mother's childrearing values, 5-18	VALUE518		VALUE518	VALUE518
Mother's well-being E201	E201	E201	E201	E201

vate talks, and helping with reading or homework. The responses ranged from 1 for *never or rarely* to 6 for *almost every day*. The items loaded between .51 and .79 on the principal component and the alpha was .71. MOMINT5 was computed as the mean of the six items for mothers who answered at least five of the items.

For resident father's activities in child-related organizations for families with children 5 to 18, the mother was asked to estimate how involved the father was in child-related organizations such as parent-teacher organizations, religious youth groups, community youth groups, and team sports. These correspond to items E1004A2, E1004B2, E1004C2, and E1004D2. The principal component had loadings of .46 to .72 but the reliability was very low, alpha = .42. The resident father's interaction/care for a child 0 to 4 was measured using a single item, M298B. This item asked the mother to estimate the hours her husband spends per day on care of the child.

Mothers' control of their child age 12 to 18, MOMCD18, was measured using four items, M330, M336, M337, and M341. These items concerned completing homework before play, restricting television time, restricting television programs, and completing chores before play. Each item was recoded so a 1 indicated *no,* 2 indicated *try,* and 3 indicated *yes.* These items loaded from .67 to .72 on the principal component and had an alpha of .65.

APPENDIX B

Additional Tables

Table B.1 Pairwise Correlations of Mothers' Well-Being With Background and Family Process Variables

Panel A: Correlates of Well-Being for First-Married and Divorced Mothers

Predictors of Well-Being	First-Married				Divorced			
	Self-Esteem	Depression	Well-Being	Health	Self-Esteem	Depression	Well-Being	Health
Sample	.02 (1,026)	.05 (1,073)	.04 (948)	−.07* (1,045)	.10** (639)	.02 (663)	.01 (601)	−.03 (632)
Marriage length	−.01 (1,025)	−.08* (1,072)	.01 (947)	−.01 (1,044)	na	na	na	na
Months since divorce	na	na	na	na	−.06 (631)	−.03 (654)	−.00 (593)	−.09* (625)
Household size	−.07 (1,026)	.06 (1,073)	−.07* (948)	−.04 (1,045)	−.09* (639)	.03 (663)	−.06 (601)	−.02 (632)
Age of youngest child	−.01 (999)	−.01 (1,046)	−.05* (942)	−.01 (1,019)	.10* (638)	−.07 (662)	.03 (600)	−.02 (632)
Household income	.08** (1,026)	−.09* (1,073)	.06 (948)	.15*** (1,045)	.15*** (639)	−.04 (663)	.09* (601)	.12** (632)
Education	.13*** (1,026)	−.13*** (1,073)	.09* (948)	.22*** (1,045)	.17*** (639)	−.08* (663)	.07 (601)	.18*** (632)
Race	.02 (1,024)	−.08** (1,071)	.08* (947)	.08* (1,043)	.02 (639)	−.03 (663)	−.05 (601)	.04 (632)
Mother's age	.03 (1,026)	−.08** (1,073)	−.02 (948)	.03 (1,045)	.06 (639)	−.02 (663)	−.06 (601)	−.01 (632)
Mother's hours employed	.01 (1,026)	−.01 (1,073)	−.09** (948)	−.01 (1,045)	.20*** (639)	−.14*** (663)	.12** (601)	.24*** (632)
Marital happiness	.23*** (935)	−.20*** (1,027)	.47*** (922)	.10*** (1,002)	na	na	na	na
Marital conflict	−.15*** (972)	.28*** (1,004)	−.22*** (885)	−.06* (995)	na	na	na	na
Marital violence	−.03 (943)	.13*** (974)	−.10** (864)	−.10** (977)	na	na	na	na
Marital stability	.23*** (955)	−.22*** (985)	.33*** (870)	.11*** (977)	na	na	na	na
Marital equity	.06* (1,002)	−.05 (1,047)	.18*** (925)	.08** (1,019)	na	na	na	na
Marital equity^2	.06* (1,002)	−.03 (1,047)	.16*** (925)	.06** (1,019)	na	na	na	na
Comparison level of marriage	−.18*** (970)	.22*** (998)	−.27*** (883)	−.06* (990)	na	na	na	na
Child well-being	.10*** (1,026)	−.11*** (1,073)	.20*** (948)	.13*** (1,045)	.22*** (638)	−.19*** (662)	−.22*** (600)	.11** (631)
Child difficulties	−.09** (1,016)	.12*** (1,063)	−.11** (942)	−.03 (1,036)	−.19*** (633)	.12** (655)	−.06 (594)	−.05 (626)
Child enjoyable times	.03 (1,021)	.01 (1,067)	.15*** (943)	.08* (1,039)	.06 (637)	−.06 (661)	.11** (594)	.01 (626)
Comparison level of divorce	na	na	na	na	.15** (463)	−.20*** (466)	.37*** (422)	.10* (455)
Cohabiting	na	na	na	na	−.06 (639)	.08* (663)	.03 (601)	−.02 (632)

Table B.1 Continued

Predictors of Well-Being	First-Married				Divorced			
	Self-Esteem	Depression	Well-Being	Health	Self-Esteem	Depression	Well-Being	Health
Interaction with nonresident father	na	na	na	na	.03 (574)	.05 (594)	−.03 (539)	.06 (569)
Conflict with nonresident father	na	na	na	na	.00 (572)	.13** (591)	.02 (539)	−.01 (566)
Dissatisfaction with child support	na	na	na	na	−.01 (574)	.08* (594)	.01 (539)	−.09* (569)
Nonresident father-child interaction	na	na	na	na	.08 (387)	.00 (397)	−.04 (368)	.04 (376)
Nonresident father's influence	na	na	na	na	.03 (415)	.05 (423)	−.07 (385)	−.00 (407)

Panel B: Correlates of Well-Being for Stepfamily and Continuously Single Mothers

Predictors of Well-Being	Stepfamily				Continuously Single			
	Self-Esteem	Depression	Well-Being	Health	Self-Esteem	Depression	Well-Being	Health
Sample	.05 (269)	.04 (275)	.01 (245)	−.01 (269)	.03 (384)	.06 (406)	−.07 (355)	.03 (376)
Marriage length	−.16** (264)	.07 (270)	−.16* (241)	−.04 (264)	na	na	na	na
Household size	−.11 (269)	.08 (275)	.01 (245)	−.02 (269)	−.03 (384)	−.04 (406)	−.05 (355)	−.05 (376)
Age of youngest child	−.02 (269)	−.01 (275)	−.05 (245)	−.10 (269)	.00 (384)	.08 (406)	.00 (355)	−.05 (376)
Household income	.07 (269)	−.11 (275)	.02 (245)	.23*** (269)	.10 (384)	−.09 (406)	.05 (355)	−.00 (376)
Education	.06 (269)	−.14* (275)	−.03 (245)	.13* (269)	.15** (384)	−.03 (406)	−.04 (355)	.22*** (376)
Race	.05 (267)	−.10 (275)	.05 (245)	.07 (269)	−.06 (384)	.05 (406)	−.01 (355)	−.05 (376)
Mother's age	−.04 (269)	−.04 (275)	−.06 (245)	.06 (269)	.04 (384)	−.08 (406)	−.01 (355)	−.12* (376)
Mother's hours employed	.05 (269)	−.03 (275)	.02 (245)	.06 (269)	.07 (384)	−.07 (406)	.08 (355)	.06 (376)
Marital happiness	.21*** (255)	−.36*** (261)	.52*** (233)	.11 (255)	na	na	na	na
Marital conflict	−.05 (253)	.25*** (256)	−.19** (229)	−.14* (254)	na	na	na	na
Marital violence	−.01 (247)	.13* (250)	−.09 (224)	−.17** (250)	na	na	na	na
Marital stability	.21** (250)	−.29*** (253)	.36*** (225)	.11 (251)	na	na	na	na
Marital equity	.17** (257)	−.20** (263)	.29*** (234)	.10 (257)	na	na	na	na
Marital equity^2	.17** (257)	−.16* (293)	.25*** (234)	.08 (257)	na	na	na	na

Table B.1   Continued

Predictors of Well-Being	Stepfamily				Continuously Single			
	Self-Esteem	Depres-sion	Well-Being	Health	Self-Esteem	Depres-sion	Well-Being	Health
Comparison level of marriage	-.09 (257)	.25*** (254)	-.31*** (226)	-.06 (252)	na	na	na	na
Child well-being	.11 (268)	-.24*** (274)	.19** (244)	.15* (260)	.18*** (384)	-.03 (406)	.17*** (355)	.11* (376)
Child difficulties	-.15* (268)	.22*** (274)	-.00 (244)	-.06 (268)	-.03 (380)	.18*** (402)	-.07 (351)	.06 (372)
Child enjoyable times	.09 (268)	.02 (274)	.10 (244)	-.06 (268)	.11* (379)	-.03 (401)	.13* (352)	.00 (371)
Cohabiting	na	na	na	na	-.04 (384)	-.04 (406)	.11* (355)	-.05 (376)
Interaction with nonresident father	-.13 (192)	-.04 (195)	-.08 (175)	.16* (194)	.14* (298)	-.01 (319)	.04 (279)	.04 (294)
Conflict with nonresident father	-.01 (191)	.18* (194)	.04 (174)	-.02 (193)	.07 (297)	-.02 (318)	.03 (278)	.15** (293)
Dissatisfaction with child support	-.12 (189)	.10 (192)	.03 (172)	-.14 (191)	-.11 (295)	.12* (315)	-.16** (275)	-.05 (290)
Nonresident father-child interaction	.01 (114)	-.17 (115)	-.04 (100)	.15 (114)	.04 (171)	-.21** (181)	.06 (157)	.21** (169)
Nonresident father's influence	.03 (117)	-.07 (118)	-.12 (107)	.07 (117)	.02 (177)	-.19** (191)	.18* (165)	.26*** (178)

The number of cases is in parentheses.
*$p < .05$; **$p < .01$; ***$p < .001$.

Table B.2   Correlates of Children's Well-Being

Panel A: Correlates of Well-Being for Children Whose Parents Are in Their First Marriage

Predictor	Global Well-Being 0-18	Adjust-ment 0-4	Adjust-ment 5-11	School Perfor-mance 5-11	Adjust-ment 12-18	School Grades 12-18
Sample	.03 (1,084)	−.15** (318)	.03 (330)	−.12* (304)	.11 (314)	−.04 (300)
Marriage length	−.16*** (1,083)	.14* (318)	.10 (330)	−.02 (304)	.16** (314)	.07 (300)
Household size	−.12*** (1,084)	−.06 (318)	.04 (330)	−.03 (304)	−.06 (314)	−.03 (300)
Household income	.03 (1,084)	.05 (318)	.08 (330)	.12* (304)	.04 (314)	.04 (300)
Education	.11*** (1,084)	.04 (318)	.12* (330)	.17** (304)	.04 (314)	.16** (300)
Mother's hours employed	.04 (1,084)	.05 (318)	.04 (330)	−.07 (304)	−.03 (314)	−.07 (300)
Race (1 white, 0 nonwhite)	−.02 (1,082)	.03 (318)	−.14* (328)	.05 (302)	−.04 (314)	−.04 (300)
Sex of focal child (1 boy, 0 girl)	−.08** (1,067)	.01 (314)	−.11* (325)	−.23*** (299)	−.06 (310)	−.17** (296)
Age of focal child	−.25*** (1,084)	−.01 (318)	−.12* (330)	−.16** (304)	.13* (314)	−.12* (300)
Marital happiness	.17*** (1,035)	.19*** (309)	.09 (311)	.08 (286)	.18** (301)	.02 (289)
Marital conflict	−.12*** (1,011)	−.29*** (301)	−.26*** (309)	−.00 (284)	−.15* (290)	−.10 (278)
Marital stability	.10** (991)	.05 (297)	.14* (299)	.05 (274)	.22*** (281)	.13* (270)
Child has enjoyable times with father	.27*** (1,052)	.22*** (312)	.18*** (320)	−.04 (294)	.25*** (299)	.07 (285)
Child has difficult times with father	−.13*** (1,059)	−.32*** (311)	−.36*** (325)	−.08 (299)	−.32*** (302)	−.13* (289)
Father active in youth organizations	.09 (489)	na	.04 (222)	.05 (200)	−.03 (199)	.00 (191)
Hours/day father cares for child	na	.00 (312)	na	na	na	na
Child has enjoyable times with mother	.27*** (1,078)	.16** (318)	.32*** (328)	.01 (302)	.25*** (310)	.14* (296)
Child has difficult times with mother	−.16*** (1,074)	−.33*** (315)	.33*** (327)	−.02 (301)	−.43*** (310)	−.14* (296)
Index of mother's interaction with child, 0-4	na	.21** (223)	na	na	na	na
Mother's support of child, 5-18	na	na	.11* (320)	.04 (294)	.08 (298)	.17** (284)
Mother's control of child, 12-18	na	na	na	na	−.11 (304)	.02 (294)

Table B.2   Continued

Predictor	Global Well-Being 0-18	Adjust-ment 0-4	Adjust-ment 5-11	School Perfor-mance 5-11	Adjust-ment 12-18	School Grades 12-18
Mother's interaction with child 5-18	na	na	.14* (315)	.06 (291)	.06 (289)	.14* (276)
Mother-adolescent disagreement 12-18	na	na	na	na	-.50*** (312)	-.27*** (299)
Mother's aggression toward child, 0-4	na	-.29*** (223)	na	na	na	na
Mother's aggression toward child, 5-18	na	na	-.26*** (320)	-.06 (294)	-.31*** (298)	-.15* (284)
Mother's childrearing values	na	-.07 (219)	.15** (305)	.03 (279)	.02 (284)	-.07 (273)
Mother's global well-being	.20*** (948)	.13* (284)	.13* (285)	.00 (263)	.25*** (272)	.08 (262)

Panel B: Correlates of Well-Being for Children Whose Mother Is Divorced

Predictor	Global Well-Being 0-18	Adjust-ment 0-4	Adjust-ment 5-11	School Perfor-mance 5-11	Adjust-ment 12-18	School Grades 12-18
Sample	.02 (676)	-.14 (101)	.11 (255)	.03 (241)	-.00 (302)	.01 (291)
Cohabiting (1 yes, 0 no)	.04 (676)	-.10 (101)	-.00 (255)	-.13* (241)	-.05 (302)	-.12* (291)
Other adult (1 yes, 0 no)	.05 (676)	.04 (101)	-.09 (255)	-.01 (241)	.11 (302)	.08 (291)
Time since divorce	.03 (676)	.09 (101)	-.03 (253)	-.03 (240)	-.00 (296)	-.05 (285)
Household size	.02 (676)	-.10 (101)	-.19** (255)	-.12 (241)	-.06 (302)	-.05 (291)
Household income	.02 (676)	-.02 (101)	.10 (255)	.16* (241)	.10 (302)	.07 (291)
Education	-.05 (676)	.21* (101)	.08 (255)	.24*** (241)	.05 (302)	.12* (291)
Mother's hours employed	-.01 (676)	-.05 (101)	.15* (255)	.15* (241)	.10 (301)	.10 (291)
Race (1 white, 0 nonwhite)	-.13*** (676)	-.04 (101)	-.04 (255)	.02 (241)	-.11 (302)	-.10 (291)
Sex of focal child (1 boy, 0 girl)	-.08* (676)	.07 (100)	-.02 (251)	-.17* (237)	-.02 (301)	-.21*** (290)
Age of focal child	-.18*** (676)	.21* (101)	-.08 (255)	-.02 (241)	.09 (302)	-.08 (291)
Dissatisfaction with child support	-.04 (607)	.14 (89)	-.05 (237)	-.11 (223)	-.06 (266)	-.02 (255)
Conflict with nonresident father	-.11** (604)	.05 (89)	-.25*** (236)	-.08 (222)	-.15* (264)	.01 (253)

Table B.2 Continued

Predictor	Global Well-Being 0-18	Adjust-ment 0-4	Adjust-ment 5-11	School Perfor-mance 5-11	Adjust-ment 12-18	School Grades 12-18
Involvement of nonresident father	-.03 (406)	-.04 (58)	.18* (159)	.17* (149)	.01 (179)	.10 (170)
Influence on child by nonresident father	-.06 (435)	-.04 (64)	-.07 (171)	.02 (160)	.01 (189)	-.06 (178)
Child has enjoyable times with mother	.20*** (675)	-.04 (101)	.26*** (255)	.13 (241)	.30*** (301)	.11 (290)
Child has difficult times with mother	-.22*** (669)	-.19 (99)	-.48*** (254)	-.21** (240)	-.47*** (298)	-.22*** (287)
Mother's support of child 5-18	na	na	.30*** (249)	.18** (235)	.19** (293)	.16** (282)
Mother's control of child 12-18	na	na	na	na	-.03 (291)	.11 (283)
Mother's interaction with child 5-18	na	na	.17** (237)	.03 (226)	.22*** (286)	-.02 (276)
Mother's interaction with child, 0-4	na	.37** (57)	na	na	na	na
Mother-adolescent disagreement	na	na	na	na	-.58*** (300)	-.35*** (288)
Mother's aggression toward child 0-4	na	-.16 (58)	na	na	na	na
Mother's aggression toward child 5-18	na	na	-.23*** (249)	.00 (235)	-.23*** (293)	-.16** (284)
Mother's childrearing values, 0-4	na	.21 (55)	na	na	na	na
Mother's childrearing values, 5-18	na	na	-.01 (234)	-.11 (221)	.16** (285)	.14* (275)
Mother's global well-being	.22*** (600)	.10 (91)	.24*** (227)	.18** (213)	.22*** (264)	.07 (256)

Panel C: Correlates of Well-Being for Children Whose Mother Has Remarried

Predictor	Global Well-Being 0-18	Adjust-ment 0-4	Adjust-ment 5-11	School Perfor-mance 5-11	Adjust-ment 12-18	School Grades 12-18
Sample	.02 (276)	-.13 (40)	-.14 (98)	-.09 (95)	-.03 (131)	-.05 (125)
Marriage length	-.05 (272)	.16 (40)	.09 (98)	.18 (95)	-.03 (128)	.09 (122)
Household size	.03 (276)	.07 (40)	.04 (98)	.09 (95)	.03 (131)	.06 (125)
Household income	.03 (276)	-.04 (40)	.10 (98)	-.07 (95)	.08 (131)	-.02 (125)
Education	-.05 (276)	-.09 (40)	-.05 (98)	.03 (95)	.07 (131)	.19* (125)

Table B.2 Continued

Predictor	Global Well-Being 0-18	Adjustment 0-4	Adjustment 5-11	School Performance 5-11	Adjustment 12-18	School Grades 12-18
Mother's hours employed	−.02 (276)	−.25 (40)	−.01 (98)	−.07 (95)	−.01 (131)	−.10 (125)
Race (1 white, 0 nonwhite)	−.01 (274)	.07 (40)	−.00 (98)	−.05 (95)	−.02 (129)	.07 (124)
Sex of focal child (1 boy, 0 girl)	−.15* (274)	.04 (39)	−.10 (98)	−.19 (95)	−.12 (130)	−.19* (124)
Age of focal child	−.35*** (276)	.02 (40)	−.01 (98)	−.12 (95)	−.06 (131)	−.15 (125)
Marital happiness	.21*** (262)	−.18 (39)	.18 (93)	.01 (90)	.11 (124)	−.01 (118)
Marital conflict	−.13* (257)	−.18 (38)	−.06 (93)	.06 (90)	−.28** (120)	−.15 (114)
Marital stability	.12 (254)	.08 (38)	−.05 (94)	−.11 (91)	.05 (116)	.03 (110)
Child has enjoyable times with father	.35*** (271)	.16 (40)	.10 (96)	.04 (93)	.19* (129)	.22* (123)
Child has difficult times with father	−.20*** (273)	−.40* (39)	−.33*** (97)	−.04 (94)	−.43*** (131)	−.07 (125)
Father active in youth organizations	.11 (188)	na	.03 (70)	.11 (69)	.16 (92)	.18 (88)
Hours/day father spends on child care	na	−.13 (40)	na	na	na	na
Dissatisfaction with child support	−.04 (194)	.11 (26)	−.02 (72)	.03 (70)	−.04 (89)	−.08 (83)
Conflict mother with nonresident father	.10 (196)	−.33 (26)	−.11 (71)	.10 (69)	.00 (92)	−.04 (86)
Nonresident father's involvement	−.04 (116)	.24 (16)	−.09 (43)	.18 (41)	−.11 (51)	−.16 (48)
Nonresident father's influence	−.09 (119)	−.32 (18)	−.09 (47)	.11 (45)	.12 (50)	−.05 (47)
Child has enjoyable times with mother	.28*** (276)	.18 (40)	.07 (98)	.12 (95)	.32*** (131)	.23* (125)
Child has difficult times with mother	−.19*** (276)	−.48** (40)	−.49*** (98)	−.15 (95)	−.50*** (131)	−.15 (125)
Mother's support of child 5-18	na	na	.07 (93)	.27** (91)	.30*** (125)	.11 (119)
Mother's control of child 12-18	na	na	na	na	.02 (128)	.09 (123)
Mother's interaction with child 5-18	na	na	−.00 (92)	.35*** (91)	.07 (124)	.10 (118)
Index of mother's interaction with child 0-4	na	.29 (10)	na	na	na	na
Mother-adolescent disagreement	−.45*** (131)	na	na	na	−.59*** (131)	−.37*** (127)
Mother's aggression toward child 0-4	na	−.12 (10)	na	na	na	na

Table B.2 Continued

Predictor	Global Well-Being 0-18	Adjust-ment 0-4	Adjust-ment 5-11	School Perfor-mance 5-11	Adjust-ment 12-18	School Grades 12-18
Mother's aggression toward child 5-18	na	na	-.18 (93)	-.17 (91)	-.30*** (124)	-.13 (118)
Mother's childrearing values, 0-4	na	.06 (10)	na	na	na	na
Mother's childrearing values, 5-18	na	na	.01 (92)	.07 (90)	.22* (120)	.06 (114)
Mother's global well-being	.19** (244)	.08 (37)	.22* (84)	-.01 (81)	.11 (116)	-.02 (112)

Panel D: Correlates of Well-Being for Children Whose Mother Has Been Continuously Single

Predictor	Global Well-Being 0-18	Adjust-ment 0-4	Adjust-ment 5-11	School Perfor-mance 5-11	Adjust-ment 12-18	School Grades 12-18
Sample	-.05 (418)	.01 (157)	.03 (156)	-.02 (152)	-.02 (64)	.06 (60)
Cohabiting (1 yes, 0 no)	.04 (418)	.01 (157)	-.02 (156)	.07 (152)	.04 (64)	-.27* (60)
Other adults (1 yes, 0 no)	-.02 (418)	-.05 (157)	-.11 (156)	-.12 (152)	.13 (64)	-.13 (60)
Household size	-.11* (418)	-.06 (157)	-.07 (156)	-.12 (152)	-.24* (64)	-.36** (60)
Household income	.05 (418)	.06 (157)	.10 (156)	.03 (152)	.29* (64)	.16 (60)
Education	.12* (418)	.20* (157)	.23** (156)	.09 (152)	.12 (64)	.25 (60)
Mother's hours employed	-.03 (418)	.07 (157)	.01 (156)	.03 (152)	.29* (64)	-.02 (60)
Race (1 white, 0 nonwhite)	.06 (418)	-.15 (157)	-.04 (156)	.08* (152)	.01 (64)	.14 (60)
Sex of focal child (1 boy, 0 girl)	-.04 (410)	-.00 (153)	-.17* (153)	-.27*** (149)	.07 (63)	-.01 (59)
Age of focal child	-.22*** (418)	.13 (157)	-.18* (156)	-.15* (152)	-.25* (64)	-.26* (60)
Dissatisfaction with child support	-.17** (326)	-.10 (124)	-.19* (131)	-.12 (126)	-.02 (42)	-.41** (40)
Conflict with nonresident father	-.02 (329)	.03 (124)	-.01 (131)	.11 (127)	-.22 (42)	-.31* (41)
Nonresident father's involvement	.09 (187)	-.08 (78)	.34** (69)	.40*** (69)	.50* (19)	.50* (18)
Nonresident father's influence	.18* (196)	-.01 (82)	.22 (72)	.18 (70)	-.08 (18)	.26 (19)
Child has enjoyable times with mother	.26*** (413)	.09 (155)	.30*** (156)	.10 (152)	.40** (62)	.14 (58)

Table B.2   Continued

Predictor	Global Well-Being 0-18	Adjust-ment 0-4	Adjust-ment 5-11	School Perfor-mance 5-11	Adjust-ment 12-18	School Grades 12-18
Child has difficult times with mother	−.05 (414)	−.20* (155)	−.41*** (156)	−.27*** (152)	−.40** (62)	−.16 (58)
Mother's support of child 5-18	na	na	.24** (148)	.30*** (144)	.21 (60)	.25 (57)
Mother's control of child, 12-18	na	na	na	na	.03 (62)	.07 (58)
Mother's interaction with child 5-18	na	na	.06 (138)	.04 (135)	−.14 (58)	.06 (55)
Index of mother's interaction with child 0-4	na	.17 (104)	na	na	na	na
Mother-adolescent disagreement	na	na	na	na	−.50*** (63)	−.12 (60)
Mother's aggression toward child 0-4	na	−.17 (106)	na	na	na	na
Mother's aggression toward child 5-18	na	na	−.15 (148)	−.03 (144)	−.13 (60)	−.16 (57)
Mother's childrearing values, 0-4	na	.16 (91)	na	na	na	na
Mother's childrearing values, 5-18	na	na	.28*** (136)	.29*** (132)	.20 (54)	.16 (51)
Mother's global well-being	.17*** (355)	.22* (132)	.11 (130)	.18* (126)	.27* (57)	−.10 (56)

The number of cases is in parentheses.
*$p < .05$; **$p < .01$; ***$p < .001$.

References

Abbott, D. A., & Brody, G. H. (1985). The relation of child age, gender, and number of children to the marital adjustment of wives. *Journal of Marriage and the Family, 47,* 77-84.

Abel, E. K., & Nelson, M. K. (Eds.). (1990). *Circles of care: Work and identity in women's lives.* Albany: State University of New York Press.

Adams, J. S. (1965). Inequity in social exchange. In L. Berkowitz (Ed.), *Advances in experimental social psychology* (Vol. 2, pp. 267-299). New York: Academic Press.

Ade-Ridder, L., & Brubaker, T. H. (1983). The quality of long-term marriages. In T. H. Brubaker (Ed.), *Family relationships in later life* (pp. 21-30). Beverly Hills, CA: Sage.

Aldous, J. (1978). *Family careers: Developmental change in families.* New York: John Wiley.

Allen, K. R., & Baber, K. M. (1992). Starting a revolution in family life education: A feminist vision. *Family Relations, 41,* 378-384.

Allen, W. (1978). The search for applicable theories of black family life. *Journal of Marriage and the Family, 40,* 117-131.

Alwin, D. F. (1986). Religion and parental child-rearing orientations: Evidence of a Catholic-Protestant convergence. *American Journal of Sociology, 92,* 412-440.

Alwin, D. F. (1990). Cohort replacement and changes in parental socialization values. *Journal of Marriage and the Family, 52,* 347-360.

Amato, P. R. (1987). Family processes in one-parent, stepparent, and intact families: The child's point of view. *Journal of Marriage and the Family, 49,* 327-337.

Amato, P. R., & Booth, A. (1991). Consequences of parental divorce and marital unhappiness for adult well-being. *Social Forces, 69,* 895-914.

Amato, P. R., & Keith, B. (1991). Parental divorce and the well-being of children: A meta-analysis. *Psychological Bulletin, 110,* 26-46.

Ambert, A. M. (1989). *Ex-spouses and new spouses: A study of relationships*. Greenwich, CT: JAI.

Astone, N. M., & McLanahan, S. S. (1991). Family structure, parental practices, and high school completion. *American Sociological Review, 56,* 309-320.

Atkinson, M. P., Blackwelder, S. P., & Risman, B. J. (1992, November). *Measuring wives' material dependence.* Paper presented at the Theory Construction and Research Methodology Workshop, annual meeting of the National Council on Family Relations, Orlando, FL.

Baber, K. M., & Allen, K. R. (1992). *Women and families: Feminist reconstructions.* New York: Guilford.

Barber, B. K., & Thomas, D. L. (1986). Dimensions of fathers' and mothers' supportive behavior: The case for physical affection. *Journal of Marriage and the Family, 48,* 783-794.

Barnett, R. C., & Baruch, G. K. (1987). Determinants of fathers' participation in family work. *Journal of Marriage and the Family, 49,* 29-40.

Baruch, G. K., Barnett, R. C., & Rivers, C. (1983). *Lifeprints: New patterns of love and work for today's women.* New York: New American Library.

Beck, R. W., & Beck, S. H. (1989). The incidence of extended households among middle-aged black and white women: Estimates from a 5-year panel study. *Journal of Family Issues, 10,* 147-168.

Bell, R. R. (1981). *Worlds of friendship.* Beverly Hills, CA: Sage.

Berg, B., & Kelly, R. (1979). The measured self-esteem of children from broken, rejected, and accepted families. *Journal of Divorce, 2,* 363-369.

Berheide, C. W. (1984). Women's work in the home: Seems like old times. In B. B. Hess & M. B. Sussman (Eds.), *Women and the family: Two decades of change* (pp. 37-55). New York: Haworth.

Berk, S. F. (1985). *The gender factory: The apportionment of work in American households.* New York: Plenum.

Bernard, J. (1972). *The future of marriage.* New York: World.

Bianchi, S. M., & Spain, D. (1986). *American women in transition.* New York: Russell Sage.

Blake, J. (1989). *Family size and achievement.* Berkeley: University of California Press.

Blau, P. M. (1964). *Exchange and power in social life.* New York: John Wiley.

Blechman, E. A. (1982). Are children with one parent at psychological risk? A methodological review. *Journal of Marriage and the Family, 44,* 179-195.

Bohannon, P. (1970). Divorce chains, households of remarriage, and multiple divorces. In P. Bohannon (Ed.), *Divorce and after* (pp. 127-139). New York: Doubleday.

Bohannon, P., & Erickson, R. (1978, January). Stepping in. *Psychology Today,* pp. 53-54, 59.

Booth, A., & Amato, P. (1991). Divorce and psychological stress. *Journal of Health and Social Behavior, 32,* 396-407.

Booth, A., & Edwards, J. N. (1989). Transmission of marital and family quality over the generations: The effect of parental divorce and unhappiness. *Journal of Divorce, 13,* 41-58.

Booth, A., Johnson, D. R., White, L., & Edwards, J. N. (1984). Women, outside employment, and marital instability. *American Journal of Sociology, 90,* 567-583.

Bould, S. (1977). Female-headed families: Personal fate control and provider role. *Journal of Marriage and the Family, 39,* 339-349.

Boyd, S. L., & Treas, J. (1989). Family care for the frail elderly: A new look at "women in the middle." *Women's Studies Quarterly, 1* and *2,* 66-74.

Bozett, F. W. (1987). *Gay and lesbian parents.* New York: Praeger.

Bray, J. (1988). Children's development during early remarriage. In M. Hetherington & J. Arasteh (Eds.), *Impact of divorce, single parenting, and stepparenting on children* (pp. 279-298). Hillsdale, NJ: Lawrence Erlbaum.

Brayfield, A. A. (1992). Employment resources and housework in Canada. *Journal of Marriage and the Family, 54,* 19-30.

Bronfenbrenner, U. (1979). *The ecology of human development: Experiments by nature and design.* Cambridge, MA: Harvard University Press.

Bronfenbrenner, U. (1989). Ecological systems theory. In R. Vasta (Ed.), *Annals of child development—six theories of child development: Revised formulations and current issues* (pp. 1-103). Greenwich, CT: JAI

Bronfenbrenner, U., & Crouter, A. C. (1983). The evolution of environmental models in developmental research. In W. Kessen (Ed.), *Handbook of child psychology: Vol. 1. History, theory, and methods* (pp. 357-414). New York: John Wiley.

Brooks-Gunn, J., Duncan, G. J., Klebanov, P. K., & Sealand, N. (1993). Do neighborhoods influence child and adolescent development? *American Journal of Sociology, 99,* 353-395.

Brown, C. (1981). Mothers, fathers, and children: From private to public patriarchy. In L. Sargent (Ed.), *Women and revolution* (pp. 239-267). New York: South End Press.

Buchanan, C. M., Maccoby, E. E., & Dornbusch, S. M. (1991). Caught between parents: Adolescents' experience in divorced homes. *Child Development, 62,* 1008-1029.

Bumpass, L. L., & Sweet, J. A. (1989). Children's experience in single-parent families: Implications of cohabitation and marital transitions. *Family Planning Perspectives, 21,* 256-260.

Burkhauser, R. V., & Duncan, G. J. (1989). Economic risks of gender roles: Income loss and life events over the life course. *Social Science Quarterly, 70,* 3-23.

Campbell, A. (1981). *The sense of well-being in America.* New York: McGraw-Hill.

Campbell, A. A., Converse, P. L., & Rodgers, W. (1976). *The quality of American life: Perceptions, evaluations, and satisfactions.* New York: Russell Sage.

Carter, B., & McGoldrick, M. (1989). *The changing family life cycle: A framework for family therapy.* Boston: Allyn & Bacon.

Cashion, B. G. (1984). Female-headed families: Effects on children and clinical implications. In D. H. Olson & B. C. Miller (Eds.), *Family studies review yearbook* (pp. 481-489). Beverly Hills, CA: Sage.

Cheal, D. (1991). *Family and the state of theory.* Toronto: University of Toronto Press.

Cherlin, A. J. (1978). Remarriage as an incomplete institution. *American Journal of Sociology, 86,* 634-650.

Cherlin, A. J. (1988). *The changing American family and public policy.* Washington, DC: The Urban Institute Press.

Cherlin, A. J., & Furstenberg, F. F., Jr. (1986). *The new American grandparent: A place in the family, A life apart.* New York: Basic Books.

Clausen, J. S. (1991). Adolescent competence and the shaping of the life course. *American Journal of Sociology, 96,* 805-842.

Clingempeel, G. (1981). Quasi-kin relationships and marital quality. *Journal of Personality and Social Psychology, 41,* 890-901.

Clingempeel, G., & Segal, S. (1986). Stepparent-stepchild relationships and the psychological adjustment of children in stepmother and stepfather families. *Child Development, 57,* 474-484.

Cochran, M., & Dean, C. (1991). Home, school relations, and the empowerment process. *The Elementary School Journal, 91,* 261-269.

Coleman, J. S. (1993). The rational reconstruction of society. *American Sociological Review, 58,* 1-15.

Coleman, M., & Ganong, L. H. (1990). Remarriage and stepfamily research in the 1980s: Increased interest in an old family form. *Journal of Marriage and the Family, 52,* 925-940.

Colletta, N. D. (1979). The impact of divorce: Father absence or poverty? *Journal of Divorce, 3,* 27-35.

Collins, A. W. (1990). Parent-child relationships in the transition to adolescence: Continuity and change in interaction, affect, and cognition. In R. Montemayor, G. R. Adams, & T. P. Gullotta (Eds.), *Advances in adolescent development: From childhood to adolescence: A transitional period?* (pp. 85-106). Newbury Park, CA: Sage.

Coltrane, S., & Ishi-Kuntz, M. (1992). Men's housework: A life course perspective. *Journal of Marriage and the Family, 54,* 43-57.

Cook, K. S., & Emerson, R. M. (1978). Power, equity, and commitment in exchange networks. *American Sociological Review, 43,* 721-739.

Cooney, T. M., & Uhlenberg, P. (1990). The role of divorce in men's relations with their adult children after midlife. *Journal of Marriage and the Family. 52,* 677-688.

Coontz, S. (1992). *The way we never were: American families and the nostalgia trap.* New York: Basic Books.

Cooper, J. E., Holman, J., & Braithwaite, V. A. (1983). Self-esteem and family cohesion: The child's perspective and adjustment. *Journal of Marriage and the Family, 45,* 153-159.

Cott, N. (1977). *The bonds of womanhood.* New Haven, CT: Yale University Press.

Coverman, S., & Sheley, J. F. (1986). Change in men's housework and child-care time, 1965-1975. *Journal of Marriage and the Family, 48,* 413-422.

Cross, W. E. (1985). Black identity: Rediscovering the distinction between personal identity and reference group orientation. In M. B. Spencer, G. K. Brookins, & W. R. Allen (Eds.), *Beginnings: The social and affective development of black children* (pp. 155-171). Hillsdale, NJ: Lawrence Erlbaum.

Curtis, R. F. (1986). Household and family in theory on inequality. *American Sociological Review, 51,* 168-183.

Damon, W., & Hart, D. (1982). The development of self-understanding from infancy through adolescence. *Child Development, 53,* 841-864.

Davis, K. (1949). *Human society.* New York: Macmillan.

Dawson, D. A. (1991). *Family structure and children's health: United States, 1988* (Vital and Health Statistics, Series 10, Data from the National Health Interview Survey; No. 1978). Hyattsville MD: Department of Health and Human Services.

Deadbeat Dads: Wanted for failure to pay child support. (1992, May 4). *Newsweek*, pp. 46-52.

Delphy, C. (1984). *Close to home*. Amherst: University of Massachusetts Press.

Demo, D. H. (1992a). Parent-child relations: Assessing recent changes. *Journal of Marriage and the Family, 54*, 104-117.

Demo, D. H. (1992b). The self-concept over time: Research issues and directions. *Annual Review of Sociology, 18*, 303-326.

Demo, D. H. (1993). The relentless search for effects of divorce: Forging new trails or tumbling down the beaten path? *Journal of Marriage and the Family, 55*, 42-45.

Demo, D. H., & Acock, A. C. (1988). The impact of divorce on children. *Journal of Marriage and the Family, 50*, 619-648.

Demo, D. H., & Acock, A. C. (1993). Family diversity and the division of domestic labor: How much have things really changed? *Family Relations, 42*, 323-331.

Demo, D. H., Small, S. A., & Savin-Williams, R. C. (1987). Family relations and the self-esteem of adolescents and their parents. *Journal of Marriage and the Family, 49*, 705-715.

Denzin, N. (1986). Postmodern social theory. *Sociological Theory, 4*, 194-204.

DeVault, M. L. (1987). Doing housework: Feeding and family life. In N. Gerstel & H. E. Gross (Eds.), *Families and work* (pp. 178-191). Philadelphia: Temple University Press.

DeVault, M. L. (1991). *Feeding the family*. Chicago: University of Chicago Press.

Dobash, R. E., & Dobash, R. P. (1979). *Violence against wives: A case against the patriarchy*. New York: Free Press.

Dornbusch, S. M., Carlsmith, J. M., Bushwall, S. J., Ritter, P. L., Leiderman, H., Hastorf, A. H., & Gross, R. T. (1985). Single parents, extended households, and the control of adolescents. *Child Development, 56*, 326-341.

Douvan, E., & Adelson, J. (1966). *The adolescent experience*. New York: John Wiley.

Dressel, P. L., & Clark, A. (1990). A critical look at family care. *Journal of Marriage and the Family, 52*, 769-782.

Duncan, G. J., & Hoffman, S. D. (1985). Economic consequences of marital instability. In M. David & T. Smeeding (Eds.), *Horizontal equity, uncertainty, and economic well-being* (pp. 427-467). Chicago: University of Chicago Press.

Duvall, E. M., & Miller, B. C. (1985). *Marriage and family development* (6th ed.). New York: Harper and Row.

Edwards, J. N. (1969). Familial behavior as social exchange. *Journal of Marriage and the Family, 31*, 518-526.

Edwards, J. N. (1991). Biosocial innovations and the family. *Journal of Marriage and the Family, 53*, 349-360.

Elder, G. H., Jr. (1984). Families, kin, and the life course. In R. Parke (Ed.), *Review of child development research*, Vol. 7, pp. 215-241. Chicago: University of Chicago Press.

Elder, G. H., Jr. (1985). *Life course dynamics: Trajectories and transitions, 1968-1980*. Ithaca, NY: Cornell University Press.

Elder, G. H., Jr. (1991). The life course. In E. F. Borgotta & M. L. Borgotta (Eds.), *The encyclopedia of sociology* (pp. 281-311). New York: Macmillan.

Elder, G. H., Jr., & Caspi, A. (1988). Economic stress in lives: Developmental perspectives. *Journal of Social Issues, 44*, 25-45.

Emerson, R. M. (1972). Exchange theory, Part 1: A psychological basis for social exchange. In J. Berger, M. Zelditch, & B. Anderson (Eds.), *Sociological theories in progress* (pp. 38-57). Boston: Houghton Mifflin.

Emerson, R. M. (1976). Social exchange theory. In *Annual review of sociology* (Vol. 2, pp. 335-362). Palo Alto, CA: Annual Reviews.

Emery, R. E. (1982). Interparental conflict and the children of discord and divorce. *Psychological Bulletin, 92*, 310-330.

Emery, R. E. (1988). *Marriage, divorce, and children's adjustment.* Newbury Park, CA: Sage.

Ferree, M. M. (1990). Beyond separate spheres: Feminism and family research. *Journal of Marriage and the Family, 52*, 866-884.

Ferree, M. M. (1991). The gender division of labor in two-earner marriages: Dimensions of variability and change. *Journal of Family Issues, 12*, 158-180.

Furstenberg, F. F., Jr., Morgan, P., & Allison, P. D. (1987). Paternal participation and children's well-being after marital dissolution. *American Sociological Review, 52*, 695-701.

Furstenberg, F. F., Jr., & Nord, C. W. (1985). Parenting apart: Patterns of childrearing after marital disruption. *Journal of Marriage and the Family, 47*, 893-904.

Furstenberg, F. F., Jr., & Spanier, G. (1984). *Recycling the family: Remarriage after divorce.* Beverly Hills, CA: Sage.

Ganong, L., & Coleman, M. (1987). Stepchildren's perceptions of their parents. *Journal of Genetic Psychology, 148*, 5-17.

Ganong, L., Coleman, M., & Mapes, D. (1990). A meta-analytic review of family structure stereotypes. *Journal of Marriage and the Family, 52*, 287-297.

Gelles, R. J. (1987). *Family violence.* Newbury Park, CA: Sage.

Glenn, E. N. (1987). Gender and the family. In B. B. Hess & M. M. Ferree (Eds.), *Analyzing gender: A handbook of social science research* (pp. 348-360). Newbury Park, CA: Sage.

Glenn, N. D. (1990). Quantitative research on marital quality in the 1980s: A critical review. *Journal of Marriage and the Family, 52*, 818-831.

Glenn, N. D., & McLanahan, S. (1982). Children and marital happiness: A further specification of the relationship. *Journal of Marriage and the Family, 44*, 63-72.

Glenn, N. D., & Weaver, C. N. (1979). A note on family situation and global happiness. *Social Forces, 57*, 960-967.

Glenn, N. D., & Weaver, C. N. (1988). The changing relationship of marital status to reported happiness. *Journal of Marriage and the Family, 50*, 317-324.

Goldscheider, F. K., & Waite, L. J. (1991). *New families, no families? The transformation of the American home.* Berkeley: University of California Press.

Gongla, P. A., & Thompson, E. (1987). Single-parent families. In M. Sussmann & S. Steinmetz (Eds.), *Handbook of marriage and the family* (pp. 397-418). New York: Plenum.

Gottman, J. M., & Katz, L. F. (1989). Effects of marital discord on young children's peer interaction and health. *Developmental Psychology, 25*, 373-381.

Gouldner, A. W. (1960). The norm of reciprocity. *American Sociological Review, 25*, 161-178.

Gove, W. R., Hughes, M., & Style, C. B. (1983). Does marriage have positive effects on the psychological well-being of the individual? *Journal of Health and Social Behavior, 24*, 122-131.

Greenberger, E., Goldberg, W. A., Crawford, T., & Granger, J. (1988). Beliefs about the consequences of maternal employment for children. *Psychology of Women Quarterly, 12,* 35-59.

Greenberger, E., & O'Neil, R. (1990). Parents' concerns about their children's development: Implications for fathers' and mothers' well-being and attitudes about work. *Journal of Marriage and the Family, 52,* 621-635.

Grych, J. H., & Fincham, F. D. (1990). Marital conflict and children's adjustment: A cognitive-contextual framework. *Psychological Bulletin, 108,* 267-290.

Guidubaldi, J., & Perry, J. D. (1985). Divorce and mental health sequelae for children: A two-year follow-up of a nationwide sample. *Journal of the American Academy of Child Psychiatry, 24,* 531-537.

Hareven, T. K. (1974). The family as process: The historical study of the family cycle. *Journal of Family History, 7,* 322-329.

Hartup, W. W. (1983). Peer relations. In P. H. Mussen & E. M. Hetherington (Eds.), *Handbook of child psychology: Socialization, personality, and social development* (pp. 103-196). New York: John Wiley.

Hauptman, A. M., & Merisotis, J. P. (1990). *The college tuition spiral: An examination of why charges are increasing* (a report to the College Board and the American Council on Education). New York: The American Council on Education and the College Board.

Hawkins, A. J., & Roberts, T. (1992). Designing a primary intervention to help dual-career couples share housework and child care. *Family Relations, 41,* 169-177.

Herzog, A. R., Rodgers, W. L., & Woodworth, J. (1982). *Subjective well-being among different age groups.* Ann Arbor, MI: Institute for Social Research.

Hess, R. D., & Camara, K. A. (1979). Post-divorce family relationships as mediating factors in the consequences of divorce for children. *Journal of Social Issues, 35,* 79-98.

Hetherington, E. M., Camara, K. A., & Featherman, D. L. (1983). Achievement and intellectual functioning of children in one-parent households. In J. T. Spence (Ed.), *Achievement and achievement motives: Psychological and sociological approaches* (pp. 205-284). San Francisco: Freeman.

Hetherington, E. M., Cox, M., & Cox, R. (1978). The aftermath of divorce. In J. H. Stevens & M. Mathews (Eds.), *Mother-child, father-child relationships* (pp. 149-176). Washington, DC: National Association for the Education of Young Children.

Hetherington, E. M., Cox, M., & Cox, R. (1982). Effects of divorce on parents and young children. In M. Lamb (Ed.), *Nontraditional families: Parenting and child development* (pp. 233-288). Hillsdale, NJ: Lawrence Erlbaum.

Hochschild, A. W. (1989). *The second shift: Working parents and the revolution at home.* New York: Viking.

Hochschild, A. W. (1992, November). *Beyond the second shift: Denying needs at home or contesting rules at work?* Paper presented at the annual meeting of the National Council on Family Relations, Orlando, FL.

Hofferth, S. L. (1985). Updating children's life course. *Journal of Marriage and the Family, 47,* 93-115.

Hoffman, L. W., & Manis, J. B. (1978). Influences of children on marital interaction and parental satisfactions and dissatisfactions. In R. M. Lerner & G. B. Spanier (Eds.), *Child influences on marital and family interaction* (pp. 165-214). New York: Academic Press.

Holmbeck, G. N., & O'Donnell, K. (1991). Discrepancies between perceptions of decision-making and behavioral autonomy. In R. L. Paikoff & W. A. Collins (Eds.), *Parent-adolescent disagreements in the family: New directions for child development* (pp. 51-69). San Francisco: Jossey-Bass.

Homans, G. C. (1961). *Social behavior: Its elementary forms.* New York: Harcourt, Brace, and World.

Homans, G. C. (1974). *Social behavior: Its elementary forms* (rev. ed.). New York: Harcourt, Brace, and World.

Huber, J., & Spitze, G. (1983). *Sex stratification: Children, housework, and jobs.* New York: Academic Press.

Hughes, M., & Demo, D. H. (1989). Self-perceptions of Black Americans: Self-esteem and personal efficacy. *American Journal of Sociology, 95,* 132-159.

Hughes, M., & Demo, D. H. (1992a, August). *Ethnic identity and self-evaluation: A study of African Americans, non-Hispanic white Americans, and persons of Mexican descent.* Paper presented at the annual meeting of the American Sociological Association, Pittsburgh, PA.

Hughes, M., & Demo, D. H. (1992b, April). *Racial inequality and personal efficacy.* Paper presented at the annual meeting of the Southern Sociological Society, New Orleans, LA.

Idler, E. L., & Kasl, S. (1991). Health perceptions and survival: Do global evaluations of health status really predict mortality. *Journal of Gerontology, 46*(2), S55-S66.

Jouriles, E. N., Barling, J., & O'Leary, K. D. (1987). Predicting child behavior problems in maritally violent families. *Journal of Abnormal Child Psychology, 15,* 497-509.

Kamo, Y. (1988). Determinants of the household division of labor: Resources, power, and ideology. *Journal of Family Issues, 9,* 177-200.

Keith, V. M., & Finlay, B. (1988). The impact of parental divorce on children's educational attainment, marital timing, and likelihood of divorce. *Journal of Marriage and the Family, 50,* 797-809.

Kidwell, J., Fischer, J. L., Dunham, R. M., & Baranowski, M. (1983). Parents and adolescents: Push and pull of change. In C. R. Figley & H. I. McCubbin (Eds.), *Stress and the family: Coping with normative transitions* (Vol. 1, pp. 74-89). New York: Brunner/Mazel.

Kinard, E. M., & Reinherz, H. (1984). Marital disruption: Effects of behavioral and emotional functioning in children. *Journal of Family Issues, 5,* 90-115.

Kinard, E. M., & Reinherz, H. (1986). Effects of marital disruption on children's school aptitude and achievement. *Journal of Marriage and the Family, 48,* 285-293.

Kingsbury, N., & Scanzoni, J. (1993). Structural-functionalism. In P. G. Boss, W. J. Doherty, R. LaRossa, W. R. Schumm, & S. K. Steinmetz (Eds.), *Sourcebook of family theories and methods: A contextual approach* (pp. 195-217). New York: Plenum.

Kitson, G. C. (1992). *Portrait of divorce: Adjustment to marital breakdown.* New York: Guilford.

Kurdek, L. (1981). An integrative perspective on children's divorce adjustment. *American Psychologist, 36,* 856-866.

Lamb, M. E. (1977). The effects of divorce on children's personality development. *Journal of Divorce, 1,* 163-174.

Lamb, M. E., Pleck, J. H., Charnov, E. L., & Levine, J. A. (1987). A biosocial perspective on paternal behavior and involvement. In J. B. Lancaster, J. Altmann, A. S. Rossi, & L. R. Sherrod (Eds.), *Parenting across the lifespan: Biosocial dimensions* (pp. 111-142). New York: Aldine de Gruyter.

LaRossa, R. (1988). Fatherhood and social change. *Family Relations, 37,* 451-457.

LaRossa, R., & LaRossa, M. M. (1981). *Transition to parenthood: How infants change families.* Beverly Hills, CA: Sage.

Lempers, J. K., Clark-Lempers, D., & Simons, R. L. (1989). Economic hardship, parenting, and distress in adolescence. *Child Development, 60,* 25-39.

Lewis, R. A., & Spanier, G. B. (1979). Theorizing about the quality and stability of marriage. In W. R. Burr, R. Hill, F. I. Nye, & I. L. Reiss (Eds.), *Contemporary theories about the family* (Vol. 1, pp. 268-294). New York: Free Press.

Lino, M. (1990). Expenditures on a child by husband-wife families. *Family Economics Review, 3*(3), 2-18.

Lino, M. (1991). Expenditures on a child by single-parent families. *Family Economics Review, 4*(1), 2-7.

Lino, M. (1993). Families with children: Changes in economic status and expenditures on children over time. *Family Economics Review, 6*(1), 9-17.

Maccoby, E. E., & Mnookin, R. H. (1992). *Dividing the child: Social and legal dilemmas of custody.* Cambridge, MA: Harvard University Press.

Mace, D. R. (1956). Married love and parent love. In S. M. Gruenberg (Ed.), *The encyclopedia of child care and guidance* (pp. 951-960). New York: Doubleday.

Maeroff, G. I. (1992). Reform comes home: Policies to encourage parental involvement in children's education. In C. E. Finn, Jr., & T. Rebarber (Eds.), *Education reform in the '90s* (pp. 157-171). New York: Macmillan.

Major, B. (1987). Gender, justice, and the psychology of entitlement. In P. Shaver & C. Hendrick (Eds.), *Sex and gender* (pp. 124-148). Newbury Park, CA: Sage.

Mancini, J. A., & Blieszner, R. (1989). Aging parents and adult children: Research themes in intergenerational relations. *Journal of Marriage and the Family, 51,* 275-290.

Martin, T. C., & Bumpass, L. L. (1989). Recent trends in marital disruption. *Demography, 26,* 37-51.

Masnick, G., & Bane, M. J. (1980). *The nation's families: 1960-1990.* Boston: Auburn House.

Mattessich, P., & Hill, R. (1987). Life cycle and family development. In M. B. Sussman & S. K. Steinmetz (Eds.), *Handbook of marriage and the family* (pp. 437-469). New York: Plenum.

McLanahan, S. (1985). Family structure and the reproduction of poverty. *American Journal of Sociology, 90,* 873-901.

McLanahan, S., & Adams, J. (1987). Parenthood and psychological well-being. *Annual Review of Sociology, 13,* 237-257.

McLanahan, S., & Booth, K. (1989). Mother-only families: Problems, prospects, and politics. *Journal of Marriage and the Family, 51,* 557-580.

McLoyd, V. C. (1990). The impact of economic hardship on black families and children: Psychological distress, parenting, and socioemotional development. *Child Development, 61,* 311-346.

Mechanic, D., & Hansell, S. (1989). Divorce, family conflict, and adolescents' well-being. *Journal of Health and Social Behavior, 30,* 105-116.

Mederer, H. (1993). Division of labor in two-earner homes: Task accomplishment versus household management as critical variables in perceptions about family work. *Journal of Marriage and the Family, 55,* 133-145.

Menaghan, E. G. (1982). Assessing the impact of family transitions on marital experience. In H. I. McCubbin, A. E. Cauble, & J. M. Patterson (Eds.), *Family stress, coping, and social support* (pp. 90-108). Springfield, IL: Charles C Thomas.

Menaghan, E. G., & Parcel, T. L. (1990). Parental employment and family life: Research in the 1980s. *Journal of Marriage and the Family, 52,* 1079-1098.

Mencken, F. C., & Acock, A. C. (1989). *Children of divorced mothers.* Unpublished manuscript, Center for Life Course and Population Studies, Louisiana State University, Baton Rouge, LA.

Michaels, J. W., Acock, A. C., & Edwards, J. N. (1986). Social exchange and equity determinants of relationship commitment. *Journal of Social and Personal Relationships, 3,* 161-175.

Michaels, J. W., Edwards, J. N., & Acock, A. C. (1984). Satisfaction in intimate relationships as a function of inequality, inequity, and outcomes. *Social Psychology Quarterly, 47,* 347-357.

Michelson, W. (1985). *From sun to sun.* Totowa, NJ: Rowman & Allenheld.

Milardo, R. M. (1987). Changes in social networks of women and men following divorce: A review. *Journal of Family Issues, 8,* 78-96.

Mirowsky, J. (1985). Depression and marital power: An equity model. *American Journal of Sociology, 91,* 557-592.

Mirowsky, J., & Ross, C. E. (1986). Social patterns of distress. *Annual Review of Sociology, 12,* 23-45.

Mirowsky, J., & Ross, C. E. (1989). *Social causes of psychological distress.* New York: Aldine de Gruyter.

Montemayor, R. (1986). Family variation in parent-adolescent storm and stress. *Journal of Adolescent Research, 1,* 15-31.

Morgan, L. A. (1989). Economic well-being following marital termination: A comparison of widowed and divorced women. *Journal of Family Issues, 10,* 86-101.

Mott, F. L. (1990). When is a father really gone? Paternal-child contact in father-absent homes. *Demography, 27,* 499-517.

Moynihan, D. P. (1965). *The Negro family: The case for national action.* Washington, DC: Department of Labor.

Neal, A. G., Groat, H. T., & Wicks, J. W. (1989). Attitudes about having children: A study of 600 couples in the early years of marriage. *Journal of Marriage and the Family, 51,* 313-328.

Newcomer, S., & Udry, J. R. (1987). Parental marital status effects on adolescent sexual behavior. *Journal of Marriage and the Family, 49,* 235-240.

Nock, S. L. (1988). The family and hierarchy. *Journal of Marriage and the Family, 50,* 957-966.

Nock, S. L., & Kingston, P. W. (1988). Time with children: The impact of couples' work-time commitments. *Social Forces, 67,* 59-85.

O'Brien, M. (1981). *The politics of reproduction.* Boston: Routledge & Kegan Paul.

O'Leary, K. D., & Emery, R. E. (1984). Marital discord and child behavior problems. In M. D. Levine & P. Satz (Eds.), *Developmental variation and dysfunction* (pp. 345-364). New York: Academic Press.

Oshman, H. P., & Manosevitz, M. (1976). Father absence: Effects of stepfathers upon psychosocial development in males. *Developmental Psychology, 12,* 479-480.

Otto, L. B. (1988). America's youth: A changing profile. *Family Relations, 37,* 385-391.

Parcel, T. L., & Menaghan, E. G. (1990). Maternal working conditions and children's verbal facility: Studying the intergenerational transmission of inequality from mothers to young children. *Social Psychology Quarterly, 53,* 132-147.

Parsons, T. (1942). Age and sex in the social structure. *American Sociological Review, 7,* 604-616.

Parsons, T., & Bales, R. F. (1955). *Family, socialization, and interaction processes.* New York: Free Press.

Pitts, J. R. (1964). The structural-functional approach. In H. T. Christensen (Ed.), *Handbook of marriage and the family* (pp. 5-124). Chicago: Rand McNally.

Pleck, J. (1985). *Working wives, working husbands.* Beverly Hills, CA: Sage.

Porter, B., & O'Leary, K. D. (1980). Marital discord and childhood behavior problems. *Journal of Abnormal Child Psychology, 8,* 287-295.

Porter, K. (1984). *The scheduling of life course events, economic adaptations, and marital history: An analysis of economic survival after separation and divorce among a cohort of midlife women.* Unpublished doctoral dissertation, Syracuse University, Syracuse, NY.

Rainwater, L. (1979). Mother's contribution to the family money economy in Europe and the United States. *Journal of Family History, 4,* 198-211.

Raschke, H. J. (1987). Divorce. In M. Sussman & S. Steinmetz (Eds.), *Handbook of marriage and the family* (pp. 597-624). New York: Plenum.

Raschke, H. J., & Raschke, V. J. (1979). Family conflict and the children's self-concepts. *Journal of Marriage and the Family, 41,* 367-374.

Raspberry, W. (1993, May 12). Bringing up fathers. *The Washington Post,* p. A19.

Robinson, J. P. (1988, December). Who's doing the housework? *American Demographics,* pp. 24-28, 63.

Rodgers, R. H., & White, J. M. (1993). Family development theory. In P. G. Boss, W. J. Doherty, R. LaRossa, W. R. Schumm, & S. K. Steinmetz (Eds.), *Sourcebook of family theories and methods: A contextual approach* (pp. 225-254). New York: Plenum.

Rollins, B. C., & Galligan, R. (1978). The developing child and marital satisfaction of parents. In R. Lerner & G. Spanier (Eds.), *Children's influence on marital and family interaction: A life-span perspective* (pp. 71-105). New York: Academic Press.

Rollins, B. C., & Thomas, D. L. (1979). Parental support, power, and control techniques in the socialization of children. In W. R. Burr, R. Hill, F. I. Nye, & I. L. Reiss (Eds.), *Contemporary theories about the family* (Vol. 1, pp. 317-364). New York: Free Press.

Rosenberg, M. (1979). *Conceiving the self.* New York: Basic Books.

Rosenberg, M. (1989). Old myths die hard: The case of black self-esteem. *Revue Internationale de Psychologie Sociale, 2,* 355-365.

Rosenfield, S. (1989). The effects of women's employment: Personal control and sex differences in mental health. *Journal of Health and Social Behavior, 30,* 77-91.

Ross, C. E., Mirowsky, J., & Goldsteen. K. (1991). The impact of the family on health: The decade in review. In A. Booth (Ed.), *Contemporary families: Look-*

ing forward, looking back (pp. 341-360). Minneapolis, MN: National Council on Family Relations.

Rossi, A. S. (1984). Gender and parenthood. *American Sociological Review, 49,* 1-19.

Savage, J. E., Jr., Adair, A. V., & Friedman, P. (1978). Community-social variables related to black parent-absent families. *Journal of Marriage and the Family, 40,* 779-785.

Sebald, H. (1986). Adolescents' shifting orientation toward parents and peers: A curvilinear trend over recent decades. *Journal of Marriage and the Family, 48,* 5-13.

Seltzer, J. A., & Bianchi, S. M. (1988). Children's contact with absent parents. *Journal of Marriage and the Family, 50,* 663-677.

Shaw, S. M. (1988). Gender differences in the definition and perception of household labor. *Family Relations, 37,* 333-337.

Skolnick, A. (1991). *Embattled paradise: The American family in an age of uncertainty.* New York: Basic Books.

Slater, P. (1961). Parental role differentiation. *American Journal of Sociology, 67,* 296-311.

Smetana, J. G. (1989). Adolescents' and parents' reasoning about actual family conflict. *Child Development, 60,* 1052-1067.

Spanier, G. B., & Lewis, R. A. (1980). Marital quality: A review of the seventies. *Journal of Marriage and the Family, 42,* 825-839.

Spanier, G. B., Lewis, R. A., & Cole, K. L. (1975). Marital adjustment over the family life cycle: The issue of curvilinearity. *Journal of Marriage and the Family, 37,* 263-275.

Spitze, G. (1988). Women's employment and family relations: A review. *Journal of Marriage and the Family, 50,* 595-618.

Stacey, J. (1991). *Brave new families.* New York: Basic Books.

Staines, G. L., & Libby, P. L. (1986). Men and women in role relationships. In R. S. Ashmore & F. K. DelBoca (Eds.), *The social psychology of female-male relations: A critical analysis of central concepts* (pp. 211-258). New York: Academic Press.

Straus, M. A., Gelles, R. J., & Steinmetz, S. K. (1980). *Behind closed doors: Violence in the American family.* New York: Doubleday.

Sweet, J. A., & Bumpass, L. L. (1987). *American families and households.* New York: Russell Sage.

Sweet, J. A., Bumpass, L. L., & Call, V.R.A. (1988). *The design and content of the National Survey of Families and Households* (Working Paper NSFH-1). Madison: University of Wisconsin, Center for Demography and Ecology.

Szinovacz, M. E. (1984). Changing family roles and interactions. In B. B. Hess & M. B. Sussman (Eds.), *Women and the family: Two decades of change* (pp. 164-201). New York: Haworth.

Teachman, J. D. (1986). First and second marital dissolution: A decomposition exercise for whites and blacks. *Sociological Quarterly, 27,* 571-590.

Thibaut, J. W., & Kelley, H. H. (1959). *The social psychology of groups.* New York: John Wiley.

Thies, J. M. (1977). Beyond divorce: The impact of remarriage on children.

Thomas, M. E., & Hughes, M. (1986). The continuing significance of race: A study of race, class, and quality of life in America, 1972-1985. *American Sociological Review, 51,* 830-841.

Thompson, L. (1991). Family work: Women's sense of fairness. *Journal of Family Issues, 12,* 181-196.

Thompson, L., & Walker, A. J. (1989). Gender in families: Women and men in marriage, work, and parenthood. *Journal of Marriage and the Family, 51,* 845-871.

Thompson, M. S., & Ensminger, M. E. (1989). Psychological well-being among mothers with school age children: Evolving family structures. *Social Forces, 67,* 715-730.

Thorne, B. (1982). Feminist rethinking of the family: An overview. In B. Thorne & M. Yalom (Eds.), *Rethinking the family: Some feminist questions* (pp. 1-24). White Plains, NY: Longman.

Thorne, B. (1992). Feminism and the family: Two decades of thought. In B. Thorne & M. Yalom (Eds.), *Rethinking the family: Some feminist questions* (rev. ed.) (pp. 3-30). White Plains, NY: Longman.

Tromsdorff, G. (1983). Value change in Japan. *International Journal of Intercultural Relations, 7,* 337-360.

Uhlenberg, P., & Eggebeen, D. (1986). The declining well-being of American adolescents. *The Public Interest, 82,* 25-38.

U.S. Department of Education. (1991). *Digest of Education Statistics.* Washington, DC: Government Printing Office.

Vemer, E., Coleman, M., Ganong, L., & Cooper, H. (1989). Marital satisfaction in remarriage: A meta-analysis. *Journal of Marriage and the Family, 51,* 713-725.

Veroff, J., Donovan, E., & Kulka, R. A. (1981). *A self-portrait from 1957 to 1976.* New York: Basic Books.

Visher, E., & Visher, J. (1983). Stepparenting: Blending families. In H. I. McCubbin & C. R. Figley (Eds.), *Stress and the family: Vol. 1. Coping with normative transitions* (pp. 133-146). New York: Brunner/Mazel.

Voeller, B. (1990). Some uses and misuses of the Kinsey scale. In D. P. McWhirter, S. A. Sanders, & J. M. Reinisch (Eds.), *Homosexuality/heterosexuality: Concepts of sexual orientation* (pp. 32-38). New York: Oxford University Press.

Voydanoff, P. (1987). *Work and family life.* Newbury Park, CA: Sage.

Voydanoff, P. (1990). Economic distress and family relations: A review of the eighties. *Journal of Marriage and the Family, 52,* 1099-1115.

Walby, S. (1990). *Theorizing patriarchy.* Oxford, UK: Blackwell.

Wallerstein, J. S., & Blakeslee, S. (1989). *Second chances: Men, women, and children a decade after divorce.* New York: Ticknor & Fields.

Walster, E., Walster, G. W., & Berscheid, E. (1978). *Equity: Theory and research.* Boston: Allyn & Bacon.

Warner, R. (1986). Alternative strategies for measuring household division of labor: A comparison. *Journal of Family Issues, 7,* 179-195.

Weiss, R. S. (1979). Growing up a little faster: The experience of growing up in a single-parent household. *Journal of Social Issues, 35,* 97-111.

Weiss, R. (1984). The impact of marital dissolution on income and consumption in single-parent households. *Journal of Marriage and the Family, 46,* 115-127.

Weitzman, L. (1985). *The divorce revolution: The unexpected social and economic consequences for women and children in America.* New York: Free Press.

White, L. K., & Booth, A. (1985). The quality and stability of remarriages: The role of stepchildren. *American Sociological Review, 50,* 689-698.

White, L. K., & Brinkerhoff, D. (1981). Children's work in the family. *Journal of Marriage and the Family, 43,* 789-798.

White, L. K., & Edwards, J. N. (1990). Emptying the nest and parental well-being: An analysis of national panel data. *American Sociological Review, 55,* 235-242.

Whitehead, B. D. (1993, April). Dan Quayle was right. *The Atlantic Monthly,* pp. 47-84.

Williams, D. G. (1988). Gender, marriage, and psychosocial well-being. *Journal of Family Issues, 9,* 452-468.

Wolchik, S., Sandler, I. N., Braver, S. T., & Fogas, B. (1985). Events of parental divorce: Stressfulness ratings by children, parents, and clinicians. *American Journal of Community Psychology, 14,* 59-74.

A world without fathers: The struggle to save the black family. (1992, May 4). *Newsweek,* pp. 16-29.

Yllö, K., & Bograd, M. (1988). *Feminist perspectives on wife abuse.* Newbury Park, CA: Sage.

Youniss, J., & Smollar, J. (1985). *Adolescent relations with mothers, fathers, and friends.* Chicago: University of Chicago Press.

Zelditch, M., Jr. (1955). Role differentiation in the nuclear family: A comparative study. In T. Parsons & R. F. Bales (Eds.), *Family socialization and interaction processes* (pp. 307-352). New York: Free Press.

Name Index

Abbott, D., 153
Abel, E., 219
Acock, A., 5, 22, 43, 45, 46, 104, 154, 189, 216
Adair, A., 189
Adams, J., 33, 154
Adelson, J., 209
Ade-Ridder, L., 152
Aldous, J., 36
Allen, K., 39, 227
Allen, W., 43
Allison, P., 23, 143
Alwin, D., 17
Amato, P., 41, 46, 141, 220, 223, 224
Ambert, A., 101
Astone, N., 208
Atkinson, M., 60

Baber, K., 39, 227
Bales, R., 39, 227
Bane, M., 10
Baranowski, M., 215
Barber, B., 190
Barling, J., 224
Barnett, R., 16, 41, 129, 190
Baruch, G., 16, 41, 129, 190
Beck, R., 209
Beck, S., 38
Bell, R., 209

Berg, B., 45, 189
Berheide, C., 90
Berk, S., 40, 72, 75, 76, 81, 83, 102, 218, 227
Bernard, J., 10, 39
Berscheid, E., 33
Bianchi, S., 19, 23, 143, 191, 197
Blackwelder, S., 60
Blake, J., 188
Blakeslee, S., 5, 224
Blau, P., 32
Blechman, E., 43
Blieszner, R., 158
Bograd, M., 98
Bohannon, P., 93, 121
Booth, A., 41, 45, 46, 92, 93, 104, 153, 220, 221
Booth, K., 22, 44
Bould, S., 60
Boyd, S., 219
Bozett, F., 24
Braithwaite, V., 190
Braver, S., 46
Bray, J., 92
Brayfield, A., 74
Brinkerhoff, D., 80
Brody, G., 153
Bronfenbrenner, U., 48, 192, 223
Brooks-Gunn, J., 192
Brown, C., 39

Brubaker, T., 154
Buchanan, C., 224
Bumpass, L., 21, 22, 44, 51, 96
Burkhauser, R., 152

Call, V., 51
Camara, K., 21, 224
Campbell, A., 35, 153
Carter, B., 36, 38
Cashion, E., 188
Caspi, A., 7
Charnov, E., 118
Cheal, D., 1
Cherlin, A., 10, 38, 92, 93, 103, 220
Clark, A., 7
Clark-Lempers, D., 22
Clausen, J., 152
Clingempeel, G., 93, 104, 191, 224
Cochran, M., 208
Cole, K., 154
Coleman, J., 4
Coleman, M., 38, 92, 96, 191, 220, 230
Colletta, N., 57
Collins, A., 211, 215
Coltrane, S., 74
Converse, P., 35, 153
Cooney, T., 27
Coontz, S., 10, 155, 176
Cooper, J., 96
Cott, N., 39
Coverman, S., 16, 73, 75, 103
Cox, M., 128, 192
Cox, R., 128, 152
Crawford, T., 19
Cross, W., 153
Crouter, A., 48, 223
Curtis, R., 61

Damon, W., 208
Davis, K., 30
Dawson, D., 228
Dean, C., 208
Delphy, C., 39
Demo, D., 5, 20, 22, 43, 45, 46, 47, 72,
    104, 146, 152, 176, 177, 189, 190,
    208, 215
Denzin, N., 1

DeVault, M., 39, 78, 84
Dobash, R. E., 155
Dobash, R. P., 155
Donovan, E., 153, 209
Dornbusch, S., 4, 21, 43, 107, 113, 189,
    224
Douvan, E., 209
Dressel, P., 7
Duncan, G., 152, 152, 192
Dunham, R., 215
Duvall, E., 36

Edwards, J., 24, 34, 45, 55, 153, 154
Eggebeen, D., 3
Elder, G., 7, 49
Emerson, R., 33
Emery, R., 45, 189, 224
Ensminger, M., 23, 141, 175, 221
Erickson, R., 121

Featherman, D., 21
Ferree, M., 7, 40, 72
Fincham, F., 45, 190, 224
Finlay, B., 21
Fischer, J., 215
Fogas, B., 46
Friedman, P., 189
Furstenberg, F., 4, 23, 38, 43, 93, 107,
    124, 143, 191, 197

Galligan, R., 154
Ganong, L., 38, 92, 96, 191, 220, 230
Gelles, R., 20, 98
Glenn, E., 35
Glenn, N., 35, 40, 41, 93, 153, 154
Goldberg, W., 19
Goldscheider, F., 80, 81, 227
Goldsteen, K., 150
Gongla, P., 152
Gottman, J., 22, 45
Gouldner, A., 32
Gove, W., 41, 150, 176
Granger, S., 19
Greenberger, E., 19, 176, 215, 222
Groat, H., 4
Grych, J., 45, 190, 224

Guidubaldi, J., 128, 216

Hansell, S., 22, 45
Hareven, T., 36
Hart, D., 208
Hartup, W., 192
Hauptman, A., 7, 77
Hawkins, A., 228
Herzog, A., 152, 153
Hess, R., 224
Hetherington, M., 21, 128, 152, 218
Hill, R., 36
Hochschild, A., 72, 84, 231
Hofferth, S., 63
Hoffman, S., 152, 153
Holman, J., 190
Holmbeck, G., 215
Homans, G., 32
Huber, J., 72, 80, 218
Hughes, M., 35, 41, 146, 153, 177

Idler, E., 146
Ishi-Kuntz, M., 74

Johnson, D., 153
Jouriles, E., 224

Kamo, Y., 75, 83, 102
Kasl, S., 146
Katz, L., 22, 45
Keith, V., 21, 223, 224
Kelley, H., 32. 156
Kelly, R., 45, 189
Kidwell, J., 215
Kinard, E., 188
Kingsbury, N., 30, 31, 224
Kingston, P., 4, 129
Kitson, G., 8, 101, 192
Klebanov, P., 192
Kulka, R., 153
Kurdek, L., 153

Lamb, M., 43, 118
LaRossa, M., 190
LaRossa, R., 53, 118, 129, 142, 181,
    190, 218

Lempers, J., 22, 44, 107, 219
Levine, J., 118
Lewis, R., 34, 35, 154
Libby, P., 228
Lino, M., 7, 8, 27

Mace, D. R., 1
Maccoby, E., 143, 224
Maeroff, G., 208
Major, B., 83
Mancini, J., 158
Manis, J., 153
Manosevitz, M., 43
Mapes, D., 92
Martin, T., 96
Masnick, G., 10
Mattessich, P., 36
McGoldrick, M., 36, 38
McLanahan, S., 21, 22, 44, 50, 53, 154,
    208
McLoyd, V., 7, 42, 107, 219
Mechanic, D., 22, 45
Mederer, H., 75, 76, 102
Menaghan, E., 19, 41, 154, 158
Mencken, F., 216
Merisotis, J., 7, 27
Michaels, J., 154
Michelson, W., 81
Milardo, R., 189
Miller, B., 36
Mirowsky, J., 41, 150, 156
Mnookin, R., 143
Montemayor, R., 128, 190, 211, 215
Morgan, L., 152
Morgan, P., 23, 143
Mott, F., 43, 44, 101
Moynihan, D., 106

Neal, A., 4
Nelson, M., 219
Newcomer, S., 21, 107, 113
Nock, S., 4, 21, 43, 107, 129
Nord, C., 4, 124, 190, 197

O'Brien, M., 39
O'Donnell, K., 215

O'Leary, K., 224
O'Neil, R., 176, 215, 222
Oshman, H., 43
Otto, L., 16

Parcel, T., 19, 41, 158
Parsons, T., 29, 30
Perry, J., 128, 218
Pleck, J., 7, 76, 118, 228
Pitts, J., 29
Porter, B., 224
Porter, K., 41, 58

Rainwater, L., 40
Raschke, H., 45, 152, 189
Raschke, V., 45, 152
Raspberry, W., 106
Reinherz, H., 188
Risman, B., 60
Rivers, C., 41
Roberts, T., 228
Robinson, J., 16
Rodgers, R., 35
Rodgers, W., 36, 152, 153
Rollins, B., 154, 190
Rosenberg, M., 146, 153, 208
Rosenfield, S., 41
Ross, C., 41, 150, 170
Rossi, A., 53, 181

Sandler, I., 46
Savage, J., 189
Savin-Williams, R., 176
Scanzoni, J., 30, 31, 224
Sealand, N., 192
Sebald, H., 17, 27
Segal, S., 191, 224
Seltzer, J., 23, 143, 191, 197
Shaw, S., 83, 90
Sheley, J., 16, 73, 74, 103
Simmons, R., 22
Skolnick, A., 9
Slater, P., 42
Small, S., 176
Smetana, J., 128

Smollar, J., 209
Spain, D., 19
Spanier, G., 34, 35, 93, 154
Spitze, G., 7, 19, 20, 40, 72, 74, 80, 158, 218
Stacey, J., 1, 9, 189
Staines, G., 228
Strauss, M., 98
Style, C., 35, 41
Sweet, J., 21, 22, 44, 51
Szinovacz, M., 83, 103

Teachman, J., 96
Theis, J., 46
Thibaut, J., 32, 154
Thomas, D., 190
Thomas, M., 153
Thompson, E., 152
Thompson, L., 40, 83, 84, 103, 131, 181, 190, 219, 228
Thompson, M., 23, 141, 175, 221
Thorne, B., 40, 72
Treas, J., 219
Tromsdorff, G., 17

Udry, J., 1-19, 21, 107, 113
Uhlenberg, P., 3, 27

Vemer, E., 96, 221
Veroff, J., 153
Visher, E., 46
Visher, J., 46
Voeller, B., 24
Voydanoff, P., 7, 72, 218

Waite, L., 80, 81, 227
Walby, S., 39
Walker, A., 40, 83, 103, 181, 190, 218, 228
Wallerstein, J., 5, 224
Walster, E., 33
Walster, G., 33
Warner, R., 75, 83, 102
Weaver, C., 35, 41
Weiss, R., 81, 152

Weitzman, L., 56, 152
White, J., 36
White, L., 55, 80, 92, 93, 153, 220, 221,
    227
Whitehead, B., 106, 219
Wicks, J., 4
Williams, D., 35
Wolchik, S., 46

Woodworth, J., 152

Yllö, K., 98
Youniss, J., 209

Zelditch, M., 29

Subject Index

Academic performance:
    effects of cohabiting partner on, 212-213
    factors associated with children ages 5-11, 206-207
    factors associated with children ages 12-18, 208-209, 211-213
    gender differences in, 208, 211
    measurement for children, 182-183
African American families, 3, 10-15
    by family type, 63-65
    limits of family development theory, 37-38
    single parents, 21
Age:
    and child well-being, 180
    and family development approach, 36-37
    children 5 to 11, 110-113, 115, 126, 132-133, 135, 204-205, 206-208
    children 12 to 18, 114-115, 208-211
    children under 5, 108-110, 114, 126, 132-133, 135, 203-204
    of children by family type, 62-63
    of mothers by family type, 61-62
Aggression. See Family conflict

Childrearing values, 108-113, 242, 243
    by family type, 107, 109, 118

    by socioeconomic status, 57-58, 107
    changes in, 17-18
    low commitment to children, 106
    measurement of, 242-243
    value of children, 4
Children's well-being:
    by family type, 183-187
    correlates of, 191-199, 269-274
    direct effects on, 201-202
    effects of family process variables on, 189-190, 194-199
    effects of family resource variables on, 188-194
    effects of marital relations on, 196
    effects of mothers on, 198-199
    effects of nonresidential fathers on, 196-197
    factors influencing, 188-190
    family composition explanation of, 42-43
    family process correlates, 191-194, 269-274
    family process versus family resources and background variables, 195, 209-210
    family resource correlates, 193-194, 269-274
    measurement of, 181-183, 257-260
    models for explaining, 199-213

Child support, 44
    effects on mothers well-being, 163
Cohabiting:
    by family type, 62
    effects on mothers well-being, 163
Compensatory factors, 43-44
Conflict. *See* Family conflict
Continuously single-parent families:
    cohabiting rate, 62
    defined, 52, 54
    factors influencing mothers well-
        being in, 164-165
    well-being of children in, 184-185
Control, 113-124
    by family type, 126-127
    in single parent families, 23, 113
    of children, 113-117
Control variables, 66-69
    description of, 68
    measurement of, 236-238
Covariates. *See* Control variables

Demographic characteristics by fam-
    ily type, 57
Disagreement. *See* Family conflict
Divorced families:
    and childrens' well-being, 184-
        185, 210-211
    cohabiting rate, 62
    defined, 51
    economic consequences for, 152
    factors influencing mothers' well-
        being in, 162-163
    interaction with nonresidential fa-
        thers in, 99

Economics. *See* Income
Educaton:
    expectations for children, 117-118,
        245
    of mothers by family type, 61
Employment. *See* Mothers' employ-
    ment
Equity theory, 33
    housework and mothers' percep-
        tions, 84, 219

mothers' perceptions by family
    type, 90, 131
summary, 226-227
See also Social exchange theory
Exchange theory. *See* Social exchange
    theory

Family composition model, 42-43, 107
    empirical evaluation of, 118
    well-being of children, 179-180
Family conflict, 45
    by gender of child, 128-129
    effects on childrens' well-being,
        45, 180, 198-199
    hypothesis, 45
    marital conflict by family type, 97-
        98
    measurement of mother-child dis-
        agreement, 247-249
    measurement of wife-husband
        conflict, 240-241
    mother-child conflict by family
        type, 128-129
    parent-child conflict, 118, 247-248
    predivorce versus postdivorce, 21
    summary, 225
    with nonresident father, 45
Family development theory, 36-38
    limitations of, 38
Family processes, 23
    and mothers' well-being, 154-157, 181
    recent changes in, 16-18
    theories of, 42
Family resource variables:
    and childrens' well-being, 181
    and mothers' well-being, 145, 236-
        238
    measurement of, 236-238
Family rules, 113-118, 243-244
Family structure effects, 23-25
    and social address, 48
    demographic changes, 11-18
    diversity and the feminist perspec-
        tive, 40
    importance of, 48
    problems attributed to nontradi-
        tional families, 3

Father's absence:
  economic effects of, 56
  See also Nonresident father
Fathers:
  economic role of, 60
  effects on well-being of children, 190
  housework performed by, 74
  housework when mother is em-
    ployed, 88-89
  relationships with children, 134-
    137, 249
  stepfather-stepchild interaction, 133
Feminist perspective, 39-42
  housework, 40, 72
  mothers' well-being, 145
First-married families, 54
  and childrens well-being, 210-211
  defined, 51
  factors influencing mothers' well-
    being, 160-161
Freudian theory, 42-43

Global well-being of children, 201-202
  and background variables, 202
  and family process variables, 202
  and family resource variables, 202
  and mother-adolescent conflict,
    129-133
  factors associated with, 201-202
  measurement of, 181

Hispanics, 10-15
  by family type, 63
  limits of family development the-
    ory, 38
Housework, 7, 71-74
  and cohabiting partners, 82
  and father's absence, 77
  and role strain, 88-91
  by employment of mothers, 85-89
  children's performance by family
    type, 80-83
  equity in, 219
  feminist perspective, 39-40
  hours spent by family type, 77, 78-83
  in traditional families, 16
  measurement of, 239

perceptions of equity, 84-85
proportional division of, 16, 75-78
structural functionalism, 30
summary, 218

Implications of study, 228
Income, 6, 44-45, 56-57
  and cost of children, 7
  and mothers' dependency, 60-61
  by family type, 57, 59
  economic deprivation, 44
  economic deprivation and well-
    being of children, 44, 180
  effects of divorce on, 7-8
  of single-parents, 7-8
  support by nonresidential fa-
    thers, 8-9

Life-cycle approach, 36-38
Life stress, 45-48
Limitations of previous research:
  control of relevant variables, 43
  failure to control for relevant vari-
    ables, 43
  few dimensions of well-being
    studied, 43
  homogeneous samples, 7
  ignore compensatory factors, 43
  lack of comparison groups, 4-5
  lack of longitudinal dimension, 5
  small samples, 7

Marital interaction, 35
Marital relations, 92-98
  adjustment, 93-97
  and feminist perspective, 40-41
  interaction, 93-97
  measurement of, 24-241
  quality, 92
  stability, 92
Mothers:
  control of children, 126
  effects on well-being of children, 190
  housework performed by, 74-76
  interaction with children, 122, 245-
    246

interaction with children by family type, 123
measures of well-being, 146
support of children,125-126
Mothers' depression:
by family type, 147
defined, 146,252
effects of processes and resource variables by family type, 168-170
model for explaining, 168-170
Mothers' employment:
and household labor, 7
and interaction with children, 7, 20
and mothers' health, 7
benefits for children, 19
effects on mothers' well-being by family type, 163
hours by family type, 61
in dual-earner families, 19
Mothers' global well-being:
by family type, 170-172
defined, 146, 253-259
effects of family process and resource variables by family type, 170
model for explaining, 170-172
Mothers' health:
by family type, 150
defined, 146
effects of family process and family resource variables by family type, 173
model for explaining, 172-173
Mothers' self-esteem:
by family type, 150, 251-252
defined, 146, 251-252
effects of family process varaibles, 167-168
effects of family process variables by family type, 167-168
model for explaining, 167-168
Mothers' well-being:
by family type, 147-151
correlates of, 157-165, 266-268
effects of family process variables on, 154-157
effects of family resources on, 151-154

factors influencing, 151-157, 165-173
family processes compared to family resources, 160
feminist perspective, 41
in continuously single-parent families, 164-165
in divorced families, 162-163
in first-married families, 160-161
in stepfamilies, 161-162
measurement of, 146
models explaining mothers well-being, 165-173
summary of effects, 174-178, 221
time since divorce, 154

National Survey of Families and Households, 26, 50
design, 51
oversampling, 52
weighting, 56, 66-67
Nonresidential fathers, 3
adverse effects of, 43
deadbeat dads, 3
effects on well-being of children, 164, 191
interaction by family type, 99-101
interaction with children, 136-139
mothers' conflict with, 100-101
mothers' satisfaction with relationship, 101-102
participation with children, 23, 43
postmarital relations with, 98-102
relationships with children by family type, 98-101, 136-139
structural functionalism, 226
support of, 23

Parent-child interaction, 118-124, 243-244
by family type, 120, 219-220
Parent-child involvement, 118-122
Physical aggression, 132-134
Postmodern families, 1
Poverty, 22-23, 44-45
by family type, 58-61
effects of divorce on, 152

in single-parent families, 22
Postmodern families, 1

Race by family type, 63
Role strain:
    and housework, 88-91
    and structural-functional theory, 90
    by family type, 88, 97, 130
    maternal role by family type, 130
    measurement of marital role
        strain, 240, 248
Rules. *See* Family rules

Sample size, 52
Sexual intercourse by family type, 95
Single parents, 20-23
    and feminist theory, 41
    and poverty, 44
    and socialization deficit, 43
    and well-being of children, 184-185
    deficit model, 107
    divorced versus continuously sin-
        gle, 8-9, 22, 60
Social exchange theory, 32-36
    and exploitation, 33-34
    comparison level and mother's
        well-being, 161
    limitations of, 35
    mothers' well-being, 144-145
    reciprocity, 32
    summary, 226-227
    See also Equity theory
Socioeconomic characteristics by fam-
    ily type, 56-65
Socioemotional adjustment, 203-206
    influences for children ages 0-4,
        204
    influences for children ages 5-11,
        205
    influences for children ages 12-18,
        208-211
    measurement for children, 182
Stepfamilies:
    defined, 52, 54
    factors influencing mothers' well-
        being in, 161-162
    marital adjustment in, 96

marital conflict in, 98
marital relations in, 92
stress in, 46
well-being of children in, 210-211
Stereotypes of family structures, 3-4
    of single parents, 38
    of stepfamilies, 38
Stress, 45-47, 180
Stress and childrens well-being:
    cummulative effects hypothesis, 46
    life stress hypothesis, 46
Structural-functional theory, 29-31
    limitations of, 31
    mothers' role strain, 144
    mothers' role strain by family
        type, 90-91
    nonresidential fathers, 226
    role differentiation, 29-30
    two parent family benefits, 30
Support, 125-126, 246

Traditional families:
    and mothers employment, 10
    breakdown of, 106
    childcare in, 16
    childrearing values in, 106
    feminist critique of, 39-40
    limitations of, 6-7, 9-12
    of the 1950s, 10
    strengths of, 1, 9-10
    structural functionalism, 30-31
Two-parent families:
    and structural functionalism, 30
    family composition model, 107
Types of families studied, 2, 24-25, 51-
    52, 234-235
    by race, 64-65
    definition of, 53-55
    restrictions on types, 54-55

Verbal agression, 132-134
    See also Family conflict

Weighting, 56, 66-67
Well-being. *See* Childrens' well-
    being, Mothers' well-being

About The Authors

Alan C. Acock is Professor and Chair of Human Development and Family Studies at Oregon State University. He received a B.S. in political science from Eastern Washington State University, his M.A. in political science from Washington State University, and his Ph.D. in sociology from Washington State University. He currently serves on the editorial boards of *Structural Equation Modeling* and *Journal of Family and Economic Issues*. His research focuses on linkages between social structure and personality, especially as they apply to intergenerational relations.

David H. Demo is Associate Professor of Human Development and Family Studies at the University of Missouri. He received a B.S. in psychology and sociology from the University of Richmond, an M.S. in sociology from Virginia Commonwealth University, and a Ph.D. in sociology and human development and family studies from Cornell University. He serves on the editorial boards of *Journal of Marriage and the Family* and *Family Relations.* His research focuses on the linkages between social structure and personality, especially the influences of divorce, family structure, and family relations on the well-being of children and parents.